Caribbean
HOME Economics
IN ACTION

BOOK 2

FOURTH EDITION

A complete health & family management course for the Caribbean

Caribbean Association of Home Economists

Claudia Brown-Wilson *Jamaica*

Penelope Harris *Guyana*

Lucille Marcelle *Trinidad and Tobago*

Latoya Reynolds *Antigua and Barbuda*

Keisha Went *Barbados*

Series Editor:

Dr Antonia Coward *Barbados*

Although every effort has been made to ensure that website addresses are correct at time of going to press, Hodder Education cannot be held responsible for the content of any website mentioned in this book. It is sometimes possible to find a relocated web page by typing in the address of the home page for a website in the URL window of your browser.

Hachette UK's policy is to use papers that are natural, renewable and recyclable products and made from wood grown in well-managed forests and other controlled sources. The logging and manufacturing processes are expected to conform to the environmental regulations of the country of origin.

To order, please visit www.hoddereducation.com or contact Customer Service at education@hachette.co.uk / +44 (0)1235 827827

ISBN: 978 1 3983 3594 3

© Caribbean Association of Home Economists 2024

First published in 1983

Second edition published in 1992

Third edition published in 2002

This edition published in 2024 by

Hodder Education,
An Hachette UK Company
Carmelite House
50 Victoria Embankment
London EC4Y 0DZ
www.hoddereducation.com

The authorised representative in the EEA is Hachette Ireland, 8 Castlecourt Centre, Dublin 15, D15 XTP3, Ireland (email: info@hbgi.ie)

Impression number   10 9 8 7 6 5 4

Year   2026 2025

All rights reserved. Apart from any use permitted under UK copyright law, no part of this publication may be reproduced or transmitted in any form or by any means, electronic or mechanical, including photocopying and recording, or held within any information storage and retrieval system, without permission in writing from the publisher or under licence from the Copyright Licensing Agency Limited. Further details of such licences (for reprographic reproduction) may be obtained from the Copyright Licensing Agency Limited, www.cla.co.uk

Cover photo © fizkes – stock.adobe.com; © mimagephotos – stock.adobe.com; © tigercat-lpg – stock.adobe.com
Illustrations by Rassie Erasmus, Stéphan Theron and Vian Oelofsen
Typeset in 10 on 12pt Helvetica Neue
Printed and bound in Great Britain by Bell and Bain Ltd, Glasgow
A catalogue record for this title is available from the British Library.

Contents

About the series 4

How to use this series 4

Section 1 Revisiting the design process

Getting to know the design process 6

Revisiting the design process 7

Section 2 Health and family ... 19

Chapter 1
Family living 20

Chapter 2
Family management 42

Chapter 3
Family economics 74

Chapter 4
Health management 86

Section 3 Food and nutrition ... 112

Chapter 5
Nutrition 113

Chapter 6
Food preparation and service 144

Section 4 Clothing and textiles ... 191

Chapter 7
Clothing and textiles 192

Appendix 1 Weights and measures 226

Appendix 2 Nutrition tables 227

Appendix 3 Height and weight tables 229

Appendix 4 Fashion silhouettes 230

Appendix 5 Glassware 232

Cookery terms 233

Glossary **234**

Index **236**

About the series

Caribbean Home Economics in Action: A complete health and family management course for the Caribbean is designed and developed by Caribbean authors for Caribbean secondary school students. This three-book course has a long history in the region and resulted from collaboration between the Caribbean Association of Home Economists and the Toronto Home Economics Association. The funding for the initial research, writing, editing and preparation of graphic material, all of which took place in the Caribbean, was granted by the Canadian International Development Agency.

Background for the writing was developed in a research project on Caribbean Lifestyle designed by members of the Caribbean Association of Home Economists and the Toronto Home Economics Association. Investigation was carried out in the territories by members of the Caribbean Association of Home Economists. The Caribbean Examinations Council Secondary Education Certificate Home Economics Syllabuses were used as a basis for the subject matter covered.

It was the objective of the Caribbean Association of Home Economists that the books' content be valuable for both classroom use and for student, teacher and home reference. It is hoped that individuals using the materials throughout the territories will be the best judges as to which segments will be used for each purpose. To that end, each segment has been revised to meet the evolving needs of the Caribbean student taking into consideration the 21st century learning environment and STEM integration.

It is hoped that *Caribbean Home Economics in Action: A complete health and family management course for the Caribbean* will find its way into the hearts of every Caribbean student in every Caribbean home.

How to use this series

In its fourth edition, this textbook remains a foundation course for the Caribbean Examinations Council Secondary Education Certificate in the three areas of Home Economics. The course is therefore written for the junior secondary student and is spread over the three books in the series. Process is the main feature that distinguishes these texts from many other Home Economics texts. The books illuminate how families deal with issues that affect them.

The substance of the text has not changed. However, the Caribbean Association of Home Economists is aware that Home Economics Education in the Caribbean is changing. Similarly, the Home Economics curriculum is focusing on developing critical thinking skills and learning about the application of technology. The book has therefore been thoroughly updated with the inclusion of current practices, materials, and features designed to enhance student learning and understanding.

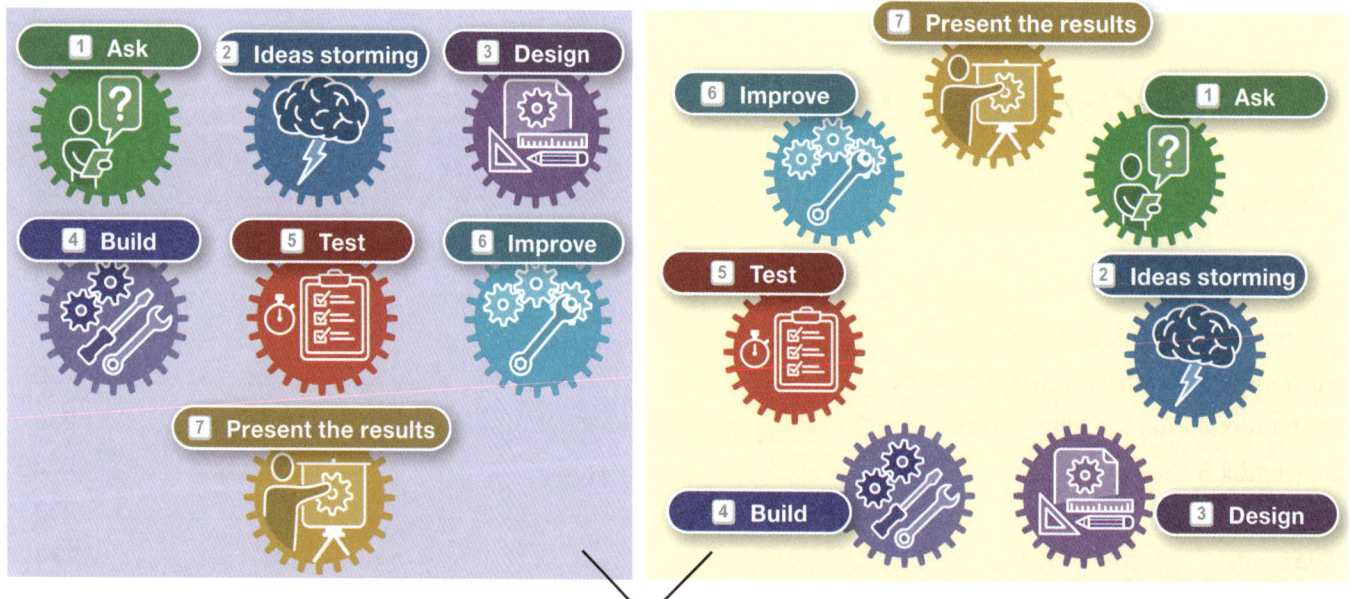

A guided approach to the application of the design process in each area of Home Economics is used to build students' confidence as they progress from apprehension about critical thinking and problem-solving processes to the mastery and autonomous thinking, which will aid in finding solutions to the challenges faced by the Caribbean.

Chapters open with objectives to stimulate student interest and focus attention on important chapter content.

In this chapter, you will:
* review the stages in the design process
* explore in greater detail how to identify a problem
* develop a design brief for the problem identified
* explore in greater detail how to generate ideas by exploring possible solutions
* explore in greater detail how to select the best possible solution
* test and evaluate the solution
* present a report.

- Research the management processes that your family makes use of daily.
- Write a paragraph about the types of decision that were considered by your family before your family housing was selected.
- Sketch your future dream house.

In order for anyone or an activity to succeed, it is important that a plan is made on what, how and by when this activity is to be achieved and what are the desired goals. If anyone tries to take up a business or a task without a goal or a plan, they will fail because they are not prepared for the processes.

Wherever possible the content is differentiated to make it more student-friendly.

ACTIVITIES

Robert is a sixth form student, who is involved in a lot of extracurricular activity at school, he is also the captain of his church Bible quiz team and plays on his community basketball team. He is also preparing for CAPE examinations. Having to do all of these activities overwhelms him at times.
1. Use the strategies outlined for good time management to assist Robert in managing his time wisely.
2. Outline at least five benefits of good time management.

Activities, which are placed in focus boxes throughout each chapter, allow students to put theory into practice. The critical thinking element of the activities allows students to apply the information they have learnt to practical situations.

What have I learnt?

Multiple choice questions
Select the letter that corresponds with your answer.
1. You find that most days are very hectic and you are not able to complete all your activities on time. What can you do to help yourself?
    - A Tell others about what you have to do.
    - B Make a checklist of what has to be completed.
    - C Make a to-do list and rank the activities in order of importance.
    - D Just go with the flow and try to complete all that you can think of.
2. Which of the following is NOT a **feature of management**?
    - A A series of continuous and related activities
    - B Works with people and resources in order to achieve goals
    - C Can be measured in terms of hours
    - D Focuses on reaching goals

Questions are placed at the end of each chapter to encourage students to probe into the chapter content, making connections and gaining insights. They also provide excellent review for examinations. Book 3 contains a variety of questions, which cover the whole course. The questions, which include matching, true/false, multiple choice, cloze passage, short answer, case study and structured essay, cater for the needs of different abilities.

Glossary

acquired immunity immunity acquired when the body produces antibodies, as a result of immunisation or a non-fatal attack of the disease

amino acid the small molecules that join together to make proteins

amniotic sac the fluid-filled bag in which a baby develops

Throughout each chapter there are red boldfaced key concepts, which are also defined in the glossary of key terms at the end of the book.

Appendix 1 Weights and measures

In this book, quantities and measurements have been given in both metric and imperial. An exact conversion does not usually give convenient working amounts, so we have rounded off the metric measures into units of 25 grams. Do not mix metric and imperial in the same recipe.

The tables below show the recommended equivalents between metric, imperial and American/Canadian (not British) standard measuring cups and spoons.

Weights and equivalent measures

METRIC	IMPERIAL	CUPS OF FAT	CUPS OF FLOUR	CUPS/SPOONS OF SUGAR
1 kg	36 oz (2 lb 4 oz)			
560 g				$2\frac{1}{4}$ cups (brown)
500 g	18 oz (1 lb 2 oz)			2 cups (granulated)
450 g	16 oz (1 lb)	2 cups		

As before, there are appendices at the end of the books. New appendices in this edition include: types of glassware, fashion silhouettes and recommended dietary allowances.

I would like to emphasise that it remains the objective of the Caribbean Association of Home Economists that these books be useful for the classroom, for the student teacher, and for home reference.

As always, we welcome comments from users of these books.

Antonia Coward
Series Editor

Section 1 Revisiting the design process

Getting to know the design process

In Book 1, you learnt that the design process is a useful approach to breaking down a problem or challenge so that a solution can be found. You were able to use the steps of the process to find and test possible solutions to problems before selecting the best one.

In this section, you will revisit the design process and take a more independent approach to its application in the search for an ideal solution to the **Do it yourself** scenario. You will be guided through some parts of the process but will have to work on your own or in a group for the other parts.

Revisiting the design process

Figure 1 Getting to know the design process

In this chapter, you will:
* review the stages in the design process
* explore in greater detail how to identify a problem
* develop a design brief for the problem identified
* explore in greater detail how to generate ideas by exploring possible solutions
* explore in greater detail how to select the best possible solution
* test and evaluate the solution
* present a report.

Reflect, research, report

The big question
Are you able to use the design process to solve/address the challenge faced by the woman in the picture below?

Breaking this down
1. What seems to be the problem?
2. Which design process steps would you take to address this problem?
3. Can you think of a new idea to address or solve the challenge identified?
4. Can you provide some possible alternatives to come to a solution?
5. How would you identify the best possible solution?
6. How can you help the woman to solve similar problems in the future?
7. What did you do to help the woman make the right decision?

Sharing the information
Think of an effective way to share your conclusions with your classmates. You could draw a comic strip or a schematic diagram or make a video using a social media format. What other entertaining and informative ways can you use to share the information about the design process with your class?

Answering the big question
Having done the research and listened to the information from your classmates:
1. Do you think that you can use the design process to solve the problem?
2. What are some of your thoughts/ideas about solving problems/challenges related to family members?
3. How would you choose the best solution for a problem?

Problem-solving tips
Think about the pros and cons of the solutions identified. This will guide your selection.

Revisiting the design process

Applying the design process

Do you remember the steps in the design process? Remember it is a sequence of activities, which help you to break down a problem and find a workable solution.

Stages in the design process

Figure 2 shows the main steps in the design process.

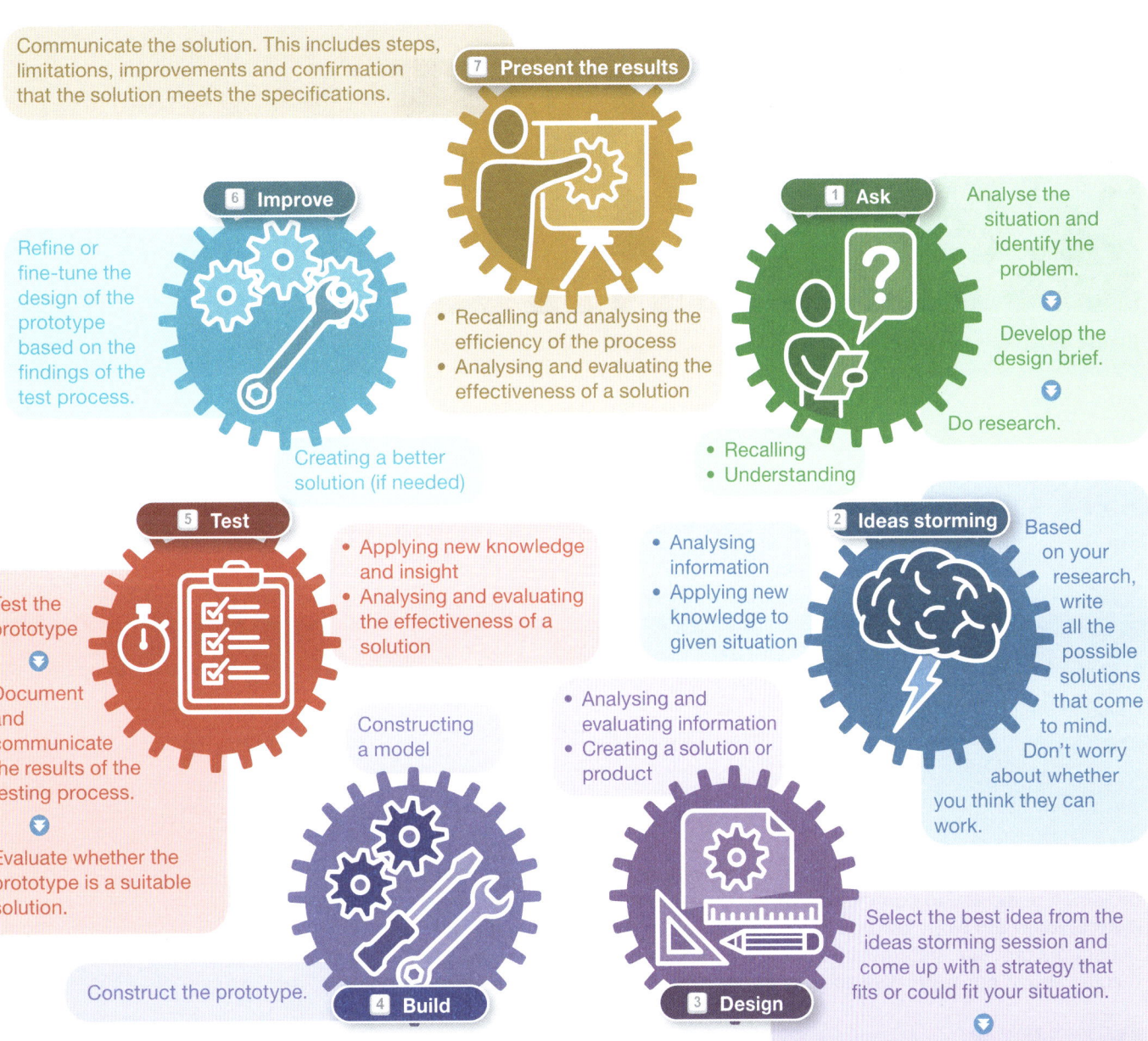

Figure 2 Stages of the design process

> **Did you know?**
> The design process is also considered an approach to learning.

The design process is a way of thinking, learning, collaborating, and problem-solving. In practice, the design process is a structured framework for identifying challenges, gathering information, coming up with potential solutions, refining ideas, and testing solutions. The design process encourages the development of inquiry skills, divergent thinking and reflection. It also promotes empathy, curiosity, creativity, innovation and constructiveness.

Figure 3 Design process thinking

STEP 1: IDENTIFYING THE PROBLEM

Figure 4 Defining the problem

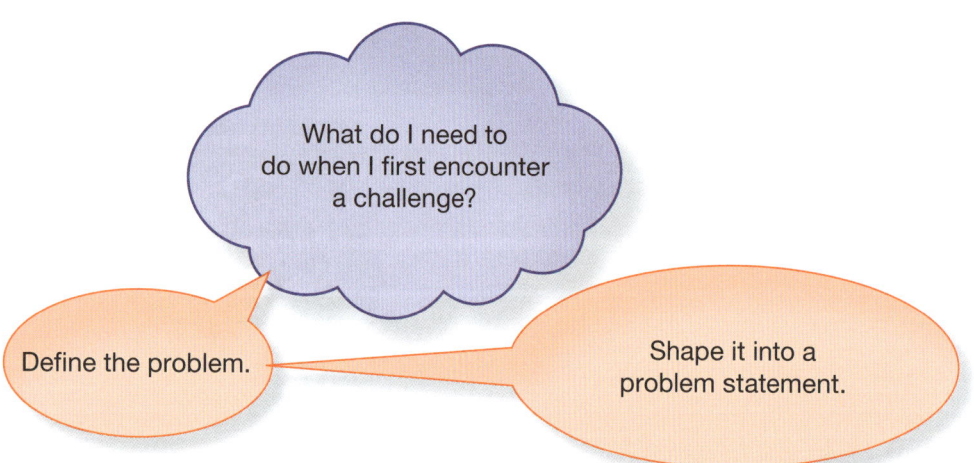

The **defining** stage ensures that you completely understand the goal of your project. It helps you to communicate your design problem and provides a clear objective to work towards. It also helps you to develop a meaningful, actionable problem statement that will guide you in the right direction while helping you to conceptualise and work your way towards a solution.

> **Consider this**
>
> Without a well-defined problem statement, it is hard to know what you are aiming for. Your work will lack focus, and the final design may not solve the problem as intended. Additionally, without a clear problem statement, it is extremely difficult to explain to your teachers and classmates exactly what you are trying to achieve.

Look at the picture below and share what it means to you with your classmates.

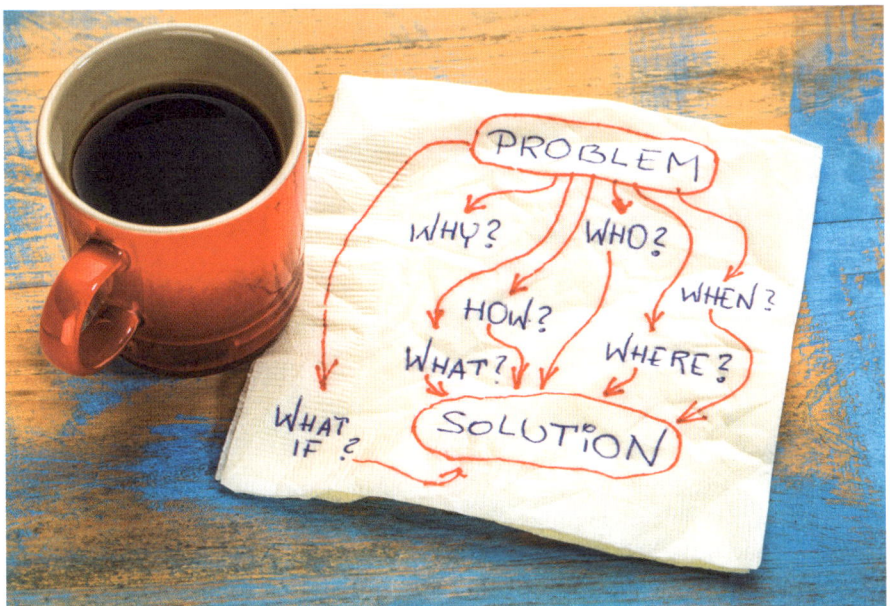

Figure 5 Question starters

- A problem statement identifies the gap between the problem and the goal of a process or product. Think of the user's problem as an unmet need. By designing a solution that meets this need, you can satisfy the user and ensure a pleasant user experience.
- A problem statement breaks down a problem so that it can be worked on by the designers. It should provide a clear description of the issue that the designer seeks to address, so that the solution is meaningful for the user.

Writing better problem statements

Problem statements can take various formats, but the end goal should be the same. Remember that your problem statement should identify the problem, mention the special conditions related to the problem if there are any and indicate what the solution should accomplish.

- From the user's perspective: As a young working professional who is trying to eat healthily, I am struggling because I work long hours and do not always have time to go grocery shopping and prepare my meals. This makes me feel frustrated and bad about myself. I need to find an efficient way to get healthy meals.
- From a user research perspective: Busy working professionals need an easy, time-efficient way to eat healthily because they often work long hours and do not have time to shop and prepare meals.
- Based on the four W's – who, what, where, and why: Young working professional struggles to eat healthily during the week because she is working long hours. Our solution should deliver a quick and easy way for her to buy ingredients and prepare healthy meals that she can take to work.

Each of the statements above addresses the same issue; however, it is done in a slightly different way. The most important thing is to focus on the users, what they need and why. Then, it is up to you how you choose to design your solution to the problem.

Problem-solving tips

The following pointers will help you to create a meaningful problem statement.
- **Be user-centric:** The user and their needs should be central to your problem statement. Avoid statements that start with 'we need to …' or 'the product should …' instead, concentrate on the user's perspective: 'Young working professionals need …' as in the examples on the previous page.
- **Keep it open:** Avoid suggesting definite solutions; instead, there should be opportunities for a solution that is innovative and creative.
- **Make it achievable:** Your problem statement should be a guide. The user's needs and goals should be specific, so that the designer does not struggle to find a suitable solution. Do not focus on multiple users' needs in one problem statement.

Do it yourself
Identify a problem in your community. In your notebooks, write your problem statements using the three different ways.

Researching solutions

After outlining the problem and stating the requirements of the ideal solutions, the next action is to conduct **research**. This will not only help to provide a better understanding of the problem but it will also expose you to potential solutions. Research may include reading articles in journals, magazines, books or on the internet to spark ideas and to consider the limitations of the possible solutions.

Research can include looking at existing designs and questioning their strengths and weaknesses.

Research is also where crucial elements of a design or solution become clear.

Doing research leads to thinking about the parts of the problem that must be addressed so that there is a meaningful solution.

Did you know?
You can identify the limits to your possible solutions and eliminate the ones that are impossible, inefficient or costly, by answering the question: *What are the limitations of this design or solution?*

Do it yourself

1. In a small group, select one of the problem statements you wrote about a challenge faced by your community and develop a research approach to find:

   a situations where there are similar challenges

   b solutions designed to address the challenges in those situations

   c the limitations of those solutions.

2. After you have conducted the research, as a group discuss the usefulness of the research and what you would do differently the next time. For example, could your group gather useful information by doing surveys or interviews?

Write a specification

After defining the problem, writing the problem statement and conducting research, the next step is to write the **specification**. The specification helps to shape the ideal solution by listing six to eight of the features required. You should also include limitations to ensure that they are always considered as you move through the process.

Do it yourself

1. In your notebook, write the specification for the challenge that you have identified in your community. These are some of the ways you can state the items on your specification:
   - The method/solution must be …
   - The solution should use …
   - Implementing the solution should be/should not be …

2. In your group, discuss what you think is likely to happen if you do not create the specification.

STEP 2: IDEAS STORMING

Once the problem has been identified and understood, the next stage of the design process involves **ideas storming**, which is a free-flow of ideas ranging from the improbable or impossible to the practical or efficient. Ideas storming is a brilliant way of allowing ideas to evolve from research and engaging with other people.

Figure 6 Ideas storming

Ideas storming best practices:

✓ focus on one problem/challenge at a time
✓ listen to input from team members or from the user
✓ document all the ideas suggested
✓ eliminate the ideas that just cannot work
✓ refine or build on the remaining ideas until you get to the limitations that cannot be resolved
✓ identify the solutions that seem feasible for the user – practical, cost-effective or innovative.

Do it yourself

1. In your group, do some ideas storming that could be implemented to resolve the challenge identified in your community.
2. After the ideas storming activity, take a moment to discuss the parts of the activity that were the most useful and what could be done differently the next time.

STEP 3: DESIGN

Selecting the best solution

Figure 7 Selecting the best solution

How do I select the best solution to design and implement when I have so many that are feasible?

Problem-solving tips

When selecting your solution, consider:
- Will the solution be beneficial to the user?
- Is it the most affordable solution?
- Is it sustainable or user-friendly?

In Book 1, you learnt that you can use a pros and cons list to help you select the ideal solution. If that list does not help to select the best solution, you can use a selection matrix from the internet to make a final decision.

Once the most feasible solution has been selected, it is time to draft a **design** for it. The design phase is where the useful information gathered is merged with the requirements of the desired outcome to create a suitable solution for the user. Depending on the problem, your design can range from a drawing of a physical product to the outline of a programme.

Do it yourself

1. Select the best solution for the challenge you identified in your community and state the reasons for that selection.
2. Design the solution.

Did you know?

Having as much information as possible about each possible solution and keeping the problem or task in mind is helpful for choosing a successful design.

The chosen design should represent the solution that you think best meets the need or solves the problem that was identified at the beginning of the design process.

STEP 4: DEVELOP A PROTOTYPE AND TEST THE SOLUTION

A **prototype** is the first working model of the solution.

It must be tested to make sure that it is functional and can address the problem in all the ways required.

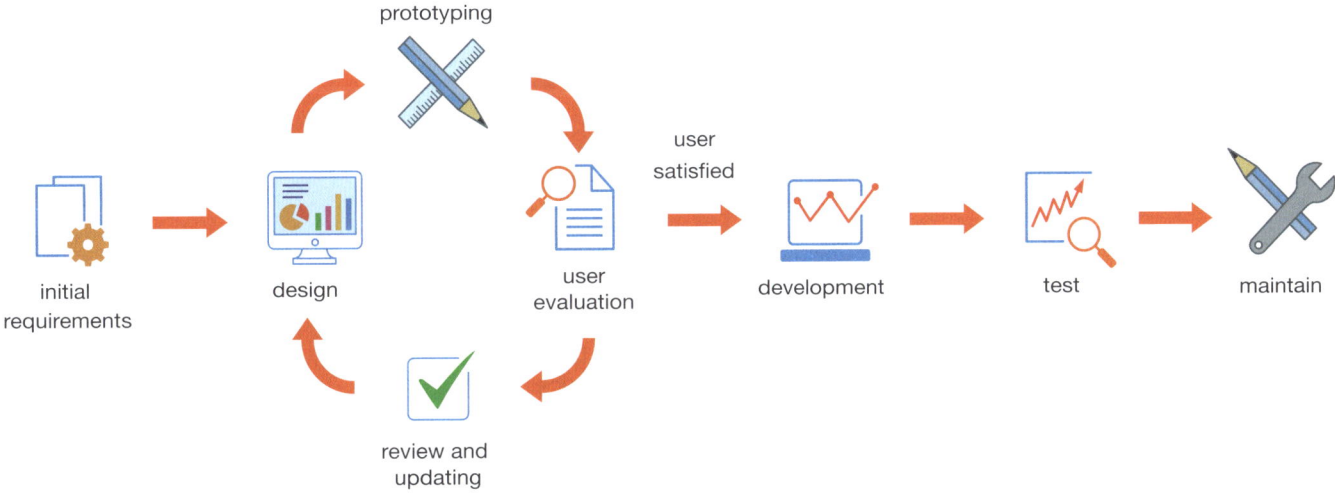

Figure 8 Prototype model

Applying the design process

Do it yourself

In your group, create a prototype (or a sketch of it) for the solution selected to address the challenge in your community.

STEP 5: TEST THE PROTOTYPE

This next stage entails testing the prototype against the specifications. This is your opportunity to make modifications to the design if it does not meet the specifications. If modifications that will improve the product cannot be made, it will mean looking for another solution.

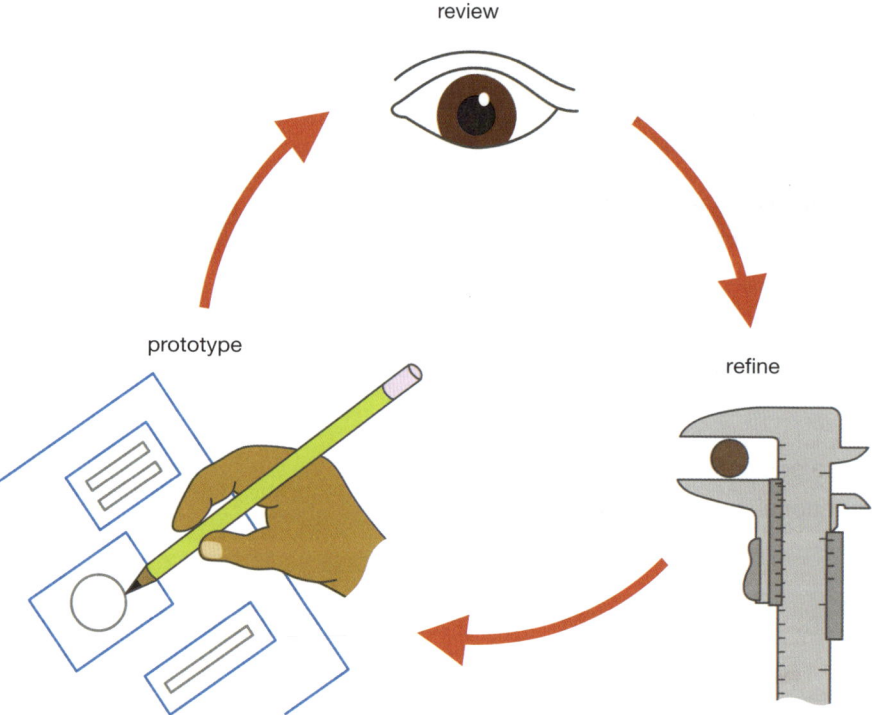

Figure 9 Prototype testing

Did you know?

The step of testing the prototype with potential users is referred to as product research. This is where you will gather feedback from your target audience or consumer on what works and what does not. This is how you identify the issues and make sure that your design is a viable solution.

Some of the steps that you need to take when testing your prototype, are answering all those important questions when you identified the problem. So, make sure that you answer the four Ws:
- WHO – ask the right people to find out if your product works and is a solution
- WHAT – ask the right questions so that you can get feedback regarding solving the problem
- WHERE – find out where this solution will work best
- WHY – remember to ask the correct questions and make a list so that you get all the necessary answers; follow up with more questions until you are satisfied that you have all the necessary information.

Do it yourself

1. Ask other groups in your class to test the prototype you designed to address the challenge in your community. Provide a feedback form that allows them to state what worked for them, as well as the flaws that need to be fixed in the design.

2. Use the feedback form to decide whether your design is viable. Can it be fixed with a simple tweak or do you need to start over again?

Problem-solving tips

The prototype must be tested against the specification each time it is tweaked because other issues that impair functionality can pop up with each adjustment. It is best to identify and correct such issues before implementation.

STEP 6: IMPROVE THE PROTOTYPE/EVALUATE THE SOLUTION

This step is about improving your prototype and may not be necessary for every project. It really depends on the results you receive from testing the prototype. If the reviews you received indicate that improvements are required, you need to look at the responses and determine exactly what needs to be corrected or changed. Also keep in mind that the product must be retested each time changes are made.

Figure 10 Improving the prototype

A final evaluation of the product or model is your evidence that the project does the job that it has been designed for. In other words, it solves or addresses the problem.

Applying the design process 17

Do it yourself

1. In your group, answer the following questions honestly:
   - Does the design meet the needs of the user?
   - Is the solution simple and easy for the user to implement?
   - Is the solution safe to use?

2. Discuss in your groups why it is necessary to perform this quality control exercise after getting satisfactory feedback on the final adjustments to the prototype.

STEP 7: PRESENT THE RESULTS

This is the final step in the design process. Here is your opportunity to provide evidence of the work you have done. You will communicate the solution to your target group. This will include the steps you took in: identifying the problem, planning and designing the model, carrying out any practical construction work and evaluating the model or design. The final steps included communicating the limitations, improvements, and providing confirmation that the solution meets the specifications identified by displaying the solution that was developed and tested.

Figure 11 Presenting results

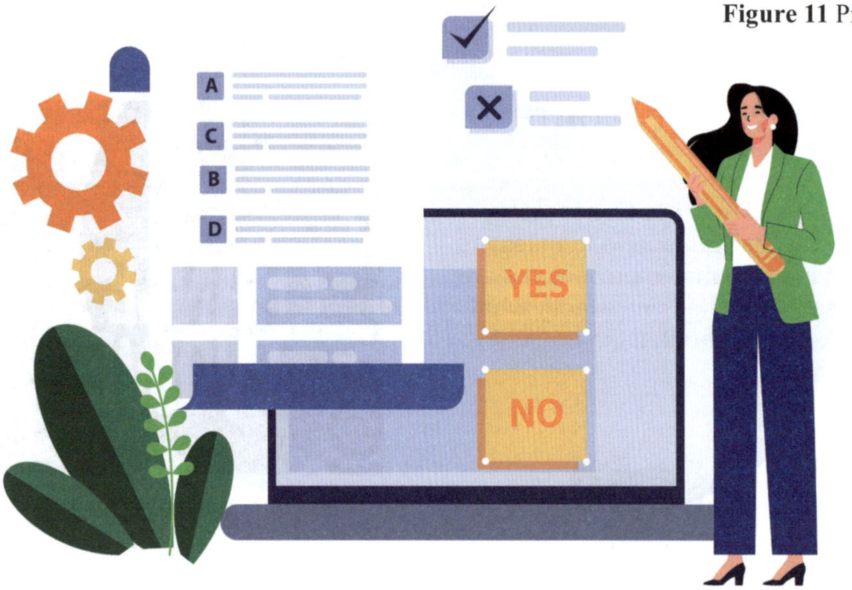

Figure 12 Communicating the results

Do it yourself

In your group, create a report for the solution you designed to address the challenge in your community, and share it with the rest of your class.

Problem-solving tips

You can be as creative as you want with a report. You can make a brochure that documents the process, limitations and shows the final solution. Your report could be a schematic chart or a documentary. The important thing is to ensure that the ideas that you want to share are clearly presented.

Section 2 Health and family

Chapter 1:	Family living
Chapter 2:	Family management
Chapter 3:	Family economics
Chapter 4:	Health management

In Book 1, you learnt about the role that the family plays in shaping its members into functioning members of the society by teaching them about values, attitudes and goals.

As you work through Section 2, you will explore how family members care for each other, live together, manage their finances and maintain their health.

Chapter 1 Family living

Figure 1.1 Not all families are the same.

Families in one form or another have existed from the beginning of time and their composition is often determined by the needs of their environment. This is true of families in the Caribbean. Caribbean families are very diverse; your family may look different from your classmates' families.

Many family practices have their roots in the past and many of these traditions/customs are practised among the Caribbean people even to this day.

- Can you list some of the family customs that your parents practise?
- What have they told you about them?
- List three things that you think you will continue to do when you are older.

In this chapter, you will:
* recognise the need to belong to a family
* identify ways to strengthen relationships with members of your own family and others
* clarify your responsibilities as a teenager
* show concern for the ageing adults in your family and community
* study the basics of population education
* become aware of the adjustments a family must make for a baby's arrival.

Family life in the past

In times gone by, most people in the Caribbean worked on sugar plantations that were owned by white men. Black people in those days were enslaved and owned by white men. The enslaved people were not free to live as they pleased. They were not encouraged to get married or take responsibility for a family of their own.

The enslaved black people were encouraged to have children, but the men among them did not have any responsibility to the children. These children were born into slavery and became the property of the slave owners at no real financial cost.

When slavery existed in the Caribbean, black people were denied the happiness and fulfilment of family life (Figure 1.2). The children of the enslaved often grew up not knowing who their fathers were. In many cases, the children were not even given the name of their father, but the name of the white man who owned the plantation. The father had no responsibility for his children. He was not expected to give them food, clothing, shelter, love or comfort.

Family ties were discouraged among the enslaved people. The children grew up mainly with their mothers, and sometimes with their grandmothers. There was no stable family life, as the enslaved people were constantly separated. During those times, black people were not happy and men probably longed to have families. The black man, therefore, was never the head of the household. He could have as many children as possible, with as many women as he chose, and no one would criticise him, since this was his main job, apart from working on the white man's plantation.

Figure 1.2 When slavery existed in the Caribbean, black people were denied the happiness and fulfilment of family life.

HOW THE PAST AFFECTS US

Many changes have taken place in the Caribbean and the world since the days of slavery. Although there have been many changes in family living since then, it appears that some habits are hard to break. These habits developed during enslavement and are responsible for the unique perspectives that some Caribbean people have on family living.

Many men in the Caribbean today continue the practice of having children with several women and do not take the responsibility of supporting them. As a result, many children today grow up mainly with their mothers and sometimes with their grandmothers. There is no father in the family and the mother figure has the sole responsibility to provide for each child.

Family life today in the Caribbean

Slavery was abolished in the Caribbean long before your parents were born, but life was not automatically wonderful for the no longer enslaved people. Even though they worked for low wages under conditions very similar to slavery, some were able to eventually own and farm land. This made it possible for people to marry and care for a family, if they wished.

> **Consider this**
>
> Did you know that when children work, it is now considered as child labour?
>
> Children born into slavery were favoured as ideal workers. Since there was no school for them to attend, they had more years to labour on the plantations.
>
> How do you think you would you cope if you had to work and not attend school?

In those early days, however, some black men found the habit of having multiple children with multiple women hard to break even though they no longer lived on the plantation. There was no thought given to how the children they fathered would be provided for or cared for or how the mothers of these children would manage the children and themselves. In the Caribbean today, this way of living is considered a demonstration of irresponsibility.

Many other changes have taken place, but some men today still behave as men did during the days of slavery. A lot of men in the Caribbean continue to have children but do not support them. In such situations, many mothers are forced to take the fathers of their children to court in order to obtain money for child support.

This behaviour deprives the child of the opportunity to grow up with both parents and experience the joys of a father's love. It also puts strain on the mother who alone must provide food, clothing, shelter, and emotional support for the child.

Many children today are born to parents who are not ready to accept the responsibilities that go along with being a parent. They cannot afford to look after them and offer them up for adoption. Some families adopt children and care for them as if they were their own. This gives many children a chance to experience family living. Some families adopt complete strangers; others adopt nieces, nephews or cousins.

Reflect, research, report

Slavery was abolished almost 200 years ago; many years before your grandparents were born. After slavery ended, the Caribbean people found new joy and freedom to love and be happy. People could now work for wages, own land, produce crops and sell in order to earn money to take care of a family.

Despite this, there are still children who are neglected and deprived of parental love and emotional care.

The big question
How can the effects of slavery on family life in the Caribbean be reduced?

Breaking this down
1. What are some of the family structures that we see in the Caribbean today?
2. How do you think slavery helped to create these family structures?
3. What is the impact of these family structures on children or their parents?
4. What kind of support do members of different family structures need in order to be responsible citizens?

Sharing the information
Think of who you want to share this information with and choose a method that will be interesting to listen to – a voice-over PowerPoint presentation, a demonstration video and so on. Remember that family can be a sensitive topic, so do not insult anyone's family structure in your presentation.

Answering the big question
Now that you have done some research and perhaps listened to presentations by your classmates, do you think that we can change how slavery has affected family life in the Caribbean?

LIVING TOGETHER

As human beings there is the natural need to belong and to be with others. Our families make us feel like we belong to a group that provides us with love, support, protection and basic needs; food, clothes and shelter.

Consider this

- What do you think would have happened to us if there were no families?
- How would you feel if you never had a family to support you?

Our family is the most valuable gift that we will ever have. It is the first group that we find ourselves in and this is where we learn relationship lessons; that is learning to respect and live with others. This is where we develop our first sense of security and trust, learn to serve one another, teach each other, and share in each other's joys and sorrows. It is the first school in which children develop the basic values of life; good manners and social graces, for example, saying, 'thank you', 'please' or 'sorry'. These values guide our behaviour throughout life.

ACTIVITIES

1. Share with the class some of the values that were instilled in you as a child.
2. Do you still believe in them or have you had a value change?

Living together is one of the most important features of the human race. You may live together in your family, where you share and care for each other, meet each other's needs and give each other love. Together you share goals, hopes, joys and sorrows. You may also share resources, experiences and talents. Family living empowers you to become the best you can be for yourself as an individual and for the success and happiness of the family. Planned family activities are important as they provide opportunities for members to interact with and learn from each other.

Figure 1.3 Family sharing the need to be together

Family life today in the Caribbean

Families help to build strong societies

Your family must relate to the community and society around you. Remember that many families use the same space, facilities, schools, clinics, shops, recreational parks and grounds.

- Families are the basic unit of any society.
- A good family creates a foundation for a successful society.
- If families fail, societies are severely affected because families maintain a productive nation.

There is a symbiotic relationship between families and societies, as both depend on each other to thrive effectively.

RELATIONSHIPS

Human beings are naturally social individuals. We spend time with other people at home, church, school and play. It is clear that forming good relationships with others will make our lives more meaningful and enjoyable.

Have you ever heard the saying 'no man is an island'? We cannot live in a bubble; we must interact with others. The more comfortable you feel around each other, the more confident you will be in voicing opinions, concerns and ideas. This kind of relationship is essential to the success of any group.

You are one of several people in your family, classroom, club or school. You are alike in many ways; you have many basic needs, values and interests. Although members might have much in common with others, each person is uniquely different. If you can understand and accept yourself as the person you are, you can begin to reach out to others. Consider that we are not all the same, and that what makes us different can be the glue that binds relationships together. Good relationships form when people have common likes, dislikes, goals and interests. For instance, most of you choose friends who share similar values and interests, hence, you expect them to give you sound advice, understand your feelings and provide approval when needed.

Your peers can help you to understand the kind of person you are, which should cause you to reflect on your own actions. This introspection allows for self-regulation and adjustments, which is a very critical step in learning how to get along with people. You should remember that no one is perfect, and that everyone has faults.

KEYS TO GOOD A FRIENDSHIP/RELATIONSHIP

A good relationship depends on trust, respect (courtesy), sharing (inclusion), and open communication in order to thrive.

Trust

Trust may be described as having a firm belief in the character, strength, honesty or truthfulness of someone who can be relied on.

Knowing you can be trusted is very important in maintaining friendship. When your friends can rely on you to keep their problems and private wishes; that's trust. When you trust your friends, you can be open and honest with your thoughts and actions because you are confident that your friends have your back. Gossip is the easiest way to lose friends. If you want to keep your friends, be trustworthy.

- Have you ever shared your friend's secret with others?
- How did it make you feel?
- Did you feel that you had betrayed your friend?

Figure 1.4 Keys to a good friendship

Sharing

Remember that each person is a unique individual and it is not healthy to be possessive of another person. You must learn to share your friends with others or be prepared to lose them. Apart from sharing your friends, you must also learn to share openly, not only your feelings but also your needs.

If you have a need, share it. You will find that people are much more attentive to your needs if you simply ask. It will be more beneficial to the relationship if individuals share openly.

Courtesy

This happens when you show a genuine interest in others and when you are considerate of the feelings of others. This means that you appreciate each other's opinions, values and wishes. This happens when both parties try to not only understand these opinions, values and wishes, but take them into account when making decisions. Courtesy also involves introducing your friends to your parents or to other friends. If you must borrow items from a friend it is your duty to return them promptly and in the same or better shape than when you borrowed them.

Consider this

Do you tell your secrets to all your friends? And do you spend a lot of time with each classmate? After you have answered these questions you may become aware of different types of friendships. Some people may be good friends with those they enjoy spending time with, others may be best friends with those they want to share a secret with.

TYPES OF RELATIONSHIP

The term *relationship* usually refers to the connection, association, interaction or bond between two or more people. There are many different types of relationships. These include but are not limited to: family, friends (best, close, casual), acquaintance and romantic relationships.

Family

The term *family* means people we are connected to through some form of kinship, whether it is through blood (parents and siblings), marriage (in-laws, step-parents), romantic relationships (girlfriend or boyfriend) or adoption. Ideally, people should have strong relationships with their families, although this is not always the case. Family members should feel love and closeness with their relatives and be able to trust them. Being part of a family also involves caring for and bonding with each other. The bond with a family plays a very critical role in the members' ability to form other kinds of relationships such as friendships and romantic relationships.

Family relationships are ideally lifelong; even if you move away from home, your family will remain a part of your life.

Consider this

How many of you travel long distances, sometimes overseas, just to be with family?

Have you ever wished that Christmas would come more than once a year because you look forward to having your relatives home for the holidays?

Friendship

Friends are people to whom we are not related, but who we choose to interact with.

Generally, our friends are people we trust, respect, care about and want to spend time with. Friendship is reciprocal; for it to exist, each person must view each other as a friend. There are varying levels of friendship, so you may feel closer to some friends rather than others.

Acquaintances

These are people whom you may encounter regularly and chat with on occasion, who are neither your friend nor relative, sometimes called distant friends. For example, your neighbour whom you say 'hello' to, a work colleague or someone you have seen a few times at the beauty salon but do not know well. Most relationships start as acquaintances but evolve into friendships over time as you get to know the person better and see them more often.

Figure 1.5 Friendship is critical to a person's well-being.

ACTIVITIES

1. Share with your classmates how one of your acquaintances became a friend.
2. Explain what caused the change.

Good or casual friends

This is a type of relationship that is not yet defined and often requires less commitment than relationships that are formal. These are people with whom you enjoy spending time. You may have similar interests such as sports. Some good friends may become best friends.

Best or close friend

A best friend is someone you like a lot and admire. You may spend a lot of time with a best friend and share secrets. It is a bond that most often exists between two friends who have a great deal of love, care, and non-romantic affection for each other.

Romantic

A romantic relationship is considered the closest type of relationship where the two people involved describe themselves as being attracted to each other or being in love. They feel a strong connection and bond between them that is not felt with anyone else.

Ending friendships

Friends grow apart for various reasons because not every friendship is lifelong. Sometimes outside elements can break up friendships. When you decide to end a friendship, you must consider the other person's feelings and explain your decision.

Some reasons for broken friendships include:

- **Wearing off.** Some friends may not seem as smart, funny and understanding as when you first met them.
- **Being used.** Some friends take all they can get from you and then move on to befriend another person. No one wants to be used.
- **Competition.** Some friends are in a constant contest to be the best or to win. This puts strain on friendships and sometimes can become painful. Friends must use competition to help their relationships and feel good about each other's successes.
- **Difference in standards.** Some friends have a drastic change in behaviour, which might not keep in line with your values, so that relationship gradually dies due to a reduction in social interaction. This fading out of the friendship is a good option for avoiding confrontation and hurt.

Older friends

Old and young can enjoy each other's company and learn from each other.

Generally, it is more common to have friends who are your peers, within your age range, but nothing is wrong with having a few friends who are older than you are. Friendships most times are about our commonalities and interests, and not necessarily about age.

As the old saying goes, 'age is nothing but a number' so friends may be any age and they all help you to grow as an individual.

As you mature, you should learn to accept your parents or grandparents and other older relatives. You can include them in games and in hobbies such as gardening, painting, quilting or in general conversation (Figure 1.6).

You may even share a room with an older relative. You can give them companionship, consideration and the respect they need. This will make them feel useful and accepted. In return, they can pass on their knowledge and wisdom and teach you traditions and skills for life. Additionally, it is believed that friendships between older and younger people help to broaden the individuals' perspective on life. This allows them to have compassion and empathy in their daily life. They will be better able to understand each other's perspective on life.

You must also consider the physical needs of older adults in your family. People are leading healthier lives and living much longer. But as they age, they might suffer from a wide range of disabilities that limit movement, speech, hearing, sight or touch. They may want to live independent lives but are unable to. This is where you as a teenager should be able to provide the necessary support to the older adults with whom you interact.

Figure 1.6 Old and young can enjoy each other's company and learn from each other.

Consider this

Observe any problems that your older relatives may have, and try to think of solutions that would help them to live happier lives by overcoming these problems.

Did you know?

Whether someone in a family is eight years old or eighty years old, they play as much a part of the family as all the other family members.

Becoming an adult

The transition from childhood or adolescence to becoming a capable adult is not necessarily very smooth.

Everyone has a different perspective of what it means to be an adult, but there are some common goals that must be achieved before one can function as an independent person. To be termed an adult, you must learn to make your way through life on your own merit, without the help of parents or guardians.

Becoming an adult is different for everyone. For some young people, it means living on your own or going away to college. For others, it means starting your first real job and becoming financially independent. No matter what the circumstances are, becoming an adult means taking responsibility for your life, for example, in the following ways:

- taking responsibility for yourself – accepting the consequences of your actions
- making independent decisions
- financial independence – paying your own way.

When do you become an adult? This may seem a long way away to you. It may surprise you to learn that you are in the process of becoming an adult right now. You may not notice the changes because they are so slow, but you can be sure that they are happening.

Figure 1.7 Becoming an adult

Consider this

- Do you think there is a certain age when someone becomes an adult?
- How can you know what that age is?
- What are the responsibilities and privileges that you associate with being an adult?

Not so long ago, parents or older relatives bought your clothes and cleaned your room. Now you may choose your own clothes, clean your room and share in other chores. You no longer envy others or worry when people are mean: you are more likely to confront them and discuss the problem. You no longer beg a parent to stop for ice cream and, although you may not exhibit the best temper when something you don't like happens, you are growing and learning.

Some people feel that becoming an adult will be awful and think they will not have as much fun as they do now. Others feel there will be no more problems once they are adults. How do you feel about it?

As you grow older, you are given more privileges. You may do odd jobs or part-time jobs to help with the family income. You may get to stay up late or sit in on an adult conversation. You may get a driver's license. You may even become a voter. Being an adult, like being a young child, is an ongoing process.

As you grow you need to remember that getting what you want does not mean an end to your problems. As you grow older you need to take more responsibility for yourself. You have to try to solve your problems, and to adjust to pressures. If you do well at school you may be pressured to keep the standard high.

> **ACTIVITY**
>
> Your sister, who just turned 22, started acting up and feels like she is above counselling from her mom.
>
> Read through the list of indicators that may be used to determine the transition into adulthood to evaluate if your sister is really an adult.

BECOMING A RESPONSIBLE ADULT

You have responsibilities to yourself as well as to the other members of your family. A family relationship is one which you usually value and hold dear. Members of the family all have needs and where possible these needs must be met. For good family relationships, each member must try to accept the others' behaviour, as long as it does not hurt anyone. Where the behaviour is affecting others, the family should meet with the member to highlight the attitude and then work with the member to help to correct the issue.

> **ACTIVITIES**
>
> 1. Do you or any member of the family make demands on your parents?
> 2. Make a list of those demands/requests and share the list with your friends.
> 3. What were your parents' responses to these requests/demands?
> 4. Do these demands below sound familiar?
>   a. May I borrow the car for tonight?
>   b. May I stay out a little later?

Figure 1.8 Making a request

Parents cannot casually accept every demand or every request you make. They need to consider how mature you are before making their decision. They may want to consider whether you are playing a supportive role that would cause them to grant you the requests. Here are a few questions that parents could consider:

- Do you complete your tasks?
- Do you react positively to parental requests?
- Are you dependable?
- Can you handle yourself in difficult situations?
- Do you carry your load of household chores?
- Do you assist the family in achieving goals?

Parents may find it difficult to honour your requests if you repeatedly score negatively on these questions. You must be willing to earn the reputation of a responsible teenager in order for your parents to consider the requests. When you perform tasks and show responsibility in your achievements then you will gain the respect of your parents and all the people around you. When you deliberately choose to ignore rules and do things that you know are wrong, you must suffer the consequences or punishment for your actions. As you assume responsibility for your actions, other people will learn that you are becoming more dependable. Maturity is a process of development, which occurs throughout your life. You may mature physically, mentally and emotionally as you grow from infancy to adulthood.

DEALING WITH STRESS

Stress is one basic element of human life. Every person suffers from stress from time to time. It can be either positive or negative and can come from internal and external pressures and conflict. Stress is simply how your body responds to changes that are challenging and demanding. Stress may also be described as a person's reaction to a situation when they feel threatened or anxious. It is a mental or emotional state or tension resulting from adverse or demanding situations. Some signs of stress may include sweating palms, biting nails, cracking knuckles, trouble sleeping or feeling overwhelmed, to name a few.

> **ACTIVITIES**
> 1. List two ways in which you feel stressed.
> 2. How did you manage the situation?

During our lifetime, we will inevitably experience both positive and negative stress.

Positive stress is usually caused by excitement over a pleasant event or happening in your life and may include success in an examination or finishing college education, or passing an interview for a job.

Negative stress occurs when you feel extremely tense, insecure or frustrated and tend to be irritable and critical. This type of stress can also result from pressure to hurry up or slow down and may be mentally and emotionally disturbing. Some of the signs of negative stress are nervousness, a pounding heart, frequent headaches, rapid breathing and inability to sleep/concentrate.

A number of factors can affect your stress level. You should try to balance your activities and plan to keep your life in order. Habits and routine may be good but may become boring over a period of time. Your self-esteem can influence how you handle stress. You also need time and space for yourself.

COPING WITH STRESS

Stressful circumstances and situations sometimes get the better of us so that we become overwhelmed and mentally drained. But we can adjust to or tolerate these stressors in order to keep a positive self-image and a state of emotional equilibrium. Here are a few coping tips you can use to deal with stress:

- Find time for relaxation – meditate, read a book, take a walk, listen to music, do something that you enjoy to get your mind off of the stress.

- Eat a healthy diet.
- Exercise daily – this helps to release good hormones in the brain and improve sleep.
- Distance yourself from the source of the stress.
- Take vacations away from home and work.
- Get enough sleep, 7–8 hours, which helps you to focus and function better, thus reducing stress.
- Talking with a trusted friend about issues will ease the pain.
- Seek counselling if necessary.

You may find several other ways of coping with stress. The important thing is that you deal with stress in a positive manner so that you can feel good about yourself. Whatever kind of stress you are going through, it is your choice as to how you will react to it.

Some people do not handle stress well and may choose negative ways to deal with it. Harming yourself, turning to drugs and alcohol or harming other people will only increase your stress level and make you feel bad about yourself. Professional help must then be sought.

Population education

Have you ever considered how the government plans for the people and resources of the country? How do they know how many people to cater for? What kind and number of schools are needed for the nation's children? These are just a few of the questions related to the population that any government will need to find an answer to. These answers can only be found through a population **census**.

A population census is the process of counting the homes and the population living in a country. This is done to determine certain characteristics such as gender, age, activity, professions, types and quality of households, size and type of housing, modes of transport, daily travel. The census is generally performed every 5–10 years (this is dependent on the country's policy), and the information gathered is of interest to respective governments at all levels.

> How often have you had to travel in a crowded bus or taxi, and wondered when the situation will change? Have you ever had to wait in a line to collect a product or to be served at a Government Agency? The real problem seems to be that there are more people than there are buses. Similarly, whenever there is not enough of a commodity/customer service agents to supply people's needs, problems develop. In several parts of the world, population growth has been so rapid that a number of commodities are in short supply. This growth in population has caused much concern. As a result, population education has become a very important study.

Did you know?
Population education is the study of the relationship between people (population) and their environment. If these two factors were always in balance, there would be no problem. But as soon as the demands of the population exceed the resources of the natural environment a population problem arises.

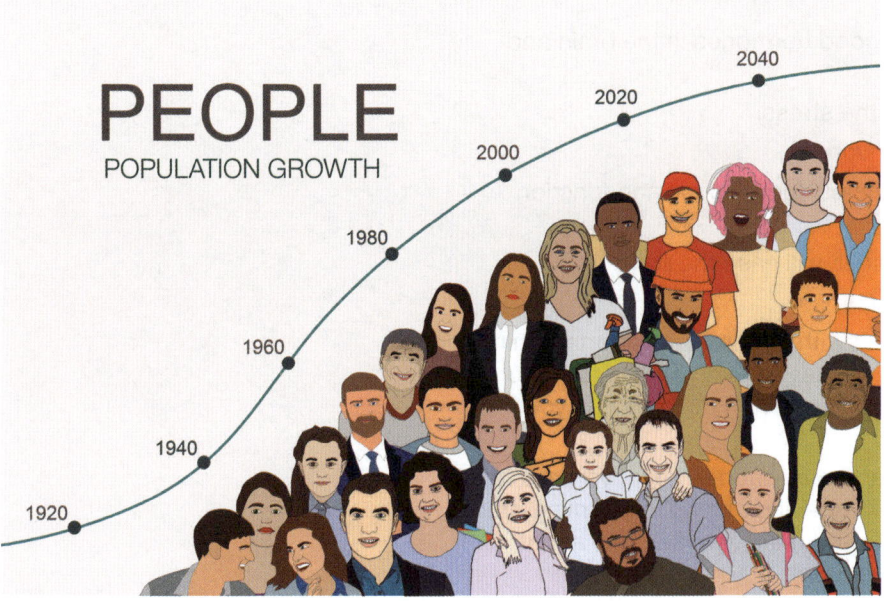

Figure 1.9 The population is on the increase.

Any study of population must have, as its key factor, a study of the family. Families must understand themselves so that they will be in a better position to cope with their resources at home and in the community. When a population is too big there is heavy demand on natural resources.

The population also affects the environment. As the population grows, there is more demand on resources. For instance, the demand for housing may require forest areas to be cleared to make land available for houses. Clearing land to build houses may seem like a logical thing to do, but it has far-reaching effects on the natural environment (such as loss of habitat for many species and soil erosion).

Plants supply us with oxygen during the day; they use the sun to help them convert carbon dioxide to oxygen and carbohydrates. Animals, including humans, take in oxygen and produce carbon dioxide. So, a balance should exist between the oxygen-producing plants and the carbon-dioxide-producing animals. However, fires, cars and factories also give off a considerable amount of carbon dioxide. If there are not enough plants to absorb all the carbon dioxide we produce, the composition of the air we breathe changes. The extra carbon dioxide in the atmosphere is causing the Earth to warm up. This is affecting the climate, and nobody knows what the result will be.

People also pollute water in rivers and streams by putting unwanted waste into them; this includes refuse, pesticides and fertilisers that run off from the land, especially in the rainy season, and seep into our water supply.

Consider this

- Can you think of other ways in which we destroy our natural environment?
- How is the environment affected?
- How can this practice be discontinued?

POPULATION GROWTH

In every country, governments try to find out how many people live in specific areas, so that they can try to provide facilities for them. How is this done? The people of an area are counted by government officers. This official count of the population is called a census and is conducted every 10 or so years. It does not always give an accurate figure, but it is a good guide.

Other ways have to be found to estimate the size of the population between one census and another. One of the methods used is the **crude birth rate** which measures the number of live babies born in one year for every 1000 people in the population. The birth rate is worked out using the following formula:

$$\text{Birth rate} = \frac{\text{number of live births in a year} \times 1000}{\text{population in the same year}}$$

The **crude death rate** can be worked out in a similar way:

$$\text{Death rate} = \frac{\text{total number of deaths in a year} \times 1000}{\text{population in the same year}}$$

Birth rates and death rates are not the only means by which a population can increase or decrease. People can also leave one country to go and live in another.

The number of people who enter a country in one year (**immigrants**) increase that country's population; those who leave (**emigrants**) help to decrease the population (Figure 1.10).

Since people come and go all the time, the population can be estimated by using a measure called the **net migration**. This is the difference between the number of people who enter the country in one year (**immigration**) and the number who leave (**emigration**).

Figure 1.10 Emigration and immigration

Birth and death rates are recorded so that accurate records can be kept.
- What is the name of the department where you receive your birth certificate?
- What other population records can be collected there?

Did you know?
The size of the population in any country is determined by four main factors:
1. birth rate
2. death rate
3. immigration
4. emigration.

Population education

Many countries are now trying to control their population by encouraging families to limit the number of children they produce. When a country becomes overpopulated, natural resources become scarce.

WHAT IS OVERPOPULATION?

Problems arise when a population makes heavy demands on natural resources. But problems also arise when the other resources of a country, such as housing, money, schools, and hospitals – in fact, all the things you need to survive – are insufficient to meet the demands of the population of that country. When this happens, the country is **overpopulated**.

Most of the problems we have in the Caribbean arise because there are more people to feed, clothe, house, educate and find jobs for, than we can comfortably look after. If these basic needs are not met, this mostly leads to social and economic upheaval in communities. As a result, it is important for every country to put strategies in place to control and plan for their citizenry.

Figure 1.11 Imbalance

Planning the family

For many years, it was the practice to have as many children as possible. Today women realise that they have other functions in life apart from having children. Research and family planning have shown how families can be planned and controlled. People can now plan to have only the number of children that they can afford.

Planning to have a child can be an exciting and delightful experience but taking on the responsibility of parenthood comes with its own hardships. Couples need to understand that parenting is a long-term responsibility and so must decide whether they are able to care for and educate their children. When children are brought into the world, they need happy, emotionally secure parents. Couples must also understand that they have to be mature enough and prepared to make responsible decisions regarding the use of their resources; money, time and **energy** in order to effectively carry out their roles as parents.

Having fewer children allows for more time and energy, and better allocation of resources. As part of planning for a family, the health of both mother and child is likely to be better when pregnancies are spaced with at least two years between each one. This is one way of improving the quality of life for individuals and families.

Family planning should be a shared experience between husband and wife because if both plan together, then it is more likely that the arrival of the baby will be a happier experience.

Consider this

Preventing teenage pregnancy should be a national priority for all countries as it impacts population control, dropout rates among high school females, health and foster care costs, and a myriad of social, economic, and developmental problems for any society.

Effective strategies for preventing teenage pregnancy can utilise family and community-based education programmes that will improve social development, responsible sexual behaviour education, and improved contraceptive counselling and delivery.

ACTIVITIES

1. Do you know anyone who started high school with you and has since dropped out due to pregnancy?
2. How did that make you feel?
3. What strategies have you put in place to ensure that you are not a victim of teenage pregnancy?

Did you know?

When deciding on a contraceptive method, it is advised to consider choosing a dual protection method, which protects people from the risk for HIV and other sexually transmitted illnesses (STIs), as well as pregnancy. Some contraceptives are only effective at preventing pregnancy, they do not protect against STIs, including HIV.

FAMILY PLANNING METHODS

Several methods of limiting or planning the size of a family are available. These methods of planning or limiting the family are called **contraception**. Contraceptives are available for males and females, and their use helps to prevent pregnancy. The choice of method for couples who are planning their family may be influenced by many factors, including their religious beliefs, individual preferences, ages and existing family.

ACTIVITIES

Create a brochure of the following contraceptive methods:
- intrauterine device (IUD) method
- hormonal methods
- barrier methods
- permanent methods of birth control
- natural or biological methods.

THE ARRIVAL OF A BABY

Although several birth control methods have been highlighted, the possibility exists that pregnancy may still occur since most of the methods cannot guarantee full protection. In the event that pregnancy occurs, the family must be prepared to accept the arrival of a new family member.

People sometimes refer to a new baby in the family as a 'bundle of joy'. This bundle of joy does not last a lifetime since raising a child also comes with challenges. To receive a newborn in the family involves serious adjustments and preparation for all family members. When parents plan for the pregnancy and the arrival of the baby, the level of enthusiasm is quite welcoming and the adjustment is positive. On the other hand, however, if the pregnancy was not planned and is unwanted, then the arrival of the baby can be quite unwelcoming for the family. Consequently, the period of adjustment can be frustrating. Such a situation can have serious effects on both the newborn baby and the family.

Parents

In Book 1, you learnt about the family life cycle, which are the stages that a family goes through during their lifetime. You also became aware that adjustments must be made at every stage in the life cycle. At the expanding stage, when the couple becomes parents, they must make several adjustments in the family relationship. In other words, they have to make significant changes to their lifestyle, as they are now required to take on roles and responsibilities that they are not accustomed to.

Adjustments include:

- sharing of household chores
- feeding the baby
- social and economic situations
- sleep patterns
- relationship.

It is critical that couples are prepared for parenthood before taking on this new role. They should have already grown accustomed to each other before bringing in a newborn because this responsibility requires serious adjustment to effectively care for the baby.

It is believed that some men in the Caribbean seem to feel that looking after babies or children is a woman's job and so might not take on the full responsibility for the care of the newborn. This task is much easier and more rewarding if both parents take a keen interest in the welfare of the child (Figure 1.12). In addition to the parents, other members in the family should also be prepared for the baby's arrival. There needs to be a period of orientation — a period when family members are told what to expect and what to do when the baby arrives.

If there is another child in the family, special care must be taken to prepare them for the new arrival. A child who is accustomed to being the baby in the family will naturally become jealous and have problems accepting the new baby unless they are actively involved in the preparation for the baby. If this is not done, the child may behave in a cruel way towards the baby. Perhaps you have seen an older child cry each time his mother picks up the baby. It is likely that this child was not prepared for the arrival of the baby, and therefore feels jealous and neglected.

Figure 1.12 Caring for a the child is much easier if both parents are involved.

ACTIVITY

Problem-solving

Imagine that a mentor whom you admire has a three-month-old baby and you suddenly realise that she communicates less with you because she has a hectic work schedule. What can you do to improve the relationship?

Preparation for baby's arrival

When a couple is anticipating the birth of their child there are number of things that must be put in place before the mother's due date. Setting up the baby's room is a fun way to help the couple prepare their home for the new arrival. As part of the preparation, the couple should get the baby's room ready by decorating and organising the space.

Baby's room

Figure 1.13 An example of a baby's room

At this stage, the baby will not be able to fully appreciate the décor of the room because all that they are interested in is food, sleep, and comfort. However, this does not mean that the room should be dull and dreary. Instead, the room should be bright and cheerful, and furniture should be placed to make caring for the baby easy.

Some essential items to have in the baby's room include a crib and a storage chest for clothes. Additionally, any surface that the baby might come into contact with should be free of sharp edges or other hazards that could cause injury.

Not every family can afford to have a separate room in the house for the baby, so one corner of the parents' room is usually arranged with the baby's furniture, clothes and other belongings. Most mothers prefer to have their babies close to them anyway. They are then able to keep an eye on the baby and it is easier to feed or change the baby during the night.

Before mother leaves for hospital

The thought of giving birth sometimes comes with some amount of anxiety especially for first-time mothers who do not know what to expect. The delivery of your baby is a time when you will likely be staying away from home for at least 24–48 hours for a normal vaginal delivery, between two to four days for a caesarean delivery and sometimes longer if complications develop during delivery.

It is also good to get the information regarding what the hospital or birthing centre will provide, so that one only packs what is necessary. Additionally, before the mother leaves for the hospital, she must make preparations for the other children in the family. Someone needs to be at the home before the mother or mother-to-be leaves to go to the hospital, because the child or children will need someone to help take care of them, especially if the father cannot manage alone.

When the baby comes home

The addition of baby to the family brings new responsibilities for the first-time parents. These responsibilities involve 'round-the-clock' care, including the tasks of feeding, changing diapers, bathing and cuddling the baby and cleaning the baby's clothing (Figure 1.14).

When the mother returns from the hospital, she will need the support of family members to assist with the regular chores and with the baby. Caring for a baby can be a challenging and demanding task, especially when combined with other responsibilities that family members may have. To make this easier, it is best for both parents to share the responsibility of taking care of the baby. This can make the tasks more fulfilling and rewarding, and it can also help to encourage siblings and other relatives to get involved and help out. By sharing the care of the baby, everyone in the family can play a role in supporting the new addition to the family and ensuring that the baby's needs are met.

The more aware and involved the siblings are, the better they will adjust to the new arrival. This acceptance helps to reduce jealous feelings and aggression towards the baby.

A baby needs all the love and attention it can get at this stage because these are the most critical years of their life. The impressions made on the child during these first years will be lasting ones.

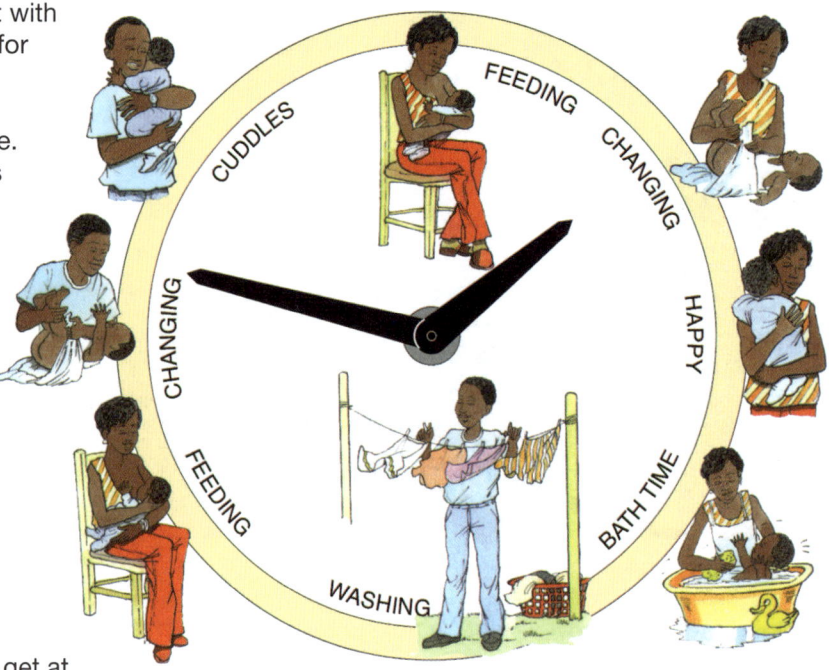

Figure 1.14 A baby involves many new responsibilities, which go on around the clock.

Baby's habits and routine

For most individuals, their lives are centred on a series of patterns and routines that they perform almost every day; eating breakfast at a certain time, reading the newspaper, tending to the garden and so on. Parents play a significant role in creating patterns in their children's lives, and these routines impact the children's development.

The habits that babies develop begin very early in their lives and were cultivated through interaction with their parents. For instance, the baby, with the mother's help, will settle into a specific feeding pattern. This means that the baby will feed every two or three hours. Sleeping and bathing will also have a specific schedule. The mother must adjust her own time schedule to accommodate her baby's schedule.

Husbands should help their wives by adjusting to new roles and responsibilities and limiting unnecessary demands. They should be fully involved in sharing tasks, which will allow for more time to be spent together. These adjustments and changes usually only last until the baby has grown up and can manage on their own. However, if there are development issues, the baby may not progress normally, which may require special care for a longer time. You will learn more about childcare and development in Chapter 4.

Family social life

With a baby in the family, parents are more restricted in their movements. The couple might be accustomed to going to parties or plays, but these activities will have to be curtailed and other means of entertainment be considered. This could include a movie night with friends, barbeques, game nights or a romantic dinner at home.

As the baby gets older, they could be left with family members in order to allow for the parents to spend some time alone.

Career corner
Social worker

A social worker helps vulnerable people in our society to work through and find solutions to the challenges faced in daily life. The support offered by social workers touches all areas of society. For example, children, at-risk youths, people who are neurodivergent (when the brain works differently to the average way), people with chronic and terminal illnesses, people dealing with loss and so on.

Pursuing a career in social work

There are several diploma and degree programmes available for people interested in a career in social work. If you want to explore social work but are not sure if it is the career for you, you can complete free online courses offered by reputable colleges and universities.

In addition to the professional qualifications required, a social worker needs to be compassionate, sensitive and passionate about their work because it requires a lot of interaction with people when they are most vulnerable or when they need guidance and direction.

Figure 1.15 A social worker interacting with a child to see how she feels

Do it yourself
DESIGN PROJECT

Your classmate, who shares your strong Christian values, confided in you that she is planning to have sex with her high school boyfriend because her friends have been sharing their exciting experiences with her. She is worried about the potential consequences of getting pregnant or contracting STIs.

Use your knowledge of contraceptive and population control to make a presentation to a group of teenagers regarding what course of action they should take to prevent teenage pregnancy.

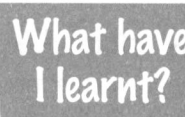

Multiple choice questions

Select the letter that corresponds with your answer.

1. Which of the following is MOST effective in reducing the population growth rate?
   A Providing access to education and family planning services
   B Encouraging healthy habits and reducing infant mortality
   C Investing in sustainable development and clean energy
   D Helping individuals and couples to make informed decisions about their reproductive health

2. Which formula represents the birth rate?
   A Number of death + emigration
   B Total number of birth + immigration
   C $\dfrac{\text{Number of live births in a year} \times 1000}{\text{population in the same year}}$
   D $\dfrac{\text{Total number of mortalities in a year} \times 1000}{\text{population in the same year}}$

3. Which of these methods of contraceptive is considered permanent?
   A Vasectomy
   B IUD
   C Diaphragm
   D Implants

4. Which is NOT a type of friendship?
   A Acquaintances
   B Family
   C Collegial
   D Casual

5. All of the following are reasons for ending friendship EXCEPT;
   A Competition
   B Gossiping
   C Wearing off
   D Standard differences

6. Which of the following statements describes a census?
   i   It is conducted every 10 years
   ii The number of live babies born in one year
   iii When people come and go in the country
   iv The official count of the population
   A i, iii
   B ii, iii
   C i, iv
   D ii, iv

7. Stress is one basic element of human life.
   Which of the following is NOT recommended for relieving stress?
   A Eat a healthy diet
   B Stay away from family
   C Find time for relaxation
   D Get enough sleep and exercise

8 Which of the following roles must new parents adjust to when the new baby arrives?
- A Cuddles
- B Changing
- C Feeding
- D All of the above

Short answer questions

1 Outline the various features in the history of Caribbean people that give them their unique perspective on family living.

2 Describe ways in which black people, during the days of slavery, were denied the happiness and fulfilment of family life.

3 Name two aspects of Caribbean life today that are likely to improve the well-being of children.

4 Explain why your family is important to you.

5 What does the emotional support of your family teach you?

6 What complaints do you have about your parents? If you were in their place, what would you do differently?

7 What are some of the traits that cause problems in making friends?

8 Why is it important that both parents are involved in the care of a child?

9 Discuss the factors that determine how a population grows/changes.

Chapter 2 Family management

Figure 2.1 Management in the family

People everywhere rely on aspects of the management processes in their daily activities without even realising it. For example, individuals and families organise their day's activities and work out a plan as to how to achieve them. The management processes assist individuals and families in managing their activities by deciding on the actions to take to ensure that tasks are accomplished. One aspect of family management is making decisions regarding the type of housing and the community where they will choose to live. Access to satisfactory housing is a basic human need for shelter. It is considered to be the fundamental factor for safety, which also contributes to the well-being of both parents and children. In Chapter 1, you learnt about family living and being a member of a family. Now we need to understand what management in the family and home means.

- Research the management processes that your family makes use of daily.
- Write a paragraph about the types of decision that were considered by your family before your family housing was selected.
- Sketch your future dream house.

In order for anyone or an activity to succeed, it is important that a plan is made on what, how and by when this activity is to be achieved and what are the desired goals. If anyone tries to take up a business or a task without a goal or a plan, they will fail because they are not prepared for the processes.

In this chapter, you will:

* demonstrate efficient use of management processes
* formulate solutions that reflect the effective use of time and energy
* demonstrate appropriate work simplification techniques
* describe the types of housing available in the Caribbean
* outline the many characteristic features of the different types of housing
* assess the family's needs for furnishing in all areas of the home
* recognise the various household tasks to be accomplished
* describe how to treat common accidents, which occur in the home.

Management process

MANAGEMENT PROCESSES DEFINED

Management processes may be defined as setting goals and using resources wisely (human and non-human) to achieve these goals.

A management process is a series of steps that are used to manage an activity or a project in order to achieve a stated goal. It involves setting goals, planning, organising, implementing, controlling and evaluating. These sets of interconnected functions are necessary, to accomplish desired objectives.

A management process is a structured, systematic and interrelated approach that individuals, families, and managers make use of as they plan the details, organise the resources, allocate resources, and control the activity to achieve optimal results.

Features of the management process
- It consists of a series of continuous and related activities.
- It focuses on reaching goals.
- It works with people and resources in order to achieve goals.

Figure 2.2 Management goals

Management processes

Management consists of five functions: planning, organising, implementing, controlling and evaluating. These functions are built on practices and theories, which help people to be successful.

Developing an understanding of these will help you to focus your efforts on activities that will be successful. Figure 2.3 shows a summary of the five functions of the successful management of activities and businesses.

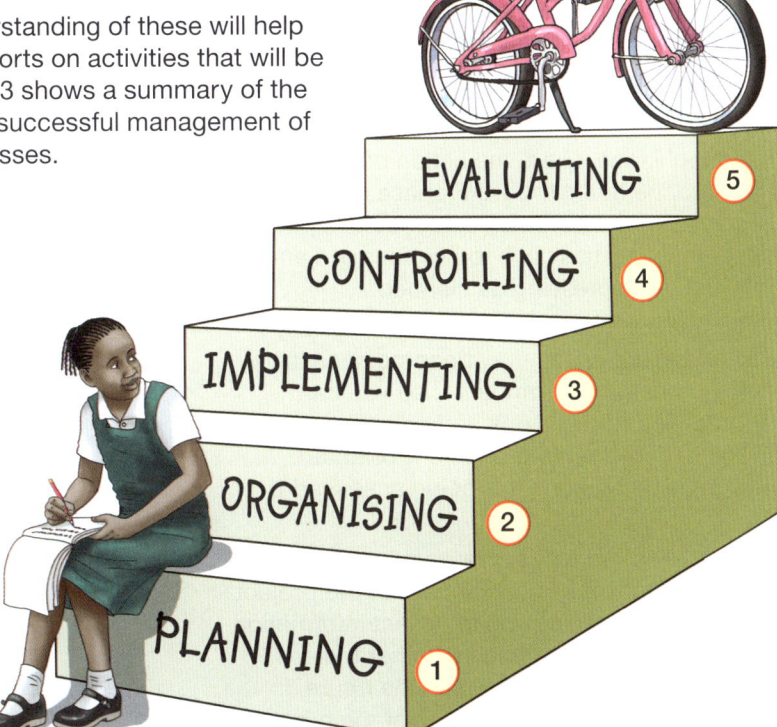

Figure 2.3 The management process

Planning: This is the first step in the management process. It involves choosing or identifying goals and developing actions to pursue them by determining the appropriate resources and strategies that are needed to achieve the goals. At this stage of the process, you have to decide on the following:

The WHAT – what your activity or project will be?

The WHY – why do you want to carry out this project or activity?

The HOW – how will this be done, what steps do you need to take?

Here are some questions you could ask yourself as you work through the planning stage:

- What project am I doing?
- Why do I need to carry out this project?
- How can it be done?
- Who will be involved?
- Where will it take place?
- When will I do it?
- What are the resources that I need to carry out this activity?
- Where will the resources come from?

These questions and answers will assist you in refining your goals and ultimately the plan of action that you develop.

Organising: Once you have decided on a project or activity, it becomes necessary to feed that plan with what it needs to function. You have to decide on the resources to be used to achieve the stated goal. These involve personnel, raw materials, tools, capital and other resources.

Organising as a function involves several elements, these include:

- identifying the activity to be carried out
- classifying and grouping the tasks in an efficient way
- identifying and providing the resources needed for completing the tasks
- creating and scheduling responsibilities by developing work teams
- assigning/delegating responsibilities based on tasks to be accomplished
- coordinating authority and responsibility relationships.

Implementing: The 'sets it in motion' stage where the action of planning and organising have now moved into the doing the work phase. This is where you are now required to carry out the activities that you have planned and organised. During this phase, the activities have to be managed and supported to ensure that the project is progressing as planned.

Controlling: Involves evaluating how well you are achieving your goals, then improving the efficiency by taking actions. It may become necessary to put processes in place to help you establish standards, so you can measure, compare, and make 'on the spot' decisions and adjustments in order to keep the project on track. Implementing and controlling are interrelated because while the work is being done it is being assessed to ensure high performance.

Evaluating: Assessing how well a project/activity achieves its objectives. It is the assessment of the relevance, effectiveness and impact of the project in relation to its stated goals. This process allows you to collect information about the project/activities, the outcome and to decide whether there is a need to make adjustments to improve its effectiveness in the future. In summary, you are assessing the strengths and weaknesses of the project in an attempt to make improvements. A checklist would be useful in assessing the effectiveness of the project.

ACTIVITIES

Your family is planning a road trip as part of their leisure activity.
* Use the management processes to effectively carry out this activity.
* Use the template below as your guide.

FAMILY ROAD TRIP				
Planning	Organising	Implementing	Controlling	Evaluating
What is to be done?	How will it be done?	How is it being done?	How well is it being done?	What adjustment can be made?
• Goals • Resources • Personnel • Schedule				

IMPORTANCE OF TIME MANAGEMENT

Figure 2.4 The clock is at the centre of time management.

Time is a treasured resource that is given equally to everyone. We all get the same 24 hours in a day. We have to decide how we manage the 24 hours in order to make wise use of our time.

It is believed that people who manage their time well are also able to manage their lives well. Have you ever wondered how some people are able to get a lot done in a day, whereas others seem so overwhelmed with work? It is as a result of how people handle their time. There is a saying; *time wasted cannot be regained.* As a result, good time management is critical to the success of daily living.

As we prepare to use time efficiently, here are a few key concepts to consider:

- Time is intangible; it cannot be touched, but can be measured in terms of hours, minutes and seconds.
- Time keeps moving forwards; it cannot move backwards as it has one direction.
- Time is the same; it is finite, everyone has the same 24 hours in one day.
- Time is irreversible; if you waste time you can never get it back.
- Time is an irreplaceable asset; it is more valuable than money.

Did you know?
People everywhere at some point in their lives have regrets about not using their time wisely. Possibly, they have not completed their assigned tasks, have missed deadlines, have been late for the bus or just have not planned their time efficiently.

ACTIVITIES
1. List two ways in which you feel stressed.
2. How did you manage the situation?

Time management
Time management is an individual's ability to use time effectively and productively. It may also be described as an approach to organising and planning how you divide your time among different activities.

Good time management principles
There are five important time management principles. These will help to keep you on track. Learn how to use them in your daily life.

1 Prioritising
Make a list of the activities or tasks to be done, then rank them in order of importance and then dedicate time for each task. You have to decide which task is most important and deal with that first. For example, if you have to prepare dinner and supervise your brother who is a toddler, you will have to decide which of the tasks is more important.

2 Keep focus

In order to achieve your goals, you have to maintain your focus. The following acronym can assist you with staying on course (DO-IT-NOW).

D = Divide big tasks into little tasks and give each part of that task a realistic timeline.

O = Organise your resources.

I = Ignore interruptions and distractions.

T = Train. Take the time to learn to do things yourself.

N = Now. Don't procrastinate.

O = Optimise opportunity. Take advantage of opportunities.

W = Watch out for time gobblers. Keep track of how much time you spend on the internet, or talking on the phone.

3 Scheduling

You have examined your list of activities and have ranked them in order, it is now time to dedicate time to each activity, as timing means efficiency. Create realistic deadlines.

It pays to complete tough tasks while you have the energy and the interest, especially in the mornings. This should allow more time for simpler tasks. For instance, you might want to complete an assignment in the morning and take up household chores later in the day.

4 Goal setting

Successful managers and families usually set clear targets and work towards achieving them. These goals are usually specific, measurable, achievable, relevant and time-bound (SMART). In order to achieve the objectives, time has to be allocated effectively for the activities.

5 Decision-making

It is important to identify exactly what needs to be done after weighing the alternatives. Put all the necessary strategies in place to achieve the objectives.

The benefits of good time management

When you know how to manage your time effectively, it will be beneficial to you in the following ways:

- more productivity and efficiency
- reduced stress
- better chances for advancement in your career
- feeling more in control on how best to use your time
- feeling more relaxed and able to think rationally.

Balance your life by spending the 24 hours that you have in a day wisely.

ACTIVITIES

Robert is a sixth form student, who is involved in a lot of extracurricular activity at school, he is also the captain of his church Bible quiz team and plays on his community basketball team. He is also preparing for CAPE examinations. Having to do all of these activities overwhelms him at times.

1. Use the strategies outlined for good time management to assist Robert in managing his time wisely.
2. Outline at least five benefits of good time management.

WORK SIMPLIFICATION AND MOTION MINDEDNESS TECHNIQUES

Working in the home involves various tedious, time consuming and wearisome tasks that require different types of skills. In order to effectively and efficiently complete these activities, it is necessary to find the easiest and quickest way to do so.

There are two approaches, which if adopted, can help families to save energy and time. These include:

- work simplification
- motion mindedness.

Work simplification is using a variety of strategies to make work easier, faster, simpler. In other words, work smarter, not harder!

Motion mindedness is based on economy of movement. This can only be achieved by understanding the movements involved in an activity and finding ways to decrease the number of movements. For example, by having all the utensils and ingredients needed for making a sandwich within reach on the kitchen counter, you reduce the number of trips to the refrigerator and cabinets.

Research is also where crucial elements of a design or solution become clear.

ACTIVITIES

Use the internet to learn more about work simplification and motion mindedness techniques. Then use that information to show how you can apply the techniques to an everyday household chore.

Housing for the family

In Book 1, you studied the way in which homes satisfy some basic needs and noted that the place a family chooses to raise their children is more than just an address or four walls; it will ultimately impact who they are, how they see themselves and who they become in the future.

Housing serves as a place where the family can come together and feel secure from the ills of the outside environment. It is a safe space to feel comfortable and to talk about anything without any judgements or comments.

Any family who is thinking about acquiring a place to live will have to explore a wide range of options, since the types, sizes and arrangements vary significantly. Having a comprehensive knowledge of the different types of houses can assist greatly in deciding which type suits your family best.

Several types of houses are available in the Caribbean. Each type has distinctive features.

Did you know?
The two main parameters that classify a home are the structure type and the style of the house. The structure refers to the type of building, like a single-family home or a condo, whereas the style refers to the architectural features and design.

Different types of houses

 single-family
 townhouse
 multi-family
 condos and co-ops

modular home   bungalow   ranch home

Figure 2.5 Different types of houses

Consider this

Whether you are planning to buy or rent a property, the first thing you should do to narrow down your search is to have a clear idea of the types of houses available to you. The following options are available in most Caribbean countries:

Single family dwelling | **Multiple family dwelling**

- bungalows
- cottages
- ranch
- split level

Overlap:
- row or terrace houses
- townhouses
- duplexes
- semi-detached houses

Multiple family dwelling only:
- apartments
- condominiums

ACTIVITIES

1.
   a. Do some research to learn what is meant by types of dwellings that are available to families.

   b. In your groups, use the information to role play one of the following scenarios:
      i. a newly married couple talking to a home loan officer about the pros and cons of purchasing a single family or multiple dwelling
      ii. parents with a pre-teen child and another on the way who live in an apartment and are considering moving to a single dwelling
      iii. a grandparent living in a ranch style house but is thinking of moving into a multiple dwelling, which still allows them to enjoy some outdoor space.

2. Imagine that you are an adult with or without a family and have set a goal to buy a new dwelling in a few years. Use the management process to show how you could buy a dwelling that is affordable and suitable for your needs.

Housing for the family

Career corner
Real estate agent

Who is a real estate agent?
A real estate agent or realtor is a licensed professional who helps people when they want to buy, sell, lease, or rent residential or commercial property.

Is a real estate agent necessary for a real estate transaction?
Real estate transactions can be time consuming, expensive and complicated, so it is best to work with people who can use their expertise to give sound advice and help you to avoid costly mistakes.

What are the qualifications needed to become a realtor?
Each country has its own requirements, which must be met before a person can legally operate as a real estate agent; however, generally most countries require successful completion of a real estate training course at a recommended training institution.

CHOOSING YOUR COMMUNITY

Wherever a family decides to live, the neighborhood or locality will depend on a number of factors. Many people like to live near their work, while others prefer any area where they can have easy access to a number of essential facilities, such as the hospital, church, supermarket and government offices. Others prefer to live in quiet areas away from the crowds.

As was mentioned in Book 1, when a family decides to set up a home, this is a major management decision. Because the housing needs of families are different, the family's values and goals will influence the type of housing selected. Other factors include those in the following text.

Environmental factor: Will there be flooding in the area during the rainy season? Is there good drainage for floodwater to run off? Will there be water problems resulting in the cost of a water tank and electrical pump? Is the area susceptible to landslides? Is the maintenance cost going to be high due to the sea blast? Will there be a threat during tropical storms?

The social environment: The social environment is of equal importance. Questions to be asked should be: Is it a location primarily for young families? Are the ideals and lifestyles of the residents similar to your own?

FURNISHING YOUR HOME

Whatever type of housing you choose, your next task is to furnish it. This can be done over a period of time and the following guidelines can help you to make good choices.

- Prioritise your needs.
- Do not buy impulsively.
- Shop around to compare prices.
- Choose a reputable dealer.
- Consider the cost of installing and operating the piece of equipment.
- Select equipment which you will be able to use and keep in good condition.
- Read all instructions carefully before purchasing. Keep them handy and read them whenever necessary.

The wrong choice of equipment or furniture will lead to a waste of money, time and energy, and a very dissatisfied family. Let us now look at some points to consider when furnishing your kitchen.

ACTIVITIES

Conduct a survey of your community (type of housing; geography/topography; demography/family types; infrastructure – schools, shops, roads). Record the type of facilities present and the adequacy of the facilities.

Figure 2.6 The homemaker's guidepost should be used when choosing items for the home.

Did you know?
Darker colours are becoming trendy for kitchens as well as stones such as granite, marble, limestone and quartz for kitchen counters and surfaces.

KITCHEN PLANNING

In the past, most kitchens were small rooms some distance away from the house. Today, the kitchen forms a part of the house and is used generally for meal preparation. It should therefore be planned to accommodate some essential kitchen furniture. The basic layout of a well-planned kitchen should follow this pattern in Figure 2.7:

Figure 2.7 The perfect work surface sequence

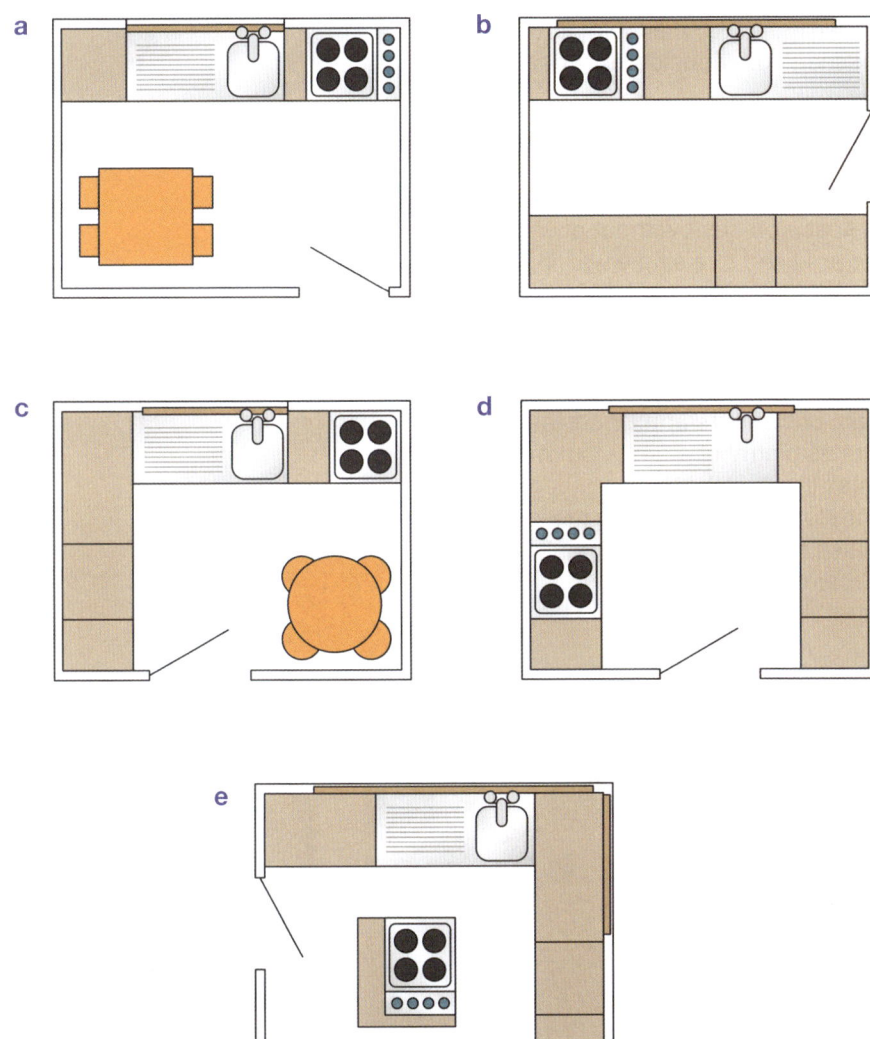

Figure 2.8 The work triangle: (a) single line or one side layout, (b) corridor/gallery layout, (c) L-shaped layout, (d) U-shaped layout, (e) island layout

Housing for the family

Principles of kitchen layout
- The kitchen should also be designed according to certain principles.
- The main items, such as sink, cooker and refrigerator should be placed to form a comfortable work triangle. See Figure 2.8 on page 51.
- The height of the work surface is important and should be considered carefully.
- The standard kitchen base unit is 900 mm (2 ft 11 in) high. This is considered the most comfortable working height for most people.
- Walls, floors and work surfaces should be hard-wearing and easy to clean.
- There should be sufficient storage space and the room should be cheerful and inviting.
- The sink, cooker and work surface can be arranged in an L-shape, a U-shape or a straight line (Figure 2.8).

Kitchen layout
Deciding on the right kitchen layout is the most important factor in ensuring an efficient and practical kitchen area. The size of the kitchen does not matter; a clever and appropriate layout will make the difference in making the most of the space. Kitchen ergonomics, which is the science of designing the environment to fit the people, should be considered when designing a great kitchen.

The work triangle measures the efficiency of any kitchen, as it creates a clear path between the area for food preparation (stove), the washing up area (sink) and the food storage area (refrigerator).

One wall or straight: This simple layout is space efficient without giving up on functionality, as cabinets and appliances are fixed to a single wall in this space-saving layout, found mainly in studio or loft spaces.

The L-shape kitchen: This layout consists of countertops on two adjoining walls that are perpendicular, forming an L. The L-shaped kitchen offers great creativity in the arrangement of appliances and work zones.

U-shape kitchen: This layout has three walls of cabinets/appliances and is great for larger kitchens. This type of layout has plenty of storage but can feel cluttered if there are upper cabinets on all three walls.

The island kitchen: A large work surface or storage area is set in the middle of the kitchen. This design incorporates a cooking surface, sink and bar. It can also be used simply as a preparation area or for dining. The kitchen space must be big enough to incorporate an island.

Figure 2.9 shows the four layouts.

One Wall

L-shaped

U-shaped

Island

Figure 2.9 Kitchen layouts

> **ACTIVITIES**
>
> Your parents are considering remodelling their kitchen to make it more ergonomically friendly.
>
> Recommend the layout that is most suitable for the space available, and for the users of the space. Justify your choice(s).

Safety features

Although the kitchen can be dangerous, accidents do not have to occur if safety practices and procedures are adhered to strictly, as these help to keep the household safe during kitchen usage.

Whatever layout is chosen, certain safety features should be kept in mind when planning it.

- Cookers should not be placed too close to windows where sudden gusts of wind may blow out gas flames, or where sparks may ignite gas containers.
- Work surfaces should be made of materials that are easily cleaned and heat resistant. Plastic laminates such as Formica are ideal. If a wooden surface is used, it should be scrubbed weekly.
- Wall surfaces should be able to withstand steam and grease. Washable gloss paints in light colours are best suited to the tropics and can easily be cleaned with soap and water.
- Floors should be level, hard-wearing and easily cleaned. Always clean spills immediately to avoid accidents.
- Ensure that all work surfaces, storage areas and floors are well lit. Fluorescent lighting is ideal for kitchens and is less expensive to use.
- There should be adequate space to prevent overcrowding of work surfaces and to ensure a neat and tidy appearance at all times.
- Fabrics for curtains and kitchen towels should be chosen wisely. Hang them carefully to avoid any accidents. Such items can make the kitchen a cheerful and inviting place for the family.

Kitchen equipment

Shopping for the right equipment for your kitchen can be a challenging task because of many options available. However, selecting the right kitchen appliances and dinnerware does not always have to be that difficult, as long as you follow some general guidelines.

The kitchen sink

Sinks are available in different arrangements of bowls and draining boards (Figure 2.10).

A modern one-piece sink and draining board is efficient, easy to clean and will not collect dirt and bacteria. The kitchen sink may be made of one of the following materials:

Stainless steel, which is resistant to rust, cannot chip, is easy to clean but expensive.

Enamelled steel, which is likely to chip but less expensive.

Plastic or fibreglass, which is not for hard-wearing, everyday use and may be damaged by very hot pans.

Whatever type of sink you choose, sink bowls should be at least 18 cm (7 in) deep.

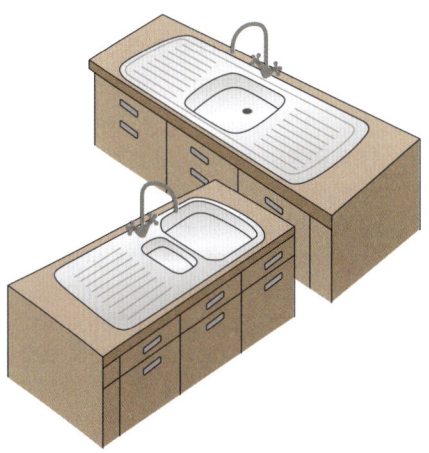

Figure 2.10 Different arrangements of bowls and draining boards

Cooking equipment

The type of cooking equipment you choose will depend on:

- Energy/fuel efficiency – the kind of fuel available in your area as well as whether the equipment chosen is energy efficient. Choosing the most efficient one will result significant financial savings.
- Amount of money available to be spent will be a deciding factor on the choice of the equipment.
- Size – this is dependent on the space in your kitchen layout, as well as your cooking needs.
- Ease of use and care – cooking equipment that you choose should be easy to use. You should also bear in mind ergonomics and ease of cleaning.

The coal pot

The coal pot (Figure 2.11) is the simplest and least expensive type of cooking equipment you can use. The fuel is charcoal, which is easily bought in most rural districts. This method of cooking is, however, only suitable for one-pot meals and limits the capabilities for meal preparation. It must also be cleaned after each use. Care must be taken to ensure that it is kept out of the reach of young children.

Figure 2.11 The coal pot

The kerosene cooker

Kerosene is a less expensive fuel than gas or electricity because the fuel that is used is kerosene oil. This type of cooker can be quite hazardous if not properly used, therefore, care must be taken when filling fuel containers attached to these cookers. The storage containers for the kerosene should be locked away as far as possible from the cooker.

Kerosene cookers (Figure 2.12) come in table-top models with two or three burners and may incorporate an oven. It is not easy to maintain an even temperature with a kerosene oven, but the hottest part of the oven will be at the top. This type of cooker has been replaced by the gas or electric cookers.

Figure 2.12 Kerosene cooker

The gas cooker

The gas cooker is more efficient than the kerosene cooker and more easily cleaned than the coal pot. Gas cookers are made of enamelled steel and are available in a variety of colours to match your kitchen décor. The models range from table-top style to others with two ovens, four to six large burners, automatic controls and clock timers. The cooker is made up of three parts.

- **The hot plate or burners.** There are usually four or six, which may vary in size and can be easily removed for cleaning.
- **The grill.** This may be found at either eye level, waist level or floor level. The top of an eye-level grill canopy can be used as a plate warmer.
- **The oven.** See Figure 2.13. This may be lined with non-stick material, or in more expensive models may have a continuous, automatic cleaning action. Some gas ovens are ignited electrically.

The hottest part of the gas oven is at the top, whereas the bottom of the oven is cooler. Foods that normally require different cooking temperatures can therefore be cooked at the same time. Some models include a removable drop-down door for easier cleaning, as well as an inner glass door so that you can watch the food while it cooks.

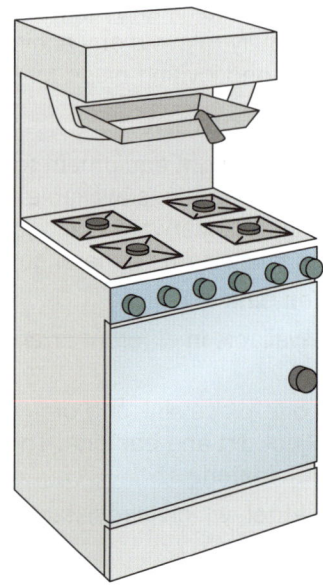

Figure 2.13 The oven

The electric cooker

The electric cooker requires users to have a reliable electricity supply. Like a gas cooker, the electric cooker (Figure 2.14) is made up of different parts.

The hot plate or burners

Electric stoves may have two to four burners of varying sizes or the same size, which are thermostatically controlled to allow food to cook at required temperatures. Use flat-bottom pans made of strong materials for the best results.

The grill: As with gas cookers, the grill can be either eye- or waist-level.

The oven: This maintains a more even temperature than gas or kerosene ovens. Automatic controls and timers are available on most models. Some have a continuous cleaning action, which maintains a high temperature. A self-locking door acts as a safety precaution during this process.

The split-level cooker

The split-level cooker can be built into the kitchen during construction. It is efficient, easy to clean and may use a combination of gas and electricity (Figure 2.15). It is practical, as the oven is usually placed at eye level, which means you do not have to bend when cooking or cleaning. However, it is twice as expensive as a conventional type of cooker.

The refrigerator

The refrigerator is the ideal place for storing food. The low temperature allows food to be kept free from bacterial spoilage for longer periods. The refrigerator maintains a temperature a few degrees above the freezing point of water. The temperature range for perishable food storage is 3 to 5 °C (37 to 41 °F). A similar device that maintains a temperature below the freezing point of water is called a freezer. Domestic refrigerators and freezers for food storage are available in a range of sizes and styles.

The refrigerator allows households to keep food fresh for long periods depending on the perishability of the food. Freezers allow people to buy perishable food in bulk for storage so that these foods can still be enjoyed even while they are out of season.

There is a wide variety of refrigerators to choose from, but your choice will depend mainly upon the needs of your family, as well as on what you can afford.

The following are important facts on the correct use of the refrigerator.

- Follow the instructions as outlined in the manufacturer's manual as a guideline for setting the temperature for the refrigerator.
- Do not overcrowd the shelves; allow for free circulation of air.
- Open the refrigerator as little as possible to avoid the growth of micro-organisms caused by changes in the temperature.
- Never put hot foods into the refrigerator, as this raises the temperature and lessens the efficiency.
- Use plastic film or aluminum foil to protect food from drying out.
- Wrap or store strong-smelling foods in covered containers to avoid absorption of odours.
- Do not refrigerate fruit such as bananas and avocado pears, as they tend to go black. Red wine, cakes and pastries should also not be stored or chilled in the refrigerator.

Figure 2.14 The electric cooker

Figure 2.15 The split-level cooker

STORAGE IN THE HOME

In a well-organised home, it is essential for everything to have its place when not in use.

Items should be stored nearest to where they are to be used. For example, supplies and equipment for food preparation should be stored near the sink and cooker, crockery and cutlery for food service near the dining area.

Some of the items that need special storage space in the home are:

- dried food supplies
- kitchen equipment
- household cleaning materials and equipment
- household linen
- books and papers
- tools
- toys and games
- unused articles
- items for recycling
- refuse for disposal.

Figure 2.16 A well-organised kitchen

General rules for safe storage

- Keep food in tightly covered containers so that it is safe from flies and other insects. Store in a food cupboard, food safe or refrigerator.
- Store kitchen utensils and tools in well-ventilated cupboards. Keep knives safely out of the reach of young children.
- Label household cleaning materials clearly and place them out of the reach of children.
- Keep flammable liquids such as kerosene and gas in tightly covered containers and store in a cool, dry place.
- Store household linen and clothes in cool, dry, well-ventilated cupboards to prevent mildew and attack by moths.
- Books are best stored in a reasonably airtight glass-fronted bookcase to keep them free from dust and insects. Old newspapers can become a fire hazard if allowed to pile up. Use them for wrapping kitchen refuse.
- Toys should be put away (into boxes) immediately after use. They can cause accidents to children, as well as adults if left lying around. Store games used by all members of the family in an area where everyone can find them.
- Articles that are not used very often should be cleaned and then stored in boxes.
- Household refuse and items for recycling should be stored in special bins used only for that purpose. These should be strong, durable and well covered to prevent flies and animals from getting into them.

ACTIVITIES

Examine your own room and note the following aspects:
* Is adequate storage space available?
* In what ways can you improve the existing storage space?

SHARING HOUSEHOLD TASKS

Most young people have some responsibility for sharing family tasks and one of the most important tasks is cleaning the house. A knowledge of basic skills combined with the wise use of time and energy will result in a clean and orderly home.

One way to accomplish this is to plan a schedule based on daily, weekly and occasional or seasonal cleaning tasks. With such a plan, every member of the family will know when each task has to be done. Everyone should have some job responsibility so that free time and relaxation can be shared by all.

Some reasons for cleaning the home regularly are:
- Clean surroundings safeguard the health of the family because it eliminates any harmful germs and insect or rodent infestations.
- Cleaning results in better indoor air quality by removing dirt and dust, leaving a trace of freshness in its wake.
- People enjoy living in clean and pleasant surroundings.
- It is easy to keep things clean if you clean often and don't let dirt build up.

Daily work routine

This involves simple household tasks that must be done on an everyday basis, for example, sweeping, dusting, preparing meals, clearing the dining area, washing dishes and making beds.

Weekly work routine

Once a week all parts of the house should be thoroughly cleaned – a task which is impossible to do every day. The amount of cleaning done each week will depend on the following:
- the size of the house and the number of people in the house
- the location of the house – whether it is in a dusty or a damp area.

Occasional or seasonal work routine

Large-scale cleaning activities are usually done on a seasonal basis for special occasions, holidays and festivals such as Christmas, Easter, Divali, Eid-ul-Fitr. Cleaning of this kind may take one week or longer. It involves thoroughly cleaning rooms and storage areas in the home. It may include removing cobwebs, scrubbing and polishing floors, changing curtains and painting furniture.

Steps for seasonal cleaning:
- Make a plan of the work to be done.
- Do not attempt to do too much work in one day. The daily work should be carried out as usual.
- Choose a convenient time when all family members can share in the work.
- Use this time to examine storage areas and get rid of those items that are no longer needed.
- Keeping things in their proper place is a good habit for all family members to acquire and should be the responsibility of everyone. This helps to keep rooms tidy and makes your home look well organised.

Cleaning individual rooms

Before you start any work routine, collect all cleaning equipment – broom, mop, duster, brush, dustpan – and any other cleaning materials you may need. When you have finished, put away all equipment in its correct place.

The bedroom

Daily work routine

- Remove all dust with a duster. Dust all ledges as high as you can reach. Dust furniture and ornaments and replace them.
- Make the bed before sweeping the floor.
- Tidy up generally and make sure that everything is returned to its proper place – shoes, clothes, books.
- It is in the bedroom that we spend most of our resting hours and you should therefore clean it daily. The bed should always be properly made up to ensure that the sleeper is comfortable (Figure 2.17).

The following steps should be followed when making the bed:

- Loosen the covers on all sides of the bed and remove along with any bedclothes and pillows.
- Straighten the mattress. Turn or air for weekly cleaning.
- Put on the bottom sheet. If this is not a fitted sheet, tuck in the ends under the mattress, mitring the corners.
- Spread on the 'top' or 'flat' sheet. Tuck in the foot end and fold back the head end leaving enough space for the pillows.
- Shake and 'fluff' the pillows. Place on the bed with the opened ends of pillowcases toward the centre of the bed – away from the door.
- A blanket is hardly ever used in our climate, so the bedspread is next spread over the bed, tucking it in under the pillows. Smooth over the bed, allowing the ends to fall evenly on the other three sides.

How to mitre

Lift the side of the sheet near the foot of the bed and lay it over the bed so that the corner hangs down in a point.

Tuck the corner of the sheet under the mattress.

Make a neat fold from the top corner of the mattress to the foot of the bed and fold the rest of the sheet under to ensure that it lies flat under the mattress.

Figure 2.17 A well-made bed

Weekly work routine

- Remove all bed linen and allow the bed to 'air' for a while.
- Clean the floor according to the type of surface or floor-covering, sweeping or vacuuming it.
- Clean windows and mirrors, tidy cupboards, dressers and drawers.
- Dust polished surfaces.
- Make the bed and do the final tidying.

Occasional work routine

- Paint or wash walls and woodwork.
- Clean, wax or repaint furniture.
- Clean storage areas, such as cupboards, bookshelves and dressing drawers.
- Remove and launder curtains.
- Replace curtains with clean ones or new ones – whichever is affordable. New curtains can make the room more attractive.

The living room

Daily work routine

If everyone puts away books, newspapers, games and toys the night before, it will lessen the work. Open all windows and empty and wash ashtrays, then proceed as for the bedroom.

Weekly and occasional work routine

Work done weekly and for seasonal occasions is similar to the routine given for the bedroom, except for making the bed and changing bed linen. Include dusting cushions, polishing wooden chairs and so on.

Dining room

Many houses in the Caribbean have the dining room combined with the living room. The general guidelines for daily, weekly and occasional cleaning of the bedroom may also be carried out here in the same way. Daily dusting, sweeping and perhaps mopping should be sufficient to keep the dining area clean.

Clear away all dirty dishes and food after each meal and make sure that no leftover bits of food are left lying around.

Clean up all spilled food immediately to discourage flies and other insects.

Remove condiments, sauces and table mats from the table and put in the cupboard or sideboard until the next meal.

The kitchen

Disease-causing bacteria can grow rapidly in food, so it is essential to keep the kitchen scrupulously clean at all times.

Daily work routine

- Put food away in clean cupboards or a refrigerator.
- Wash dishes and cooking utensils and store them in a clean, safe place.
- Wipe counter surfaces and cabinets, as well as the cooker, refrigerator and sink, which should also be kept free of smells.
- Mop or sweep the floor.
- Empty the refuse bin. Wash kitchen bins and reline them with newspaper or other suitable bin liner.

Daily care of sink

- Use a sink tidy or drain protector to trap small pieces of food and to prevent blockage in the waste pipe.
- Always wash the sink thoroughly to remove excess soap and cooking odours.
- Rinse and wipe draining boards. If one is very dirty, scrub with a detergent and a net cloth or scrubbing brush.
- Rinse the soap dish and sponge or net cloth. Dry well and replace.

Weekly care of sink

- Clean the sink according to the material it is made of to remove any stains, food marks or built-up scum.
- Pour a small quantity of washing soda down the waste pipe, followed by some boiling water to dissolve grease and grime.
- Rinse well and rub the taps with a soft cloth to bring up a shine.
- Always leave clean water in the U-bend to trap any unpleasant smells from outside drains. A little household chlorine bleach poured into the waste pipe and overflow and left overnight will destroy harmful bacteria.

Daily care of coal pot
- Remove the coal pot to an outside area.
- Spread newspaper around the coal pot. Remove the ash carefully and wrap in a newspaper.
- Dust the chimney area with a stiff-bristled brush.
- Wipe the inside and outside of the coal pot with some crumpled paper.
- Refill the coal pot with coals.

Daily care of gas or electric cooker
- Turn off the gas or electricity after use.
- Wipe all spills with a damp cloth after cooking.

Daily care of kerosene cooker
- Use a special rag for cleaning after turning off the burners.
- Remove spot marks with a damp cloth wrung out in detergent. Rinse well.
- Make sure that all burners are tightly closed.
- Refill the kerosene container.

Weekly care of cooker
- Turn off the gas, electricity or kerosene at the main tap or switch.
- Collect a bowl of warm soapy water, a net cloth and scouring powder.
- Mop up spills; then remove all detachable parts and wash thoroughly.
- Rinse well and dry with a clean cloth. Replace all parts; relight all burners to dry out all parts thoroughly.
- Rinse the cleaning cloth and scourer and leave to dry.

Daily care of refrigerator
- Special care is important when using a refrigerator if it is to be a safe place to keep food.
- Cover all foods to prevent drying out and loss of flavour.
- Wipe all bottles before putting them in.
- Wipe all spills immediately.
- Check the contents and remove any food that is no longer fit for use.

Occasional care of refrigerator
- Turn the control knob to the off position. Remove the plug or turn off the gas jet.
- Remove all food and keep it in a cool place.
- Allow the freezing compartment to defrost. A bowl of hot water placed in the compartment will help to melt the ice quickly.
- Remove all shelves; leave the door ajar.
- Wash the inside and the door with a bowl of warm water and 15–25 ml (1–2 tbsp) of bicarbonate of soda. Rinse well and dry. Wash and dry other parts, such as ice trays, shelves and so on.
- Rub the chromium trim with a soft dry cloth.
- Refill the ice trays. Replace all food in clean containers.
- Switch on the electric current or the light gas jet.
- Reset the control knob.

Daily care of kitchen bin

Empty the contents of the kitchen bin into an outside storage bin or burn it. Reline the bin with newspaper.

Weekly care of kitchen bin

Empty the refuse bin and wash the inside and outside of the bin with warm, soapy water and a little disinfectant or household bleach. Dry thoroughly. Reline with newspaper.

The bathroom and toilet

Many of today's homes have a bathroom inside the house, which includes a toilet and a shower or bathtub. In other homes, the toilet and shower may be separate units located outside the house. These areas need to be cleaned frequently to keep them germ-free and pleasant. All members of the family should be responsible for leaving the rooms clean after use.

Daily care of bathroom

- Allow fresh air to pass through freely.
- Clean the hand basin and bath with cleaning agent that is suited to the material from which they are made. A little chlorine bleach can be used to remove stains.
- Rinse all toothbrush mugs and soap dishes. Dry and replace.
- Replace covers on toothbrushes, as well as on toothpaste.
- Wipe mirrors and remove wet towels.

Weekly care of bathroom

- Mop floor or scrub them if necessary.
- Clean walls with a cloth or brush. Use a chlorine bleach or a disinfectant.
- Pour a little chlorine bleach or other disinfectant into the waste pipe of the basin and bath.
- Wash all towels, mats, rugs and cloths. Replace when dry.

Daily care of toilet

Flush regularly after use.

Brush the inside of the toilet bowl with a suitable commercial toilet cleaner and a lavatory brush (Figure 2.18). A small amount of chlorine bleach may be used to remove stubborn stains. Never mix cleaner with bleach since the mixture will produce toxic fumes, which are harmful. Do not use disinfectant if you have a septic tank, as this destroys the good bacteria.

Weekly care of toilet

- Mop and scrub the floors and walls. Use a disinfectant or chlorine bleach to destroy bacteria and remove unpleasant odours.
- Replenish the toilet paper.
- Wash the inside of the bowl and clean around the outside of the bowl with a detergent or disinfectant solution.

Figure 2.18 Clean the toilet bowl

It is important to clean the home regularly if a family wishes it to remain in good condition for a long time. The working efficiency of a home is lowered if its surfaces and contents are not well cared for. This is another way for a family to manage its resources.

In addition, the position of your body when you carry out these chores – standing and bending – is very important. Poor posture can contribute to backache and tiredness.

> **ACTIVITIES**
>
> 1. Conduct a survey of the household tasks that your classmates like to do and those that they least like to do. Discuss ways in which the tasks that are least liked could be made easier.
> 2. Investigate and make a list of the types of chore to be done in your household on a daily and weekly basis. Indicate how these tasks can be shared by suggesting a suitable schedule for one month. Try it out. Evaluate its effectiveness after this period.
> 3. You want your bedroom to take on a new look for the Christmas holiday. Identify those areas that you would give specific attention to and say how you would carry out each task to give your bedroom a clean, orderly and pleasing appearance.
> 4. Choose a room in your home and show how you would reorganise the existing storage areas so that the best use is made of the available space.

Stain removal

A **stain** is an unwanted discolouration usually caused by an accident. Removing a stain can be a tedious activity, especially if you do not know the correct method of removing it. This may be made easier if the cause of the stain and the fibre content of the fabric are first identified.

Table 2.1 General guidelines for removing stains

1	Remove any surface deposit.
2	Rinse the stained item in warm or cold water according to the type of stain.
3	Treat the stained area with the recommended stain remover. If the stain persists, place a clean absorbent pad under the fabric on the other side of the stain.
4	Sponge the stain with more stain remover.
5	Rinse with clean water and blot dry.

Follow the points below for good results.
- Always treat stains as soon as possible to prevent the stain from setting into the fabric.
- Always spot-test solvents on a small area of the garment (hems or seam) before proceeding.
- Try the simplest method first.
- Keep stain removers out of the reach of children, as some can be poisonous.
- Never use stain-removing chemicals near an open flame, as some are flammable.
- If using a chemical stain remover on a fabric that is not colourfast, check the effect of the stain remover on the seam allowance, hem or cuff on the wrong side of the article.
- If the stain remover is to be applied to a small area, place the fabric over a pad of absorbent material such as cotton wool or towelling.
- To avoid an unsightly ring in the area of the stain, place the stained area face down onto a pad and work from the wrong side of the stain and from the inside of the stain towards the outside.
- Never use acetone (nail polish remover) on acetate rayon, as it will damage the fabric.
- Never use hot water on bloodstains, as it will set the stain in the fabric making it difficult to remove.

Figure 2.19 Stain removal

METHODS OF STAIN REMOVAL

Sponging and soaking

Sponging involves the use of a damp sponge or piece of absorbent fabric such as a towel to remove soil from the fabric. The damp sponge is rubbed along the surface of the fabric to be cleaned, then rinsed, wrung and rubbed again on the fabric. **Soaking** is the immersion of the fabric in liquid.

Non-washable fabrics

1. Remove any surface deposit.
2. Use cold water and sponge gently without saturating the fabric.
3. When possible, stretch the fabric over a container such as a bowl or bucket, and pour cold water from a height of ¾ to 1 m (2–3 ft) through the stained part of the article.

Washable fabrics

Chemical action

With this method, the chemical reacts with the stain to form a new compound. The compound takes on a new characteristic and may become invisible. Or it may become soluble, so that it can be washed away.

Enzyme action

This treatment is used mainly on protein-based stains such as blood and egg. Enzyme treatment products can be obtained from supermarkets and pharmacies. Enzyme treatments are also included as an ingredient in some washing powders ('biological washing powders'). The enzyme acts on the stain by digesting the protein in the stain. Any residue is then easily washed away.

ACTIVITIES

1. In small groups, use the internet to create a brochure on stains and stain removers.
2. Collect a number of articles that are stained.
   a. Identify the stains and the fibre content of the articles.
   b. Determine the stain removers and the correct procedure to be used for each article.
   c. Treat the stain and launder the articles.
   d. Write a brief report on the procedure carried out and the results of the exercise.

Table 2.2 General guidelines for removing specific stains

STAIN	MATERIALS REQUIRED	PROCEDURE
Ball point ink	Methylated spirits, bleach	Place a pad beneath the stain. Dab the stain with methylated spirits. Blot between applications. If stubborn, use diluted bleach. Wash as usual.
Blood	Cold water, enzyme detergent, common salt, ammonia	Soak in cold water with enzyme detergent. Wash as usual. Use other stain removers if the stain is stubborn.
Chewing gum	Ice, egg white, carbon tetrachloride	Harden gum with ice, scrape to remove excess, remove the remainder with stain remover. Wash as usual.
Chocolate	Borax, ammonia, aerated water	Rinse the area with cold water and dab on the selected stain remover. Wash with detergent and rinse thoroughly.
Cola, soft drinks	Glycerine, warm water, enzyme detergent	Mix glycerine and warm water. Wash with enzyme detergent and the water mixture.

ACTIVITIES

STAIN	MATERIALS REQUIRED	PROCEDURE
Egg	Cold water, salt, enzyme detergent	Soak area in 1 pt cold water and 1 tsp salt. Wash with enzyme detergent.
Fruit juice	Borax, cold water, milk, hydrogen peroxide, white vinegar	Soak in cold water or milk. If necessary, sponge with the selected stain remover. Wash as usual.
Grass	Methylated spirits, eucalyptus oil, glycerine, hydrogen peroxide	Place a pad beneath the stain. Dab the stain with the selected stain remover. If the stain is stubborn, use hydrogen peroxide. Wash as usual.
Grease from food, gravy	Blotting/absorbent paper, warm iron, talcum powder, washing soda, ammonia, commercial grease solvent, dishwashing liquid	Place the paper or powder over the stain and iron with a warm iron OR treat with another stain remover. Wash with detergent as usual.
Ice cream, milk	Borax, grease solvent, enzyme detergent	Rinse area with cold water and dab on the selected stain remover. Wash with enzyme detergent and rinse thoroughly.
Iodine	Cold water, detergent, ammonia, alcohol	Rinse the stain immediately. Dab the stain with stain remover, place a pad beneath the stain. Blot between applications. Wash as usual.
Lipstick	Grease solvent, bleach	Moisten with stain remover. Wash as usual. Use bleach if the stain is stubborn.
Mildew	Sour milk, bleach, lemon juice, enzyme detergent, warm water	Moisten with stain remover. Leave in the sunlight or use enzyme detergent. Wash as usual.
Mud	Detergent	Brush when dry. Wash as usual.
Mustard	Glycerine, ammonia, detergent	Sponge with glycerine or detergent solution. Wash as usual. Use ammonia solution if stubborn.
Nail polish	Nail polish remover (not for acetates)	Dab the stain with the selected stain remover, remove any excess. Place a pad beneath the stain. Blot between applications. Wash as usual. If the fabric is acetate rayon, take it to a dry-cleaner.
Oil from machinery	Sugar, cold water	Make a paste from sugar and water. Cover the stain. Wash as usual.
Paint	Turpentine, benzene, paraffin	Moisten with a stain remover. Wash as usual.
Rust	Salt, lemon or lime juice, cold water	Moisten with a stain remover. Wash as usual.
Scorch marks	Hydrogen peroxide, borax, ammonia	Moisten with a stain remover. Wash as usual.
Shoe polish	Ammonia, methylated spirits, bleach	Place a pad beneath the stain. Dab the stain with stain remover. Blot between applications. If the stain is stubborn, use diluted bleach. Wash as usual.
Tar	Turpentine, benzene, paraffin	Moisten with a stain remover. Wash as usual.
Tea, coffee, cocoa	Cold water, washing soda, detergent, borax, bicarbonate of soda	Rinse the stained area with cold water and dab on the selected stain remover. Wash with detergent and rinse thoroughly.

Safety in the home

In Book 1, you learnt how accidents in the home are caused and how to prevent them. Even in the safest home, accidents do sometimes occur. It is therefore critical that you understand how to prevent these accidents from occurring, as well as how to treat them when they cause injury to a child or adult.

Before studying this, you should reread the section in Book 1 on 'Safety in the home'. Remember – 'prevention is better than cure'.

FIRST AID

As the name implies, first aid is the first help and attention given in the case of an accident, using facilities and materials available at the time. In simple accidents, all that is necessary is first aid, but if the injury is serious, call a doctor and/or ambulance immediately.

On arriving at the scene, the first aider should take the following action:

- Look at the situation and come to a decision for each problem.
- Give immediate treatment, remembering that there may be more than one injury and that some may require more urgent attention than others.
- Remain calm and confident.
- Talk to and reassure the victim if conscious at the time of treatment.
- Handle the victim carefully and gently at all times and move them as little as possible.
- Ensure that the victim is taken without delay to a hospital if the problem seems to be serious.
- Send a brief written report to the doctor, stating the nature of the accident and any treatment that may have been given to the victim.

The first-aid box/kit

Every household, school and place of business should have a first-aid box (Figure 2.20).

This first-aid box/kit should be easily accessible by adults, but out of the reach of children. It should be painted red with a white cross in order to be easily identified.

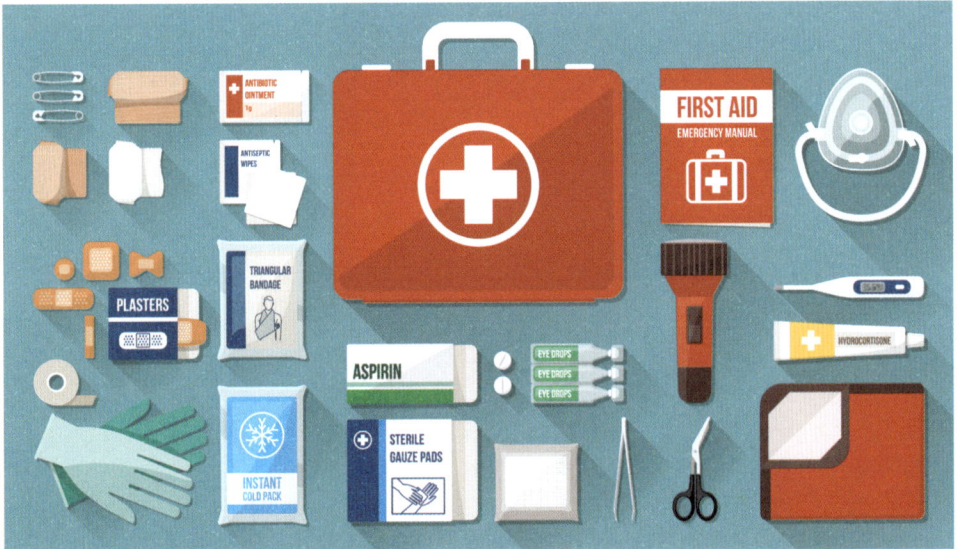

Figure 2.20 The first-aid box

The contents of the first-aid box may vary, but the following is a useful list:

1. a variety of clean rolled bandages varying in width from 1 cm (½ in) to 10 cm (4 in) – they may be bought from a pharmacy or made from clean strips of linen or cotton
2. triangular bandages
3. boric lint (gauze)
4. cotton wool
5. tincture of iodine
6. scissors
7. safety pins
8. adhesive dressings
9. tweezers
10. aspirin or similar pain-killing tablets
11. a graduated medicine glass
12. a clinical thermometer
13. enamel bowl
14. eye bath
15. an antiseptic
16. hydrogen peroxide

Rules for keeping a first-aid box/kit

- Keep an adequate supply of first-aid materials.
- Keep it clean.
- Keep any bandages neatly rolled.
- Check supplies occasionally and dispose of those that have passed the 'best before date' or 'expiry date' given by the manufacturer, and replace as necessary.

How to apply basic first aid

You will now look at the signs and symptoms of some common accidents and how they can be treated.

Shock

It is always wise to treat the victim of any accident in the home for shock, even if the person does not seem to be shocked. Small babies and children, especially, may suffer shock following what appears to be only a minor accident.

Signs and symptoms

The victim may:

- have a pale face
- have rapid and shallow breathing
- feel sick
- shiver and feel cold, but is not sweating
- feel weak, giddy or faint.

Treatment

- Reassure and comfort the victim.
- Sit the victim down on a chair or lay them with their feet on a pillow or cushion and their head turned to one side (Figure 2.21).
- Loosen any tight clothing.
- Cover the victim with a blanket.

- Check for the cause of the shock and treat it if possible.
- Give the victim a warm drink – not alcohol or water – when they begin to recover.

Burns and scalds

As you saw in Book 1, burns are a leading cause of accidental deaths in the home.

Signs and symptoms

- There may be redness and/or swelling of the area and sometimes blistering.
- The victim may be in shock.
- In the case of a house fire, the victim's clothing may be burning.

Treatment

- Remove the victim from the source of the burn or scald. If any clothing is on fire, smother the flames by either dousing with water or other non-flammable liquid, or wrapping the victim in a rug, blanket or coat (Figure 2.22). Do not let the victim rush into the open air.
- Gently hold the burnt part under running cold water or immerse it in cold water for 10 minutes to alleviate pain.
- Remove anything of a constrictive nature, such as bangles, rings, belts or shoes, from the burnt area before it starts to swell.
- If the burn is bad or is in the mouth or throat and the victim is conscious, give sips of cold water at frequent intervals.
- Cover burns with sterile dressing to exclude air. Do not apply any lotions, ointments or oil dressings. Do not prick blisters, touch or breathe over the burn.
- If the burn is severe, call a doctor or transport the victim to a hospital.

Cuts and scratches

The causes are many and varied.

Signs and symptoms

There may be pain and bleeding at the site of the wound.

Treatment

- Bathe the wound gently in clean water, removing any dirt.
- Apply dry dressing of white lint or sticking plaster.
- If the bleeding is severe, raise the limb as high as possible, and press a pad of clean material or your hand directly on the wound for 5–15 minutes. Never use dirt, kerosene, lime or coffee to stop bleeding.
- If the wound is caused by an animal bite, or by rusty items such as nails, knives or galvanised iron, or has been contaminated by soil, there is a risk of tetanus infection. Consult a doctor immediately.

Poisoning

Swift action is necessary with poisoning, as every second of delay could do more harm.

Signs and symptoms

- There may be vomiting.
- A rash may appear after several hours.
- The victim may complain of stomachache, headache or stomach cramps.
- The victim may have pain in the throat.
- The victim may experience a high temperature and/or drowsiness.
- The victim may have burnt lips, especially when the substance taken was very strong or corrosive.

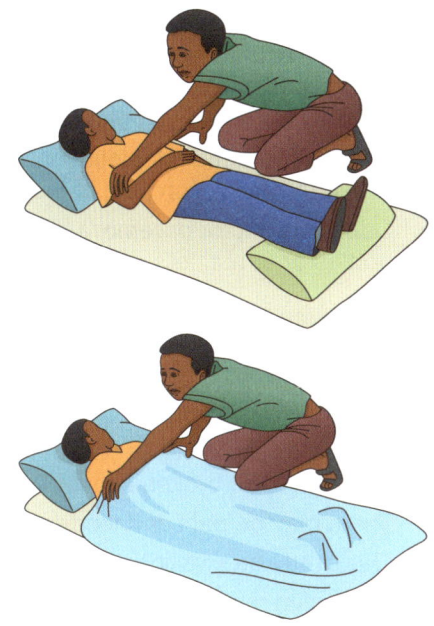

Figure 2.21 Make sure a victim of shock is kept warm

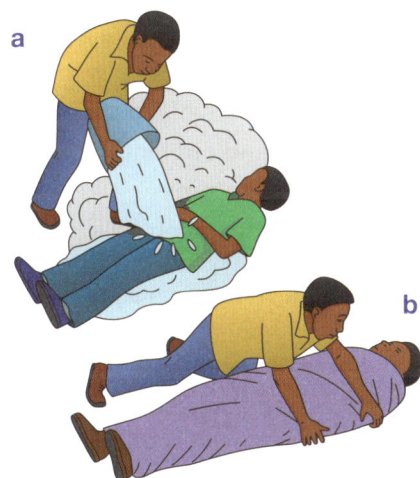

Figure 2.22 If clothing is on fire, either (a) douse the victim with water or (b) wrap tightly in a blanket

Safety in the home

Treatment

- Ask the victim what poison was taken. If they are unconscious, you may see an empty container or bottle that contained the poison. If so, an antidote may be given on the label. Follow the instructions.
- Have the victim drink plenty of water or bicarbonate of soda diluted in water, to induce vomiting of the poison. Follow this with a drink of milk.
- Consult a doctor or remove the victim to a hospital. Keep any empty bottles or containers and a sample of the vomit to give to the doctor.

Falls

The very young or older members of the family are especially likely to be injured by falls.

Signs and symptoms

- These depend on what part of the body is affected by the fall, whether any bones are broken and if the injury is merely a sprain.
- There may be pain and tenderness at the site of the injury.
- There may be swelling.
- The victim may find it impossible to move the injured part of the body.
- A limb may look noticeably different – for example, a foot turned out at an unnatural angle.

Treatment

- Do not move the affected part; doing so will risk further injury to the victim (Figure 2.23).
- Leave the victim where the accident occurred, unless in danger of further injury, and cover with a blanket.
- Seek the advice of a doctor immediately.

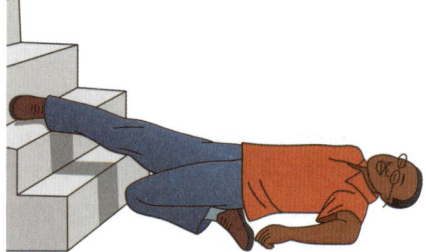

Figure 2.23 If a person has had a fall, do not move the affected part, such as a leg, to see if it is broken

Suffocation and choking

Signs and symptoms

In general, these are obvious, as the cause is usually apparent. For example, a child with a plastic bag over its head is in danger of suffocation, or someone choking on a piece of food will have great difficulty in breathing and may be blue around the lips and mouth.

Treatment for choking

- Remove any objects from the mouth, such as food, dentures or false teeth and encourage the victim to cough.
- If this does not dislodge the obstruction, perform the **Heimlich manoeuvre** (Figure 2.24). Grasp the victim from behind with one of your fists, thumb side in, placed just below the victim's breastbone, with the other hand placed firmly over the fist. Next, pull your fist firmly into the top of the abdomen in an attempt to dislodge the object. If repeated attempts do not free the airway, an emergency incision in the windpipe may be necessary.
- Place a choking child over your knee with the head down and slap them smartly between the shoulder blades.
- In the case of a baby, give five slaps on the back and then use one finger to try to remove the object. If the object is still present, place two fingertips on the lower half of the baby's breastbone, give five sharp thrusts into the chest and check the baby's mouth again. Repeat the procedure if not cleared, or take the baby to a doctor.

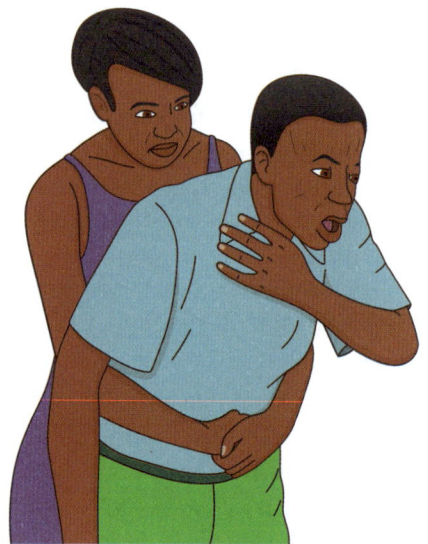

Figure 2.24 The Heimlich manoeuvre – treatment for an adult who is choking

Treatment for suffocation

Remove the obstruction – pillow, plastic bag, whatever it is.

Victim should be reassured if conscious and breathing normally. If breathing has stopped, try artificial respiration.

Artificial respiration

Cardiopulmonary resuscitation (CPR) is a lifesaving technique that is useful in many emergencies, such as a heart attack or near drowning, in which someone's breathing or heartbeat has stopped. This is also called 'mouth-to-mouth breathing' and involves transferring air from your lungs into the victim's lungs. Quick action is important at this stage. However, you should not practise this technique until you have been shown how to do it properly by a qualified first-aid instructor.

- Lay the victim down flat (Figure 2.25).
- Place one hand under the victim's neck and the other hand on the forehead, then tilt the head backwards. Next, push the chin upwards.
- Remove any obstruction in the mouth or throat.
- Pinch the victim's nostrils together with one hand, open your mouth wide and breathe deeply into the victim's open mouth. You will soon see the victim's chest rise. Remove your mouth and breathe out. Take another deep breath and breathe into victim's mouth again.
- Repeat this exercise 15 to 20 times a minute until normal breathing resumes, or until expert medical help arrives.
- For very small children or babies, breathe very gently into their mouth and nose, about 20 times a minute.
- Place the victim in the **recovery position** (Figure 2.26) once normal breathing resumes (continues).
- Call the doctor.

Electrocution

Signs and symptoms

- The victim may have stopped breathing.
- Burns may be present at the points of entry and exit of the electric current.
- The victim may be in shock.

Treatment

- Turn off the electricity at the main switch or remove plug from socket.
- Never touch a person who has been electrocuted, as the current will pass through your body too.
- Use a wooden implement, such as a broom handle (Figure 2.27) or other wooden instrument to push the victim away from the source of power.
- A length of rope may be looped around the feet to pull the victim away.
- Never use anything made of metal or anything that is wet.
- If the victim is not breathing, apply artificial respiration.
- Call the doctor or rush the victim to the hospital.

Remember that accidents do not happen on their own – they are caused by and can happen to people of all ages. Many accidents in the home occur through carelessness and thoughtlessness. They can often be prevented, for example, by wiping up a spill immediately or removing a toy that has been left on the floor. 'Better safe than sorry' should always be the household motto in an attempt to have a safe home.

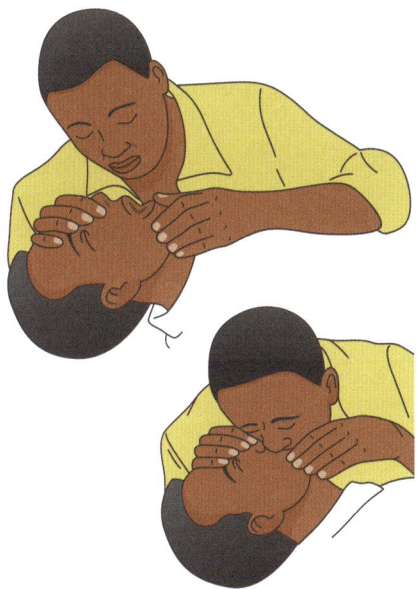

Figure 2.25 Artificial respiration

Figure 2.26 The recovery position. Lay the victim down on his side and gently bend one arm and leg to prevent him from rolling over onto his back.

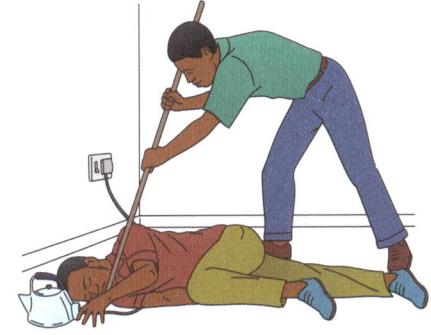

Figure 2.27 When a person has been electrocuted, never touch them yourself. Instead push them away from the source of electricity with a broom handle or other wooden implement.

ACTIVITIES

1. Observe the type of accidents that occur over a four-week period in your household and record how each was handled.
2. Organise a visit to a main electrical department outlet. Record all the information and tips given on the hazards of electricity. Compare these with what you are presently practising in your home. Identify the changes that would be necessary to ensure safety.
3. On one of your weekly shopping trips with an older member of your household, select the items necessary to set up a first-aid kit for the home. Encourage other members to make and design the box appropriately before packing it. Store the kit in a safe place.

Subject link

Technology can be used to provide programmes for designing kitchen layouts.

Mathematics concepts such as measuring and calculation will be required when redesigning the kitchen.

Design project

Your family started out as a four-member unit but soon became six members because your aunt who was a single mom emigrated and her two children were left in your parents' care. This has resulted in a serious space challenge in the small three-bedroom house that houses your parents, your brother and you. The limited storage spaces now have to be shared among six of you. Use the appropriate management processes when making decisions.

1. Make a list the main items requiring storage space in your household.
2. Suggest where and how they can be stored to ensure a well-organised home.
3. Recommend three multi-purpose furniture items that could serve dual purposes and where each item could be placed.
4. Prepare a list of tasks to be done routinely by members of the household to ensure a well-organised and clean environment. List tasks under the following headings; daily, weekly, monthly and seasonally.
5. Report your findings to your classmates.

Multiple choice questions

Select the letter that corresponds with your answer.

1. You find that most days are very hectic and you are not able to complete all your activities on time. What can you do to help yourself?
   A Tell others about what you have to do.
   B Make a checklist of what has to be completed.
   C Make a to-do list and rank the activities in order of importance.
   D Just go with the flow and try to complete all that you can think of.

2. Which of the following is NOT a **feature of management**?
   A A series of continuous and related activities
   B Works with people and resources in order to achieve goals
   C Can be measured in terms of hours
   D Focuses on reaching goals

3. Work simplification is _____
   A an approach that requires an awareness of the movements involved in doing a task.
   B adopting the simplest, easiest and quickest method of doing the work.
   C doing two tasks at the same time in the same area.
   D trying out better ways of doing a task.

4. Which of the following is NOT a management process?
   A Coordinating
   B Organising
   C Implementing
   D Evaluating

5. This house is all on ground level. It is a _____
   A terrace.
   B bungalow.
   C palace.
   D semi-detached.

6. Identify the type of house in the picture on the right.
   A Ranch
   B Cottage
   C Townhouse
   D Duplex

7. Which of the following types of housing will you be most likely to share a wall with one neighbour?
   A Cottage
   B Bungalow
   C Ranch
   D Terrace

8   Someone who enjoys having lots of neighbours very close to their house would likely to want to live in which of the following?
    i   Terrace
    ii Townhouse
    iii Apartment
    iv Cottage
    A   i and ii
    B   ii and iii
    C   i and iii
    D   ii and iv

9   Which type of dwelling provides the most privacy of any type of housing?
    A   Townhouse
    B   Cottage
    C   Co-operative
    D   Condominium

10 This kitchen layout requires three full walls of the room.
    A   L shaped
    B   U shaped
    C   Island
    D   Galley

11 This layout is perfect for a kitchen that will get a lot of use and needs a great deal of space.
    A   L shaped
    B   U shaped
    C   Island
    D   Galley

12 This layout plan is nice for a kitchen where a lot of entertaining might be done.
    A   L shaped
    B   U shaped
    C   Island
    D   Galley

13 This kitchen layout is a good solution for a narrow kitchen.
    A   L shaped
    B   U shaped
    C   Island
    D   Single wall

14 Which of the following is the most popular material used for tools and equipment in the kitchen?
    A   Stainless steel
    B   Aluminum
    C   Glass
    D   Cast Iron

15 Which of the following temperatures allows food to be kept free from bacterial spoilage for longer periods?
    A 3–5 °C
    B 10–15 °C
    C 37–41 °C
    D 20–30 °C

16 Household tasks must be done on a regular basis. Which of the following is NOT a routine for cleaning?
    A Daily
    B Weekly
    C Spring
    D Seasonal

17 Which of the following is not recommended for removing a bloodstain?
    A Turpentine
    B Lime juice
    C Hydrogen peroxide
    D Cold salt water

Short answer questions

1 Give a brief description of three different types/categories of houses.
2 State the two most popular types of housing in your community.
3 Outline at least five safety features to observe when planning a kitchen. Give reasons for each feature.
4 List four types of cooking equipment.
5 Make a list of tasks to be done on a daily and weekly basis in your household.
6 Explain the meaning of 'first aid'.
7 State five items that are to be included in a first-aid kit and suggest when and how each should be used.
8 Your sister cut her finger while trying to open a can of baked beans. Explain the steps you should take to treat such an injury.
9 Explain what is meant by the 'Heimlich manoeuver'.

Chapter 3 Family economics

Do you know anyone who does not like to spend money? Most of us start to spend when we are small children and continue to spend throughout life. Spending seems to come naturally, but controlling our spending is not so natural for everyone. Therefore, by managing income with spending you can avoid money problems and work towards a secure financial future.

- Have you ever had a disagreement over money?
- Do you have a problem with saving money for unexpected events?
- How do you manage to keep spending under control?
- How does advertising influence your shopping habits?

In this chapter, you will:

* become aware of the benefits of making a budget
* categorise family expenditure such as food, clothing, housing
* distinguish among the various types of savings and investment institutions
* appreciate your role as a consumer
* assess the factors that influence consumer spending
* examine the functions, advantages and disadvantages of advertising
* investigate the various methods of paying for goods.

Managing family income

BUDGETING

Budgeting is a method of money management that helps you to control the spending of income. A budget is a plan outlining expected income and expenses over a specific period.

Governments budget for a year or more. But most families normally budget for a month or a week.

There are many reasons for preparing a budget. Some of these are:

- Clarity of your income and expenditure and helps you live within your means.
- Control over your money by providing spending limits and avoiding unnecessary expenditure.
- Achievement of your goals by allocating money towards specific financial goals.

MONTH: JANUARY 2022			
INCOME	$US	EXPENDITURE	$US
Mother	$600	Rent	$450
Brother	$200	Food	$300
Father	$900	Clothing	$150
		Insurance	$100
		Savings	$150
		Transportation	$150
		Utilities – electricity, water, telephone	$100
		Debts – loans	$200
		Miscellaneous	$100
TOTAL	$1700	TOTAL	$1700

Figure 3.1 A sample family budget for one month.

- Allowing you to prepare for emergencies by setting aside money regularly to build an emergency fund.
- Deciding what you must spend your money on and allocating money towards the things that are needed.

There are two distinct categories of expenditures in a budget:

1. **Fixed expenditure**: expenses that are constant and remain the same for each month. Fixed expenses often include rent or mortgage payment, loan payments, insurance premiums, school fees, utilities (for example, internet or cable), and savings.
2. **Flexible expenditure**: expenses that are variable from month to month based on lifestyle choices, usage or need. Flexible expenses may include groceries and dining out, healthcare, transportation, utilities such as electricity or telephone, clothing and personal care items, household repairs, entertainment and holidays.

Your monthly spending pattern may vary due to special events or unexpected occurrences. A good practice to prepare for these activities is by spending less during the months leading up to a known event. To allow for unexpected occurrences, you should include a regular amount in the budget as 'miscellaneous'. Your budget should be regularly reviewed to better manage your income and adjust to changing situations.

Some factors which may cause monthly expenses to change, include festivals like Christmas, Carnival, or Divali; the reopening of school and needing to pay for uniforms, textbooks, transportation, electronic devices; life events such as weddings, funerals, births of family members; illness involving doctor's visits or hospitalisation; inflation – increase in the price of groceries, transportation, utilities; or lifestyle changes such as healthier eating habits or joining a gym.

ACTIVITIES

Draw up a budget for your family. Show the expenditure against the income and indicate where improvements in spending can be made to help balance the budget.

Preparing a budget

Here are some steps to follow:

1. Identify and total all sources of income to know your monthly earnings.
2. Collect information on all expenses and categorise into fixed and flexible.
3. Create a plan for savings towards specific goals and emergencies.
4. Allocate money to category of expenses and savings.
5. Add up all expenditure and compare to total income.
6. If expenses exceed income, adjust your flexible expenses.
7. Review your budget regularly to ensure that you are staying on track, however, be prepared to adjust for unexpected expenses.
8. Compare your actual spending against your budget at the end of each month and if necessary, adjust for the following month.

FAMILY EXPENDITURE

Basic needs such as food, housing, clothing and healthcare must be met first. The remainder is divided between other necessities, by priority:

- food
- housing
- essential clothing
- healthcare
- household expenses – electricity, cleaning, repairs, telephone, furniture
- fares – travel, car
- insurance – house, contents, life, and so on

Managing family income

- education, sport
- personal – toiletries, extra clothes, books, hobbies
- non-essentials – entertainment, holidays, pets and other luxuries
- savings – (a) for emergencies, (b) for luxuries.

Food

Budget experts have discovered that the smaller our income, the greater the percentage that we spend on food. Whatever the size of the family's income, the important thing is to spend it wisely.

Spending the food dollar wisely:

- *Plan meals for the week before going grocery shopping.* This reduces the chance of food waste.
- *Base menus on advertised specials.* Become familiar with prices so that you can tell which specials represent genuine savings.
- *Make a shopping list of the ingredients you need, based on your meal plan.*
- *Avoid items that you or your family members do not enjoy.* Even at bargain prices, items that you have to throw away are a waste of money.
- *Shop only once a week.* More frequent trips should not be necessary. With cooking and/or proper storage, most food items (including perishables) should keep at least this long.
- *If possible, go shopping when shops are not crowded.* This will give you time to read labels, compare prices, and avoid long queues at payment points.
- *Avoid grocery shopping when you are hungry.* That way you will be less likely to make unplanned purchases.
- *Look out for sales and discounts.* Do not buy items you don't need because they're on sale.
- Get the most nutrition for your money. Buy foods that are both high in nutrients and high in calories (Figure 3.2 and see page 130 'How is energy measured?').
- Minimise food waste by being mindful of food expiration dates and using up perishable items before they go bad.
- Buy items like beans, pasta, or rice in bulk so that you can save money in the long run.
- Limit using processed foods as they are likely to be less nutritious and more expensive than whole foods.
- Cook most of your meals at home and limit eating out, which may be convenient but more expensive.

Figure 3.2 Remember the six food groups and try to eat some of the foods in each group every day.

Housing

In the Caribbean, most people who live in villages own their homes. People in urban areas more frequently rent homes. Rented homes are usually near businesses, markets, schools and hospitals, so people renting these homes must pay more rent than they would for the same type of house in the country. In individual budgets, the most costly item is probably the rent or home loan payment.

Factors which account for the cost of renting a house are:
- location (urban, suburban or rural)
- type of house
- size of house
- quality of house

- community facilities
- paved areas and landscaping.

When a house is being bought, the home loan repayment of one family can be greater than that of another family because of:
- the size of the property involved
- the area (this affects house prices)
- the type of home loan
- the amount of home loan that is left to be paid.

Clothing

The decision to make or buy clothing can affect family expenses. Custom-made clothing is produced at home or by a dressmaker or tailor. Ready-made clothing is usually factory produced and is bought at the shop.

Spending the clothing dollar wisely:
- Upon entering a shop, go to the rack or department that features garments in your price range. Ignore displays of high-cost merchandise.
- Consider factory outlets where factory overruns and seconds are sold at bargain prices.
- Visit discount shops – many of them have upgraded their clothing department and now offer stylish, fashion-oriented items.
- Shop at garage sales and thrift shops where some real bargains can be found.
- Emphasise one or two colours so that your new purchases and your existing clothes can be coordinated or harmonised. This technique helps you to build a wardrobe with many mix-and-match possibilities.

Healthcare

Healthcare is a critical expense as more people are becoming ill and require medical attention. You should always try to prepare for healthcare costs by planning and budgeting for routine and unexpected medical expenses.

Healthcare costs can be managed by:
- Maintaining a healthy lifestyle to decrease the risk of non-communicable diseases.
- Choosing a health insurance plan that satisfies your needs and fits your budget.
- Preventative care such as vaccinations and annual check-ups can help catch health issues and reduce long-term expenses.
- Utilizing 'Health and Wellness Fairs' where a range of medical screening and services are offered free of charge.
- Seeking assistance from social programmes if you have high medical expenses.

Personal needs

Items that are used for regular personal body care are commonly known as **toiletries**. They help to maintain a clean, well-groomed body. Some items, such as bath soaps, body lotions, toothpaste and shampoo may be shared with other members of the family. Other items, such as a toothbrush and deodorant, are personal and should not be shared with others. Deodorants should only be used when the body is freshly washed (Figure 3.3).

Fuel

Whenever you cook, you use a certain amount of fuel; for example, gas, electricity, charcoal, wood or oil. Fuel can be a very expensive item in the family budget.

Family members can save towards healthcare by becoming members of a **health insurance scheme**. Through this scheme, a specific amount of money is paid to the scheme on a monthly, quarterly or even yearly basis, or as the contributor might find it financially convenient.

Figure 3.3 However much you spend on deodorants, they will not make a dirty body smell good!

Things you can do to avoid wasting fuel:
- Include one-pot dishes in your meal planning. This saves fuel because you can cook it all in one saucepan on one burner.
- When baking, fill all the shelves with food that can be baked at the same time.
- When you put a saucepan on the cooker, control the flame. The flame should only be under the pan, not up the sides.
- Turn down the flame as soon as the food in the pot comes to the boil.
- Use pressure cookers and slow cookers, which are more energy efficient than stovetop cooking.
- Clean and maintain the oven and stove regularly to ensure they are working efficiently.
- Plan meals that utilise raw ingredients or require less cooking time, for example sandwiches or salads.
- Cover pots and pans to help food cook faster and reduce cooking time and fuel use.

Transport

Whether you use your own vehicle or public transport, transport costs money. In some rural areas transport facilities may be limited, so the cost of transport tends to be high.

Spending the transport dollar wisely:
- Plan your routes and try not to make unnecessary trips.
- Consider walking or cycling short distances.
- Carpool with family, friends or work colleagues to split fuel cost.
- Use public transport options like water taxis or buses which can offer significant savings.
- Maintain your vehicle regularly to improve fuel efficiency and prevent costly repair.

ACTIVITIES

1. Investigate and record:
   a. the basic national insurance contributions in your country.
   b. the basic and upper rates of income tax.
   c. the current rate of interest for savings at commercial banks.
   d. the current rate of interest for home loans at commercial banks.
2. Visit a supermarket and select any five items to study. Write the names of the items and for each, write down the information that is on the label.
3. Compare shopping in a supermarket with shopping in a small grocery shop, using the following headings: (a) 'Comfort and convenience', (b) 'Value for money' and (c) 'Quality of goods and variety'.

SAVINGS AND INVESTMENTS

Saving is probably the most important single item in a personal or family budget. Making up and keeping a budget will allow many people to save who otherwise would encounter financial problems every year. There are two different forms of saving – short-term and long-term. Within these two categories, there are many valid reasons for saving.

Did you know?
Saving means to set aside a part of your income for future use, while investment is putting your saved money into financial products, which will hopefully make a profit.

Reasons for saving
- **Emergencies.** The term 'emergency' extends to a wide range of circumstances, from unemployment to medical bills not covered by health insurance. To protect yourself in such situations, you should have an emergency fund.
- **Expensive purchases.** Some items are so expensive that payment cannot usually be made from current income. For most people, these items include a house, a car and major appliances. To purchase these, most people must either borrow money or save money.
- **Recurring expenses.** These include real estate taxes and insurance premiums. Since the amounts needed are usually known in advance, you can set aside small amounts over a long period of time, so that your budget will not be exceeded when these large bills are due.
- **Retirement.** For most workers, retirement income is generally inadequate. To meet their expenses, people must supplement their income with savings.
- **Special goals.** Most people have special goals that go beyond acquiring the mere necessities of life. These include saving for a university education, marriage, travel, hobbies and setting up a business.

Saving guidelines
For most people, a savings account in a bank is the first step towards realising long-term goals. Here are some practical hints to help you move in that direction.
- **Start now.** Make a decision and act on it.
- **Plan to save a realistic amount.** Allow enough money to pay current expenses and bills.
- **Save regularly and consistently.** Try to save the same amount every month.
- **Keep your savings goal in mind.** This will help to confirm your decision to save.
- **Place your savings in a savings account.** Your money will earn interest, and your savings will be safe.
- **Only carry with you the amount of cash you need each day.** With less cash available for impulse buying, you may have more cash available for saving.
- **Use a combination of savings accounts.** You should not keep all your money in an account that allows you to make withdrawals whenever you choose.

Savings institutions
Savings should be placed in a financial institution where they will earn interest. When deciding which institution, you should consider three important factors.
- **Safety.** Deposits should be insured.
- **Liquidity.** The ease with which an individual can turn invested assets (like savings) into cash in hand is called **liquidity**. Some accounts are highly liquid – money can be withdrawn from them immediately.
- **Earnings.** All savings institutions do not offer the same interest rate.

Financial institutions that are available to family members for savings and investments include the following:

Commercial banks

Commercial banks offer the full range of banking services. Although they are looked upon as the chief source of loans to businesses they also make home loans. There are two basic types of account.

- **Current account:** You have the use of a cheque book but your money earns no interest – in fact you pay the bank fees and charges.
- **Deposit account:** Money can be deposited or withdrawn at any time. Such accounts are mainly used to save money. Interest is paid automatically into the account. When money is deposited directly to the bank, a deposit slip is used (Figure 3.4). Cash dispensing machines such as the automatic teller machine (ATM) allow you to deposit or withdraw cash at any time of the day or night.

Mutual savings banks

The word 'mutual' indicates that a bank is owned by its depositors. As owners, they receive dividends instead of interest. A **dividend** is a share of the profits paid in proportion to the share of ownership. Mutual savings banks offer all the traditional banking services, as well as residential and commercial loans.

Credit unions

A credit union operates as both a savings and lending institution for the benefit of its members. By encouraging its members to save collectively, a credit union builds up a fund that can be used for loans. The loans, in turn, earn interest from which the credit union's expenses are paid.

Savings bonds

A **savings bond** is a promise made by a cooperation or government to pay the investor a certain amount of money, plus interest, at a specific time in the future. When government tax receipts are insufficient to finance programmes, the government must borrow money. One of the ways it does this is by selling savings bonds.

Shares

Some people invest their money by buying shares in large companies or banks. If the company has profits, the shareholders receive some of the profits in proportion to the number of shares they hold. On the other hand, the company may not make any profit and the value of the shares may decrease, so buying shares can be a risky way of saving.

> # Career corner
> ## Bank teller
> Bank tellers are customer service and finance professionals who assist customers with monetary transactions like withdrawals, transfers, deposits and foreign exchange. Their job role may involve providing customer information on bank products and services such as loans, account types, credit cards and interest rates. Skills that can help you become a successful bank teller are communication skills, customer service skills, cash handling and mathematical skills, documentation and data entry skills.

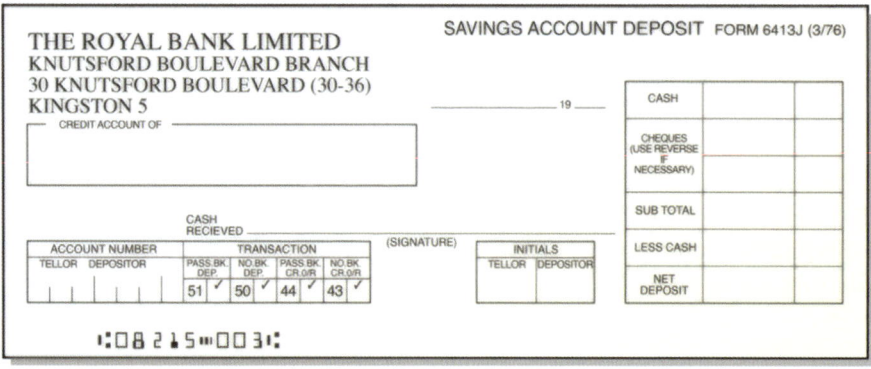

Figure 3.4 A savings account paying-in slip

Co-operatives

A co-operative is a form of business organisation in which people become members, usually by depositing a small sum of money or by buying shares. To be eligible for membership, a person must be connected with or belong to the group of people for whom the benefits of the co-operative are meant. A co-operative gives members a financial advantage in buying the goods and services that they want, at cost.

ACTIVITIES

1. Make a list of all the ways in which your family could improve its method of saving.
2. Design a poster to show the danger of keeping cash in the house.
3. Do friends or co-workers in your community get together to save money? What is this called? How does it work? What are the disadvantages?
4. Collect samples of deposit and withdrawal slips from several banks. Complete the information required on each.

Who is the consumer?

A consumer is anyone who uses goods and services to satisfy personal needs and wants. Consumers' needs and wants are influenced by their goals, values, lifestyle, peer pressure and effects of advertisements. A **need** is something that is necessary for maintaining a basic standard of living. It is an essential item for survival and well-being. For example, food, water, clothing, shelter, healthcare. A **want** is a non-essential item or service that may improve the quality of life. It is a desire for something, but not essential for survival. For example, dining out, designer items, leisure activities.

The consumer process involves several persons:
- the manufacturer who makes the goods
- the retailer who sells the goods
- the consumer who buys and uses the goods.

Consumers are the end-users in the chain of production: manufacturers make the goods; retailers sell the goods; and consumers buy the goods.

Sometimes more than one brand or make is available of the same item. As a consumer, you may need to ask yourself the following:
- Do I buy the cheapest one?
- Is it the packaging that is most attractive?
- Are the labels stating the contents similar?
- Which one contains more for the same price?
- Is this the product I saw advertised?
- Is this the one that my friend recommended?

Whatever the final choice is, you should make sure you base your decision on: Do I really need it? Can I afford it? Is it worth the money? Could I get a better bargain? However, if you have bought the item and are still not satisfied with your purchase, you do not have to remain silent as a consumer. Instead, you should return to the place of purchase and politely and carefully point out your problem.

Did you know?

As a consumer, you have certain rights. **Consumer protection** refers to the laws, regulations, and practices designed to safeguard the rights and interests of consumers and is essential for maintaining trust in the marketplace and ensuring that consumers can make choices with confidence. Consumers are protected from:
- unfair trade practices, misleading advertising and unethical behaviour
- online scams and financial fraud
- faulty goods or low-quality products and services
- dangerous products
- incorrect labelling, ingredient lists or usage instructions
- unlawful organisational practices.

Table 3.1 Consumer rights and responsibilities

Consumer rights	Consumer responsibilities
• *Right to safety.* Consumers should be protected against goods that are hazardous to health or life.	• *Responsibility to use products safely.* Consumers should use products as they were meant to be used and follow recommended procedures for care and maintenance.
• *Right to be informed.* Consumers should be protected against fraudulent or misleading advertising, labelling or sales practices. They should be given the facts to make informed choices.	• *Responsibility to use information.* Consumers should look for information about products they plan to buy and use it to compare and evaluate different brands and models.
• *Right to choose.* Consumers should be assured access to a variety of goods and services at competitive prices.	• *Responsibility to choose carefully.* Consumers should use their buying power intelligently to encourage ethical business practices and safe and reliable products.
• *Right to be heard.* Consumers should be assured that their interest will be considered in the making of laws.	• *Responsibility to speak up.* Consumers should keep themselves informed on consumer issues and let public officials know their opinions.
• *Right to redress.* Consumers are entitled to swift and fair remedies for consumer problems.	• *Responsibility to seek redress.* Consumers should let businesses know when their products and services do not measure up to expectations. They should pursue legal and other available remedies when problems do arise.
• *Right to consumer education.* Consumers should be taught about the market system. They should know how to work within that system to get the greatest possible satisfaction for each dollar spent.	• *Responsibility to learn.* Consumers should take advantage of every opportunity to develop consumer skills.

LOOKING AT ADVERTISEMENTS

The main purpose of advertising is to sell products. It is one of the most important ways in which someone who has something to sell can communicate with as many potential buyers as possible.

Functions of advertising

The functions of advertising are:
- to tell the consumer about new products
- to persuade you to buy goods; this increases sales
- to promote the brand name and good image of the manufacturer
- to give information about products and services.

Advertisements appear in many places, especially the following:
- on radio and television commercials
- on billboards and bus shelters
- in magazines and newspapers
- through person-to-person communication
- in direct-mail letters and leaflets
- through samples of products
- on social media platforms.

Advantages of advertising

Some advantages of advertising are as follows. Advertising:
- informs us of new products and services
- creates jobs by employing large numbers of people and by increasing sales of consumer goods

- provides important information on our rights and entitlements, for example social welfare
- keeps down the costs of newspapers and other media
- is useful when we want to buy, sell or rent goods, for example houses, cars.

Disadvantages of advertising

Some disadvantages of advertising are as follows. Advertising:

- increases the cost of many consumer goods
- persuades people to buy things they cannot afford
- targets children and young people who may not judge it critically
- often shows unrealistic lifestyles and can make you feel dissatisfied with life
- can be misleading and often exaggerates (Figure 3.5).

GOING SHOPPING

One of your main problems as a consumer is choosing from the large variety of selling establishments that compete for your dollars. Most of your shopping will be done in **retail shops**, which are business establishments that sell goods and services to the general public. Retail shops differ in the way they operate, the merchandise they sell, the services they give and the prices they charge.

Figure 3.5 Learn to be alert to the claims of advertisements.

Guidelines for shopping

- Shop at places that have a quick turnover.
- Make a shopping list before you shop.
- Explore different shops to compare prices; the wider your choice, the more satisfactory your purchase will be.
- Read labels so that you will have a clear idea of the contents.
- Obtain a guarantee for the goods you buy, whenever possible.
- Always ask for a demonstration when you buy any mechanical or electrical goods. Find out arrangements for servicing and repairs.
- Check measurements, sizes and quantities before you leave the shop.
- In a supermarket, check that the cashier strikes the correct prices on the cash machine.
- Check to see that you are given the correct change, as mistakes can be difficult to correct once you leave the shop.
- Keep the receipt; it is proof of your payment in case you want to return the goods.

Paying for goods

There are three types of goods that all consumers use:

- consumer goods, for example, food, clothing, toiletries, alcohol, tobacco and perfumes
- consumer durables, for example, refrigerators, cookers, washing machines and freezers
- capital goods, for example, house, land, business, jewellery and other investments.

There are several ways of paying for these goods. The method chosen depends upon the nature of the purchase and the money available.

Career corner

Creative development professional

Creative development professionals put together the visuals for online advertisements, magazine and newspaper advertisements, television advertisements, or brochures and corporate reports. Workers with these jobs tend to have strong attention to detail and communication skills, as well as creativity and training in the specific disciplines required. The position usually requires a bachelor's degree in a specific creative field, such as marketing, graphic design, or fine arts.

Methods of payment

Table 3.2 Methods of payment

Method of payment	Advantages	Disadvantages
Cash – physical currency such as coins and banknotes	Quick and easy, no processing fees	Not suitable for large purchases, risk of loss or theft
Cheques – written orders for a bank to pay a specific amount from the writer's account to a payee	Useful for large payments, can be mailed	Processing time, risk of bouncing if insufficient funds
Prepaid cards – cards preloaded with a set amount of money, usable until the balance is reduced	No need for a bank account, useful as gifts, controlled spending	Limited balance, not always reloadable
Debit cards – plastic cards linked to a bank account allowing direct withdrawal of funds	No interest charges, immediate deduction from account, convenient	Limited to available bank balance
Credit cards – plastic cards issued by banks for purchases on credit	Builds credit history, convenient for online and large transactions	Interest charges if not paid in full
Bank transfers – electronic transfer of funds from one bank account to another	Secure, suitable for large transactions	Requires accurate bank details, may incur fees, processing time varies
Mobile payment – payments made through mobile apps	Convenient, secure, contactless	Requires internet access, not accepted everywhere, dependent on smartphone
Direct debit – an authorisation that allows a company to take money directly from a customer's bank account on a regular basis	Ensures timely payment, convenient, ideal for recurring payment	Requires trust in the payee, involves a setup process
Digital currencies – used for transactions via blockchain technology	Secure, low transaction fees, global acceptance in some online stores	Requires digital literacy, not widely accepted
Wire transfer – transfer of funds between banks through a network	Suitable for large sums, secure, fast for international transactions	Requires accurate banking details, high fees

Buying on credit

Credit card is one of the most common forms of buying on credit. Consumers can make purchases up to a certain credit limit and must repay the borrowed amount. Other options include:

- Lay-away plans: consumers make a series of payments on an item but cannot take the item away until the total cost has been paid.
- Rent to own: consumers are allowed to rent an item with the option to buy after a certain period. The consumer owns the item after completing all payments.
- Buy Now, Pay Later: consumers are allowed to purchase an item without making an initial payment and pay for the item in instalments.
- Instalment loans: consumers repay these loans in fixed monthly payments over a specified period, examples are personal loans, student loans, vehicle loan, mortgage.
- Hire purchase: consumers usually pay a deposit and then repay in smaller regular instalments until the debt is repaid. The consumer can use the product while making repayments, but does not own the product until the full amount is repaid. This is often used for expensive purchases such as cars.

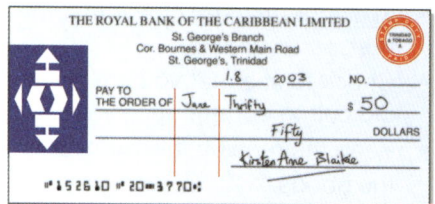

Figure 3.6 Paying by cheque is convenient. A crossed cheque is a sensible security measure.

Figure 3.7 A credit card is a safe and convenient way of paying for goods.

Buying on credit gives flexible payment options. It is convenient and often faster and helps to build positive credit history. Purchases are more affordable since the cost can be spread over a period. However, consumers also have to pay interest and fees, which increases the purchase cost and there is a higher total cost than the cash price. Some credit agreements may include hidden costs. Credit can lead to financial mismanagement and defaulting on payments could result in repossession.

Online banking

Online banking (also called internet banking, e-banking, web banking or virtual banking) is quick, usually free and allows you to perform tasks such as paying bills and transferring money without having to visit or call your bank. Online banking relies on an internet connection. If your internet is not strong or disrupted by a power outage, your ability to access your account might be affected. Privacy and security are major concerns with online banking because valuable information is always prone to hacks. Be sure to follow the guidelines provided by the bank to safeguard your information.

ACTIVITIES

1. Design an advertisement for the sale of some school shoes.
2. Discuss with a classmate the questions that you must ask yourself as a consumer of goods and services.
3. Listen to some radio and television advertisements and name three things they all have in common.

What have I learnt?

Multiple-choice questions

1. The most likely purpose of budgeting is _____
   A estimating your income.
   B planning and control of income and expenditure.
   C spending the food dollar wisely.
   D determining your needs.
2. A type of savings account where money can be deposited or withdrawn at any time.
   A Regular savings
   B Current account
   C Fixed deposit
   D Savings bond
3. Dividends are a characteristic of _____
   A safety deposit.
   B deposit account.
   C mutual funds.
   D current account.
4. Which of the following is not true about advertising?
   A Persuades you to buy the product
   B Decreases the cost of consumer goods
   C Can be misleading and often exaggerates
   D Promotes the good image of the manufacturer
5. Electronic transfer of money from one bank account to another is a description of _____
   A mobile payments.
   B prepaid cards.
   C bank transfers.
   D digital currencies.

Short answer questions

1. 'Expenditure should never exceed income.' Comment on this statement.
2. Describe two ways by which a family might reduce its expenditure in order to keep within its budget.
3. List the major areas of expenditure to be accounted for when planning a family budget.
4. Explain to a friend why it is a good idea to make your own clothing.
5. What basic factors should you consider, and why, when deciding where to invest regular savings?
6. List three forms of buying on credit. Explain why a family might use one rather than another.
7. List three advantages and three disadvantages of buying by credit.
8. Describe the saving guidelines that family members should consider.

Design project

Mr and Mrs Smith and their nine-year-old twins Sonny and Sally recently moved into their first home. After a couple of months, the family realised that their budget hadn't helped at all since they were spending more than what was budgeted, and their emergency expenses fund was not building up as they'd hope. The family was eating out regularly and household items and clothes for the twins were purchased on impulse.

1. Develop a plan which would help the family to make the budget work, as well as to keep it running smoothly.
2. Create an advertisement for an online platform to sell the items purchased on impulse.

Who is the consumer?

Chapter 4 Health management

Figure 4.1 Health management

You know that being healthy depends on how you live and that it is more than preventing illnesses. The absence of disease requires prevention and control of diseases and establishing a healthy environment.

Have you ever had a runny nose and an aching, stuffy head that made you feel so miserable that you could hardly think straight or even clearly? If you have, you were probably suffering from a disease – one called the 'flu'.

- Can you name a disease that is evident in your country?
- Do you know the possible causes of this disease?
- Name two practices that will protect you from getting this disease.

In this chapter, you will:
* outline the nature of diseases
* devise a plan for the control of communicable diseases
* become aware of the importance of a healthy environment
* increase your understanding of the various changes that take place during the growth and development of a baby after birth
* recognise the important aspects of care required to maintain babies in good health.

Consider this

A disease is a condition that prevents the body or part of it from working properly. When the body is not working properly, we say that we are ill. Most people become ill at some time in their lives. Some recover quickly, but others are crippled or killed by their disease. If you want to learn to protect yourself from diseases, you need to understand how they are caused, how they are spread and how they can be prevented.

In this section, we are going to identify the different types of disease, what causes them, how they are spread and most importantly how they can be prevented. Let's start by finding out more about diseases.

What is a disease?

Reflect, research, report

Did you know that diseases prevent our bodies from working properly? There are many types of disease that cause illness in people. Some people recover easily but others can be crippled or die from a disease.

The big question

How can you protect yourself and your family from diseases?

Figure 4.2 displays some different types of disease, along with the main causes.

Breaking this down

1. Identify the different diseases in Figure 4.2.
2. Select one disease that you know occurs in your community and find out how it is spread.
3. Research the occurrence of the same or a similar disease in another country. Was the government of the country able to contain the disease? How did they do so?
4. How did the citizens respond to any programmes implemented by the government?
5. What can you take away from how that country handled the disease, to use in your own situation?

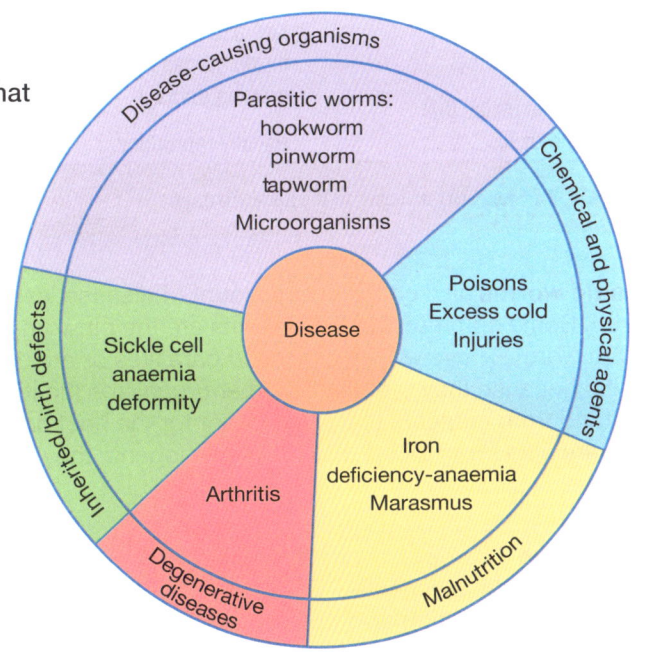

Figure 4.2 The main causes of disease

Sharing the information

Think of an effective way of sharing your findings with your family to convince them to prevent a disease and present this to your classmates. You could make an infographic of a schematic diagram. You could even make a short video using a social media platform or any other method that would work with your family.

Answering the big question

Having done the research and listened to the information from your classmates:

1. Do you think you can protect yourself and your family from disease?
2. What suggestions can you and your classmates make to prevent the spread of diseases in your community?

CAUSES OF DISEASE

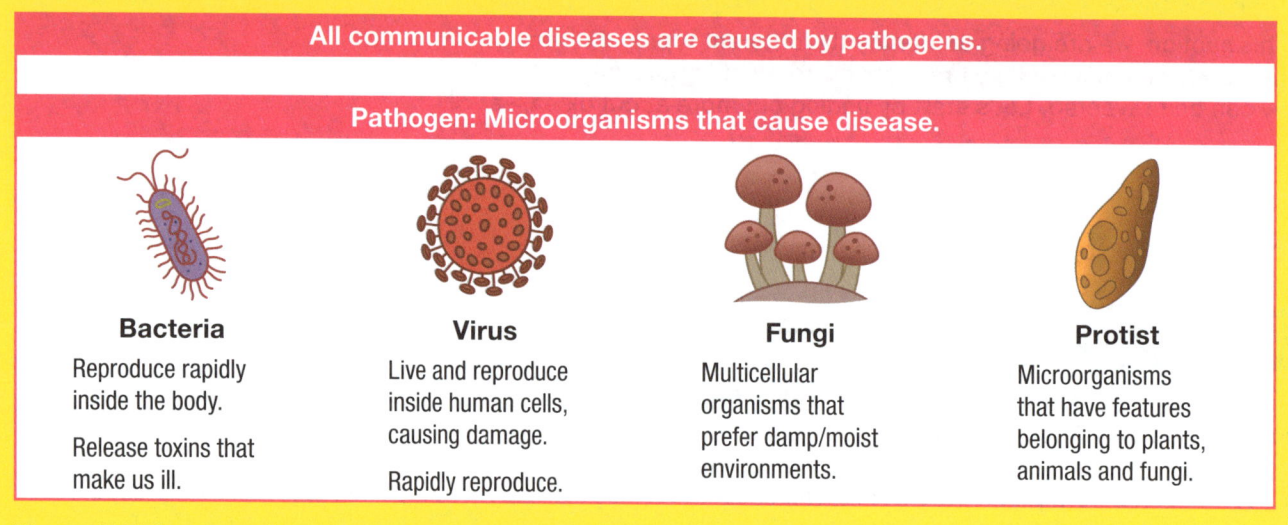

> **Did you know?**
> Most diseases known to the world are caused by **microorganisms**. These are tiny living things that cannot be seen by the naked eye. Sometimes we call them germs. Four of the most common classes of microorganisms or germs are viruses, bacteria, protozoa and fungi. Although some microorganisms cause disease, many are harmless. Those that do the body harm are called **pathogens**.
>
> All communicable diseases are caused by pathogens.
>
> Pathogen: Microorganisms that cause disease.
>
> **Bacteria** — Reproduce rapidly inside the body. Release toxins that make us ill.
>
> **Virus** — Live and reproduce inside human cells, causing damage. Rapidly reproduce.
>
> **Fungi** — Multicellular organisms that prefer damp/moist environments.
>
> **Protist** — Microorganisms that have features belonging to plants, animals and fungi.

Figure 4.3 Micro-organisms that cause disease

Parasitic worms also cause a fair amount of disease, especially in children. Some common parasitic worms are the pinworm, hookworm and tapeworm. These worms are called parasites or are described as parasitic because they live in or on other organisms (hosts), feeding on and benefitting from nutrients that were meant for the host organisms. Parasitic worms are also living things, but unlike pathogens, they are visible to the naked eye.

As seen in Figure 4.2 on page 87, **degenerative** disorders, chemical and physical agents, inherited defects and malnutrition also cause diseases. However, there is a major difference between these factors and the disease-causing organisms. Pathogens and parasitic worms can be caught or passed on by people or things, but the others cannot be passed on. Consequently, diseases caused by organisms are termed **communicable diseases**, and diseases resulting from the other factors are called **non-communicable diseases**. Figure 4.4 provides a classification of the different types of disease that makes it easier to understand.

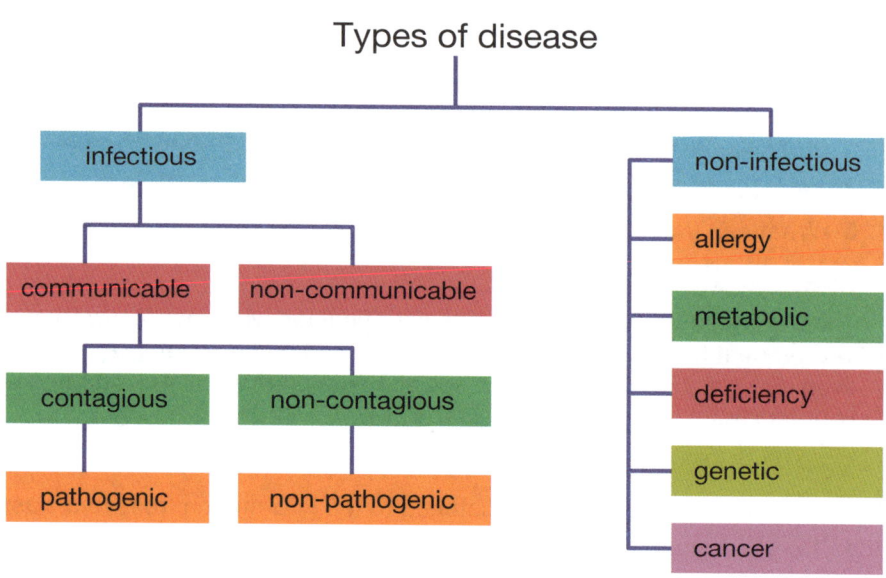

Figure 4.4 Classification of the different types of disease

HOW COMMUNICABLE DISEASES ARE SPREAD

Communicable diseases can be spread in five different ways, as shown in Figure 4.5.

airborne transmission	contaminated objects	food and drinking water	animal-to-person contact	insect bites

Diseases can be spread when an infected person coughs, sneezes or exhales onto another person.	Touching contaminated objects soon after an infected person has done so can spread diseases.	Diseases can be spread through contaminated food and drinking water.	If an infected animal bites or scratches you, you have become exposed to the disease.	Diseases can be transmitted through insect bites, especially insects that suck blood.

Figure 4.5 How communicable diseases are spread

By water. Although the water in streams and rivers may seem clear and tasteless, it can be a source of disease. Animals, sewage and waste matter (Figure 4.6) that has been poorly disposed of, can contaminate our waters. People who use untreated river or stream water for drinking, bathing or cooking are therefore exposed to waterborne germs. Two diseases that are spread in this way are typhoid and dysentery. Some parasitic worms, for example, hookworms, can also be transmitted by way of infested waters.

Figure 4.6 Poor disposal of refuse can contaminate water supplies.

By food. Food can become a source of disease if it is exposed to germs, comes from an unhealthy animal, or is stored under unsuitable conditions. For example, salad vegetables may be contaminated with waterborne germs if they are irrigated with or washed in contaminated water, and cooked food can cause food poisoning if exposed to insects or infected food handlers. Two microorganisms commonly spread by food are Salmonella and *E. coli*. Two parasitic worms that spread through food are the tapeworm and pinworm.

By air. Every time you cough, sneeze, talk or even breathe naturally, you send tiny droplets of moisture into the air. People suffering from a common cold, influenza or tuberculosis also send droplets of these pathogens into the air every time they cough, sneeze or breathe. When people with communicable diseases live or work in crowded, stuffy rooms their germs are more easily spread to others.

By direct contact. Diseases, such as gonorrhoea and syphilis (venereal diseases), ringworm and smallpox are spread by physical contact, i.e. through touching the infected person (as in the case of measles), handling the clothing of the infected person (as in the case of smallpox), or having sexual intercourse with the infected person (as in the case of gonorrhoea and syphilis).

By vectors. A **vector** is any insect or other animal that carries disease-causing organisms from one person or animal to another. The common housefly can spread many different germs, including germs that cause cholera, polio and dysentery. Certain species of mosquitoes spread malaria, and rats are known to spread food-borne diseases, infectious jaundice and the bubonic plague. Pets can be vectors. This is why, on entering a country animals may be quarantined.

Vectors spread germs in a number of ways. Some spread germs by biting the victim or by injecting germs into the victim's bloodstream, while others vomit germs onto food. In other instances, the germ may be lodged in the fur or on the feet of the vector and get transferred as the animal walks. In the case of the bubonic plague, the vector (the rat) was not the actual carrier of the germ but the host of a parasite (the flea) that transmits the disease. Diseases that are spread by direct or indirect contact with people or organisms are described as **contagious diseases**.

How do pathogens and parasites cause disease?

Most pathogens and parasites must enter the body to cause disease. Some cause disease by their mere presence in the body. Others cause disease by feeding on nutrients meant for us, or by producing **toxins** (poisons). When a person's body is invaded by pathogens, the condition is called an **infection**. When the body is invaded by parasites, it is called an **infestation**. An outbreak of disease that spreads rapidly, infecting lots of people in the population, is called an **epidemic**. When the epidemic spreads to several countries, it is described as being a **pandemic** disease.

The body's natural defence against disease

Infection caused by airborne transmission

Infection caused by contact and faeces

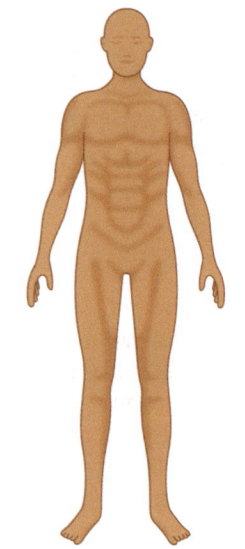

Infection caused by contaminated water

Infection caused by pathogens in bloodstream and tissues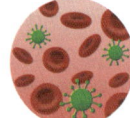

Figure 4.7 Human pathogen transmission

> **Consider this**
>
> Your body is wonderfully made. It has several natural ways of preventing the entry of pathogens and many other ways of protecting itself against disease if germs should enter it.
>
> 1 **Can my skin act as a barrier to germs?**
>
>   Yes, think of the skin as a type of armour. It provides a physical barrier to germs (for more details see Book 1). The only way germs can get past this shield is through cuts or scratches.
>
> 2 **Are there protection mechanisms in the body that trap germs and prevent them from entering the body?**
>
>   Yes, **tiny hairs and the sticky mucus** that coat the walls of our nostrils, throat and other body cavities, help to trap germs and prevent them from entering further into the body.
>
>   Other body secretions such as tears, sweat, urine and saliva help by washing away germs. They also contain salts and acids that either kill or slow down the growth of some microorganisms.

Consider this

3 **What happens if organisms get past these protection mechanisms in the body?**

When determined organisms get past these defences, protective substances inside our bodies, for example, white blood cells and antibodies, take over. They fight and destroy germs. If a person is able to fight and kill invading germs without becoming ill, we say that person has **immunity** to that germ or disease.

4 **What can I do to help protect myself from getting infected with communicable diseases?**

Your ability to fight some communicable diseases is also helped by good nutrition. In Book 1, you learnt that vitamins and minerals help to protect the body against infection. In Book 3 you will see that deficiency diseases such as energy-protein malnutrition and anaemia can be prevented through healthy eating.

Figure 4.8 Regular immunisation can protect against diseases.

Did you know?

Immunity can be either natural or acquired. **Natural immunity** is inherited from our parents or ancestors. **Acquired immunity** results when we receive immunisation vaccines, or our bodies succeed in producing antibodies following a non-fatal attack of a disease. Immunisation vaccines may be given orally or by injection in the form of antibodies or harmless doses of the germ. In the Caribbean, babies are immunised against tuberculosis, polio, measles, diphtheria, whooping cough and tetanus.

Hygiene

While the body has its own natural defences against disease, we all know that it is far better to prevent disease. In Book 1, you acquired some skills in disease prevention as you studied personal hygiene. Now you will see how hygiene in the home and surroundings can help in the battle against disease. Since pathogens and vectors flourish in warm, damp, dirty places our hygiene plan will aim to do away with as many of these conditions as possible.

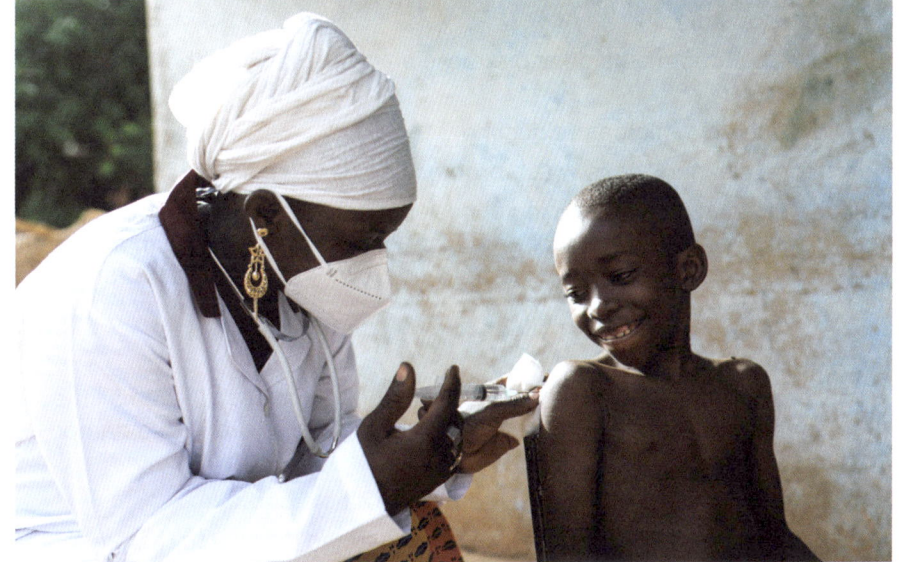

Figure 4.9 A boy being immunised in a health clinic.

What is a disease?

Hygiene in the home

To prevent diseases from spreading, it is important that our homes are kept clean and free from germs. **How do we achieve that? Here are some tasks that will help in keeping our environments germ free:**

- Sweeping, dusting, mopping and scrubbing are simple ways of removing dust, dirt, grime and other soils that can attract germs and vermin to your home.
- Each one of these cleaning procedures must be carried out in a specific manner if they are to be effective.

Figure 4.10 The correct equipment to clean effectively

ACTIVITIES

1. Observe the tasks that your family does in your home for one week. Describe whether your family performs these tasks effectively.
2. Which of the tasks do you help with in your home?

Here are some instructions that will help you and your family to clean effectively.

Sweeping

Use a long-handled broom for large rooms and a short-handled broom for small areas.

- Shut windows and doors if it is windy.
- Remove rugs or mats.
- Stand behind the broom and sweep smoothly away from or across you, with the head of the broom down, so that dust does not get all over you (Figure 4.11).
- Work methodically towards the door if you are sweeping the whole room or house.
- Gather the dust to one spot and collect it in a dustpan. Sometimes it is easier to use a hand brush for this. Wrap the dust in paper and throw it into the dustbin.
- Shake the broom outside and remove any fluff. Hang up the brooms and dustpan.
- Allow dust to settle before dusting.

Note: For a cleaner sweep, wash brooms and brushes occasionally.

Walls. Walls may need sweeping occasionally. For this, you will need a special long-handled broom, or an ordinary sweeping broom with a duster tied over it. Remove all wall decorations first. Work from top to bottom using even strokes.

Figure 4.11 Sweep dust and dirt away from or across your body.

Dusting

- Have two clean dusters. If you prefer, dampen one slightly with a little water or liquid furniture polish. Dust will cling more readily to a damp duster.
- Fold in the corners of the cloth so that it forms a pad.
- Use the damp duster to gather the dust and the dry one to restore polish.

- Rub polished surfaces well.
- Work methodically around the room, dusting high places first. Pay particular attention to doors and ledges.
- When dusting furniture with ornaments, do the ornaments first and lay them aside.
- Shake dusters frequently outside. Look out for open windows and passing people.

Note: For a cleaner job, wash dusters when they become dirty.

Rugs and carpets may be dusted by shaking, beating or brushing with a hard brush or broom. This dispersal method is not the best, as much of the dust may be blown back into the house. The vacuum cleaner is the easiest, cleanest method of removing dust, but needs electricity. The dust is drawn into an enclosed bag or compartment by suction. Empty and clean frequently. The vacuum cleaner is also useful for dusting rough surfaces.

Figure 4.12 Dampen the duster with liquid or furniture polish.

Figure 4.13 Using a vacuum cleaner is the cleanest method of removing dust.

Mopping

A dry cotton mop can be used to remove dust from polished surfaces and vinyl or linoleum floors. The dust is collected in the mop head and disposed of by shaking out of a window or door. These mops usually have wide, flat swivel-type heads.

Figure 4.14 Dry cotton mop

Figure 4.15 Mop for wet wiping

Mops for wet wiping may be made of cotton or sponge. When cleaning large areas it is most convenient to use them with a special bucket fitted with a strainer for squeezing out excess water. A more recent invention is the sponge mop with a self-squeezing device. This is ideal for smooth surfaces.

- Sweep the floor.
- Prepare a bucket with water and a grease remover such as soap or detergent.
- Wipe methodically towards the door in manageable patches, using a wet mop first, then drying off with a mop that has been squeezed to remove excess water.
- After use, rinse the mop thoroughly in clean hot water. Shake open the mop head then leave it to dry. Store with the head standing uppermost, if possible. Occasionally the plain wooden handle may require scrubbing.

What is a disease?

Scrubbing

- Sweep or dust the surface that is to be cleaned.
- Dampen the surface.
- Scrub with a cleaning agent and scrubbing brush along the grain of the wood (not against or across it) until it is clean.
- Rinse with a clean cloth, lightly wrung out in clean water.
- Dry with a clean absorbent cloth.
- After use, rinse scrubbing brush and cloth, and put out to dry.

Every room in the home should be kept scrupulously clean. This can be a simple task if every family member helps. This gives them a sense of cleanliness and helps to develop a spirit of cooperation. If rooms are cleaned often, dust and dirt will not accumulate and cleaning becomes easier.

Figure 4.16 Family members work together in helping to keep the house clean.

Removal of refuse

> **Did you know?**
> Your household produces two types of refuse – organic and inorganic.
> **Organic refuse:** Chicken skin, plantain skin, fruit peelings and leftovers from meals. They are given this name because they are all perishable. If organic refuse is not properly disposed of, it develops bad smells and becomes a breeding ground for harmful microorganisms. Organic refuse also attracts pests and vermin.
> **Inorganic waste:** Waste that will not decay, for example, plastic containers and bottles, and the bottles and tins that once contained foodstuffs.

Every family should have a bin for the collection of refuse. It may be metal or plastic, but it must have a lid that can be closed properly. In some countries the law demands that bins be fitted with disposable plastic bags, which can be tied and removed when they are full. In other cases, refuse is placed in small plastic bags before being put into the bin. Both systems are recommended, as they are more sanitary than putting waste directly in the bin. Plastic bags also make the removal of waste and the cleaning of bins less messy.

Figure 4.17 Place refuse in plastic bags before putting them into the bin.

All bins should be kept where prowling animals cannot upset them easily, and it is a good habit to empty them daily. Since conditions within most bins are ideal for the growth of germs and vermin, they should be washed and disinfected at least once a week. Rounded corners make cleaning and disinfecting easier.

Figure 4.18 Bins should be cleaned regularly.

> **ACTIVITIES**
>
> 1. Keep a record of the waste your family produces in one week. Separate it between organic and inorganic waste.
> 2. Make suggestions on how your family can separate their organic and inorganic waste.
> 3. Find out if there are any waste management initiatives in your community and share the information with your class.

Getting rid of vermin

Rats, mice, cockroaches, bugs, ants, beetles, fleas, houseflies and other household pests often carry germs that cause disease. You can keep your home free of pests by maintaining sanitary conditions in and around your home.

Figure 4.19 Pest control

Figure. 4.20 The housefly

The following measures will help to maintain good sanitation in your home.

- Wash dirty dishes and clear away scraps of food or crumbs after every meal.
- Cover and store food carefully.
- Clean and spray storerooms, store cupboards and other storage areas regularly.
- Dispose of rubbish in a proper manner. This prevents insects and pests from breeding or living in them.

Get rid of mice, rats, beetles, cockroaches, moths, houseflies, bedbugs and fleas. The housefly is one of the most dangerous of household pests.

- Hang in the sun or wash sheets and blankets every week and sun mattresses occasionally.
- Air pillows frequently.
- Stop up cracks and holes where roaches, bedbugs and other insects can hide.

Note: Do not let pets lick children or climb onto beds. They can also spread disease.

Figure 4.21 Getting rid of vermin

What is a disease?

Hygiene in the surroundings

It is also important to maintain a healthy environment. Your environment includes the area around your home and in your neighbourhood. A clean environment is pleasant to be in but, more importantly, it safeguards your physical well-being. Pests, vermin and germs cannot exist in clean conditions. Here are some suggestions for keeping your surroundings clean and disease free.

- Sweep the yard and surrounding area often.
- In many places the local health authorities collect refuse regularly. If there is no refuse collection or recycling facility in your community, burn or bury refuse in a spot far away from houses and rivers or streams where people collect drinking water.
- Weed grassy areas and dispose of cut grass. Insects, rats and mice use grass dumps to nest.
- Get rid of receptacles such as tins, coconut shells, broken calabashes and old containers. They collect water and can form excellent breeding places for mosquitoes.
- Repair cracks in paving as they also hold water.
- Latrines or outhouses should be built so that animals cannot reach the faeces. A deep hole with a well-built hut over it works well, placed at least 19 metres (21 yards) from the house and kept well covered.
- Clean drains often and keep them free of stagnant water. They are good breeding grounds for ringworms and mosquitoes.
- Do not rear animals close to the house (Figure 4.22). The dung encourages flies, roaches and rats and the smell can be very unpleasant.
- Have walkways paved if possible. Sweep and wash frequently to prevent a build-up of moss.
- Keep flower or kitchen gardens to add to the attractiveness of your surroundings.
- Some flowers also repel insects.

No matter how small and humble your home may be, you and your family are better protected against disease if it is kept clean and tidy.

Figure 4.22 Rearing animals near the home

Figure 4.23 Keeping animals in the backyard can be a health hazard.

The community's role in the fight against disease

Does your country have organisations that help to safeguard the nation's health? Is the safety of your water system overseen by a special organisation? Most countries in the Caribbean have authorities that work to safeguard the health of the nation. These include Public Health Departments and Water Authorities. In addition, many countries receive assistance from international organisations that oversee world health. The World Health Organization (WHO) is one. It was formed by the United Nations Assembly in 1948. The aim of WHO is to attain the highest level of health for all people throughout the world. WHO is involved in activities such as immunisation, health research and the training of health workers.

ACTIVITIES

1. Name three international organisations that are involved in the fight against disease in your country. State their general responsibilities.
2. Plan a campaign against disease in your school.
   a. Formulate five hygiene rules that will help to improve the sanitation of classrooms.
   b. Identify three changes that can be made to the school building or its facilities to improve the sanitation of the school environment.

What is a disease?

Child growth and development

Each month, one of the two ovaries in a female releases a ripe egg called an **ovum**. Each ovary contains about 200 000 egg cells, but only one will ripen each month in one ovary. The ripened egg or ovum is released into the fallopian tube that leads from the ovary to the uterus. Each fallopian tube is about 10 cm (4 in) long.

If sexual intercourse takes place while the ripened egg is in the fallopian tube, it is likely that some of the many millions of sperms that were deposited in the vagina during ejaculation by a male partner will find their way to the fallopian tube. Here, only one sperm will unite or fuse with the ripened egg. When this happens, **fertilisation** or **conception** has occurred. Several changes will take place in the growth and development of the fertilised egg until the baby is ready to be born.

FROM CONCEPTION TO BIRTH

The fertilised egg travels slowly down the fallopian tube and embeds itself in the lining of the uterus. The process takes about seven days. The woman is then said to be pregnant. At this stage, the undeveloped offspring is just a mass of cells, invisible to the naked eye, and is called an **embryo**. This developing organism will go through several changes during the period of pregnancy, which usually lasts for 40 weeks (Figure 4.25).

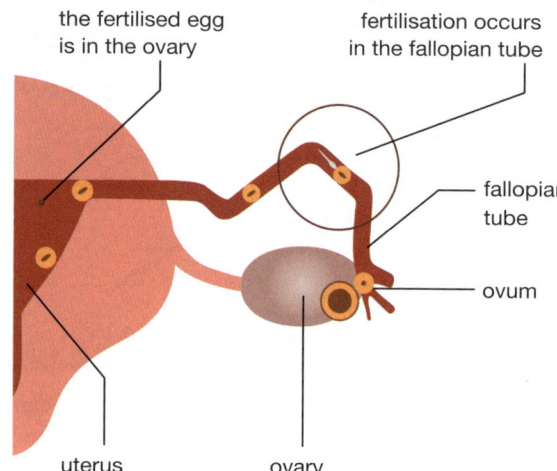

Figure 4.24 Fertilisation or conception takes place between the egg and the sperm.

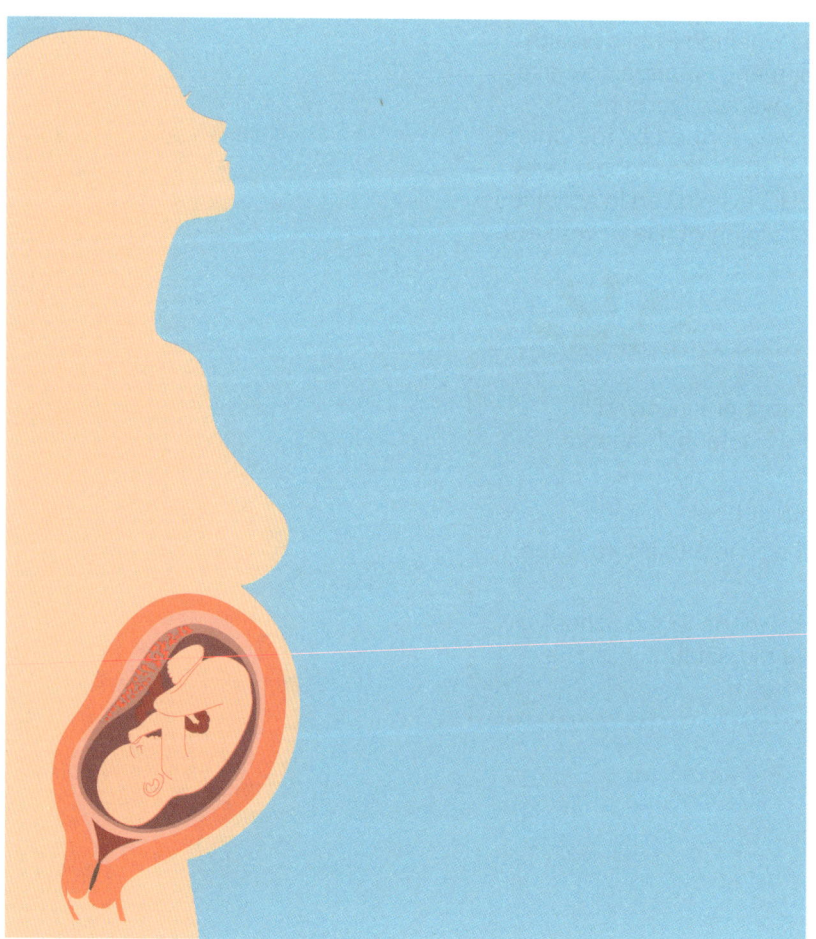

Figure 4.25 The developing foetus

CHANGES DURING PREGNANCY

At 6 weeks

The embryo, which is only 6 mm (¼ in) long, is beginning to take the shape of a human being inside a bag of fluid called the **amniotic sac**. Although it is not yet recognisably human, limb buds, which will develop into legs and arms, are appearing. The head begins to take shape and there is a bulge for the heart. At this embryonic stage, all the vital structures and internal organs, such as spine, eyes, brain and heart, begin to form.

At 8 weeks

All the major internal organs of the embryo are now formed and the heart is beating strongly. The limbs continue to develop and the face has some recognisable characteristics: nostrils, eyes and mouth. Although the embryo at this stage has a fairly large head in proportion to its overall size, it is still very small – about 2.2 cm (⅞ in) long.

At 12 weeks

After the twelfth week of pregnancy the embryo is called a **foetus**. Although the head is still overlarge, the foetus is recognisably human. The face is properly formed and eyelids are present. The external genital organs are appearing, though it is still too early to tell the sex of the baby. At this stage, the foetus is about 6.5 cm (2½ in) long and weighs only 18 g (½ oz).

At 16 weeks

The uterus (womb) is beginning to make a bulge and the mother's abdomen becomes visibly larger. At this stage, all the limbs of the foetus are properly formed with fingers, toes and nails. The sex of the foetus can now be identified by the doctor, although it is only about 16 cm (6¼ in) long and will normally weigh about 135 g (4¾ oz). The foetus moves its limbs quite vigorously, though the mother may not yet be able to feel the movements.

At 20 weeks

The foetus begins to grow rapidly. Its length is about 25 cm (10 in) and it weighs about 340 g (12 oz). Hair appears on the head and the mother can now feel the movements of the foetus. The growth rate of the foetus can be checked regularly by qualified people at pre-natal clinics.

At 24 weeks

The skin of the foetus is wrinkled because it lacks fat. It is also covered with fine, downy hair. At this stage the foetus is about 32 cm (13 in) long and will normally weigh about 565 g (1¼ lb).

At 28 weeks

The foetus is covered with a creamy, waxy substance called vernix, which protects it from the surrounding fluid. At this stage, its length is 37 cm (14½ in) and will normally weigh about 900 g (2 lb).

At 32 weeks

The baby is now perfectly formed and its head is in proportion with its body. At this stage the baby is about 40.5 cm (16 in) long and weighs about 1.6 kg (3½ lb).

At 36 weeks

The baby is now almost fully mature and has filled out with the laying down of more fat. It measures 46 cm (18½ in) and weighs 2.5 kg (5½ lb).

At 40 weeks

The baby is now fully developed and ready to be born. At birth, the average baby is about 50 cm (20 in) long and normally weighs about 3.4 kg (7½ lb). But there are wide variations in birth weight and a normal, healthy baby may weigh as little as 2.5 kg (5½ lb) or as much as 4.5 kg (10 lb) or more.

Child growth and development

GROWTH AND DEVELOPMENT AFTER BIRTH

Growth and development of the baby does not stop at birth but will continue throughout life until the baby reaches the stage of adulthood. After birth, it is important to take the baby for regular health checks. Changes in weight, height, size and general physical development of the child can be checked by medical personnel at childcare clinics in many health centres. Post-natal care is as important for the child after birth as pre-natal care is before birth.

Figure 4.26 Growth and development after birth

Baby's weight and height

During the first week of life it is normal for a newborn baby to lose a few pounds, but the weight is usually regained after the tenth day. From then on, the average weight gain is 142–170 g (5–6 oz) a week. At one year old, the baby will have tripled its birth weight.

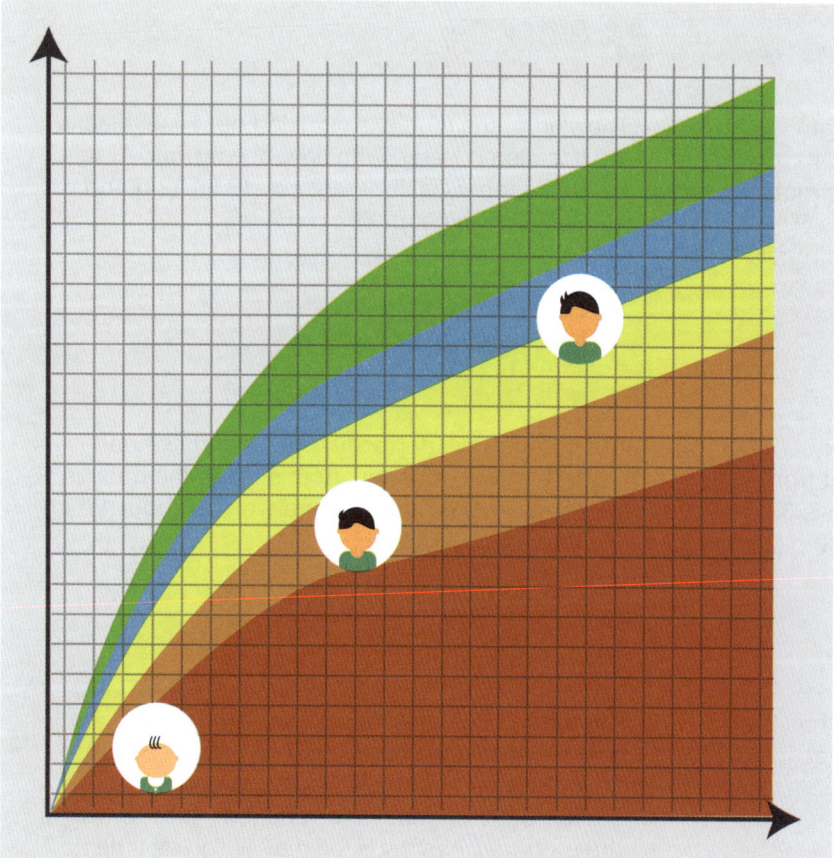

Figure 4.27 Growth chart indicating height and weight of babies

A child between the ages of one and three years is commonly called a toddler. The average toddler gains about 3.2 kg (7 lb) in the second year and 2.2 kg (5 lb) in the third year. After this, the body weight increases comparatively slowly until adolescence is reached.

As with weight gain, a baby's increase in height (or length) is greatest during the first six months of life. After that, growth slows down gradually.

Figure 4.28 A toddler interacting with her mother

Baby's head

At birth, a baby's head is about 33 cm (13 in) in circumference. The size of the head increases rapidly during the first year to about 46 cm (18 in) by the time the baby is one year old. During the next 11 years, growth in head size is much slower. The circumference increases by only about 7.5 cm (3 in).

It used to be thought that the size of the head determined the degree of intelligence of a child. Research has shown, however, that the size of the head has nothing whatsoever to do with intelligence.

Figure 4.29 Measuring a baby's head circumference

Baby's limbs

During the first year of life, the baby's appearance changes dramatically as the proportions of the body even out. The narrow shoulders of the newborn infant broaden and the large abdomen becomes flatter. The fingers and toes lengthen and fill out so that they lose their claw-like appearance. The palms of the hands broaden and the feet become larger in length and width.

At this stage the young baby is top heavy and has difficulty controlling its body, particularly the head. For the first few weeks, the baby's head will flop like a rag doll unless supported. Therefore, it is very important to support the baby's head when it is still very young (Figure 4.30).

The baby will topple over easily whenever it is placed to sit or stand, or it attempts to crawl or walk. The small hands and feet make the baby appear clumsy, as the hands are not yet strong or large enough to hold or grasp objects. Muscle control or coordination is not very good either.

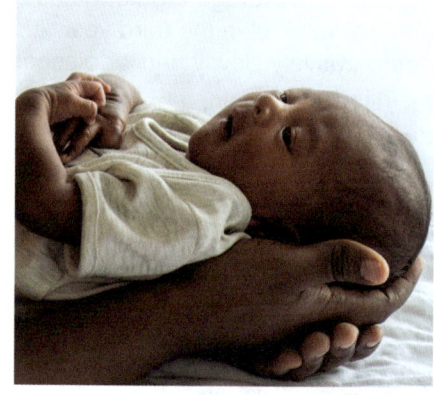

Figure 4.30 Holding a baby's head when it is still very young

Baby's bones

At birth, a baby's bones are not yet fully hardened. The bones in the skull are not even fully joined, which allows for growth of the brain during the first year of life. At the top of the baby's head there is a diamond-shaped area called the **fontanelle** or soft spot. The spot is not really soft at all, but unlike the rest of the head it is not covered by bone but by a tough membrane.

The hardening of the bones starts soon after birth and ends between the ages of 16 and 18. The healthy growth of bones depends on the correct diet, which should be particularly rich in calcium, phosphorus and vitamin D. This is why it is very important for a mother to increase her intake of these nutrients during pregnancy and lactation (breast-feeding).

FONTANELLE

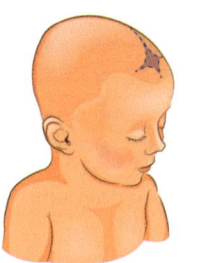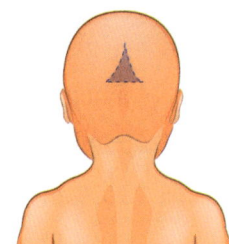

Figure 4.31 The fontanelle, the soft spot on the baby's head

Baby's teeth

During the sixth month of life, the first of the 20 milk teeth will appear, usually at the front of the mouth. These are temporary teeth. The erupting or breaking through of the milk teeth is called teething.

During teething, the baby may feel out-of-sorts and the gums may become sore and the cheeks red. Once the tooth has come through the gum, however, the baby will feel better. The remaining temporary teeth will appear one by one over the next two years. These temporary teeth are soft, small and have shallow roots.

At about the age of 6 or 7, the temporary teeth will gradually fall out and be replaced by a permanent set of teeth. Permanent teeth are usually all in place by the age of 13.

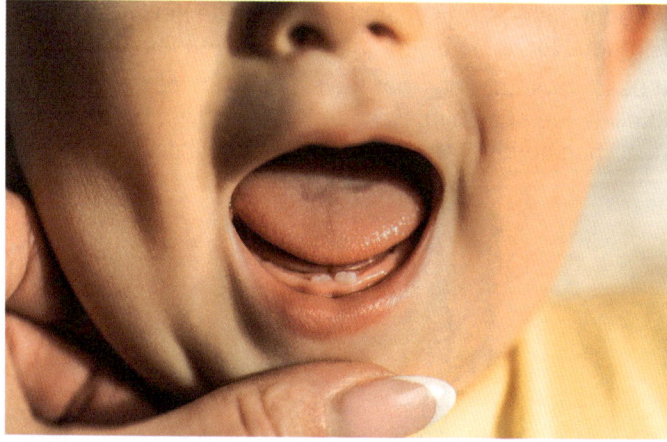

Figure 4.32 Teething baby

The healthy growth of the baby's teeth also depends on the mother's diet, which should be rich in calcium and phosphorus during pregnancy and lactation. Even the temporary teeth can suffer from decay if they are not taken care of properly. Children who are allowed to eat too many sweets can lose their temporary teeth. This can affect the proper growth of the permanent teeth.

Caring for baby's teeth

- Use special soft toothbrushes, which will not damage the baby's gums.
- Start brushing the teeth as soon as the baby will allow it.
- Use a toothpaste containing the mineral fluoride, which helps to prevent tooth decay.
- Teach children to brush their own teeth as soon as they are able to.
- Do not allow children to eat too many sweets. Encourage them to eat fresh fruits instead. Their teeth will last longer.

Figure 4.33 Teach children to take care of their teeth.

Baby's physical progress

During the first 12 to 20 months, a baby makes more physical progress than at any other time in life. The following gives some of the major landmarks in that progress. However, all babies are different and some may do things earlier or later than others.

From birth to 3 months. The newborn baby has primitive or automatic reflexes, most of which will gradually disappear.

- *Grasp reflex.* If a finger or object is put in the hand, the baby will automatically clench its fist around it. A baby's grasp will be very strong for about three months.
- *Walking or stepping reflex.* Babies whose bare feet are put on a flat surface when they are picked up, will automatically make walking or stepping movements (Figure 4.34). This reflex is lost after two months.
- *Sucking, swallowing and rooting reflexes.* These reflexes enable babies to feed as soon after birth as possible. Gently stroking the baby's cheek with the nipple or the teat of a bottle will cause the baby's head to move in the direction of the touch.

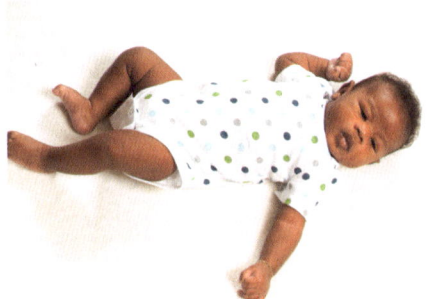
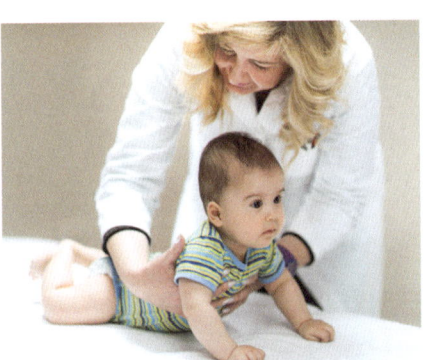
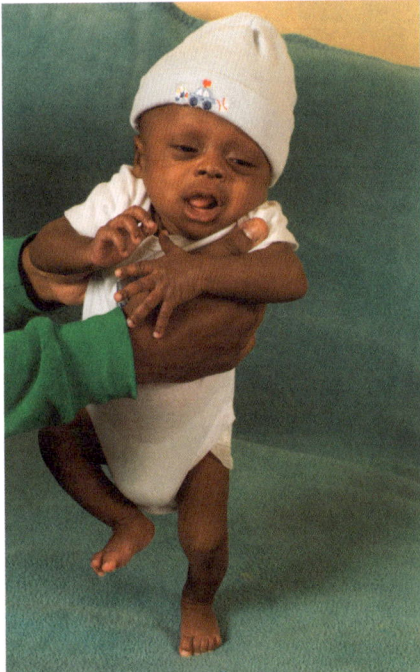
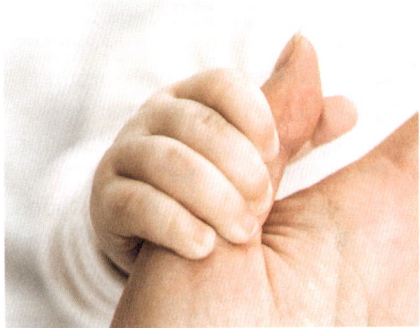

Figure 4.34 Automatic reflexes of newborn babies

Child growth and development

At about two months, the baby's eye muscles begin to focus together properly. The baby no longer squints or looks cross-eyed. During this stage babies will smile, gurgle with joy and respond automatically to their mother's voice.

At 3 to 6 months. Coordination improves and babies can sit up with support (at about 5 months), roll over, and can use the whole hand to grasp a toy. They are visually alert. At this stage babies suck anything they can get hold of (Figure 4.35).

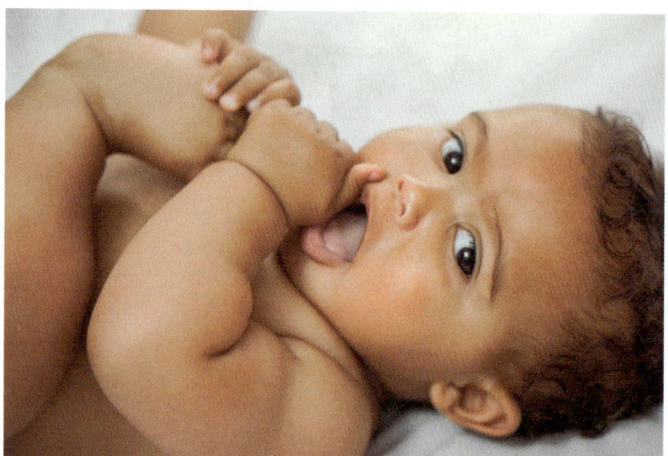

Figure 4.35 At 3–6 months, babies suck anything they can get hold of

Figure 4.36 A baby will try to walk at between 6 and 9 months old

At 6 to 9 months. Babies can sit up unaided for about 10–15 minutes and may also start to crawl and stand while holding on to something, or even try to walk (Figure 4.36). They can pick up small objects between the finger and thumb and will try to hold a spoon. At this stage, babies can understand simple everyday words such as 'bye-bye', 'no' and 'hello'. They also like to imitate sounds made by their parents.

At 9 to 12 months. Babies can sit on the floor without support; drop and throw toys; walk around furniture while holding on and stepping sideways; stand alone for a few moments or even walk. They can understand simple instructions, such as 'Give it to Daddy', 'Where is your cup?'. They can drink from a cup and chew soft food.

At 12 to 15 months. Babies will probably take their first few steps alone, usually quite suddenly. They can go up and down stairs; can feed themselves (Figure 4.37) and can string two or three words together, such as 'Mummy sit'. At this stage, babies love listening to nursery rhymes and other songs, and simple stories.

Figure 4.37 A one-year-old baby likes to feed himself.

ACTIVITIES

1. Visit a clinic where mothers take their babies and ask the nurse or doctor to let you record the activities that take place. Talk with some of the mothers and find out what services they get from the clinic, during and after their pregnancy.
2. Observe a toddler for half an hour. Record the age of the toddler and all activities engaged in during your observation. Indicate which activities seem to have some link with learning about the surroundings. Compare your record with two other classmates and report to your class.

Childcare

Young children should naturally eat when they are hungry and sleep when they are tired. Newborn babies naturally sleep a lot. They also need plenty of care and personal attention. Plenty of sleep, fresh air and sunshine, good nourishment and protection against disease all help to ensure babies' good health. This section will deal with some important aspects of the care babies must have in order to be in good health.

Sleeping

A newborn baby sleeps about 19 hours daily. By age one, the baby sleeps for only about 12 hours. This pattern continues until the child is about five or six years old. After this, the child will sleep for 9 or 10 hours daily.

Newborn babies will sleep for short periods of two or three hours. When not sleeping, they are usually feeding. By age one, the baby may take a nap in the morning and again in the afternoon, in addition to night-time sleep. After the second year, the baby may give up the morning nap.

The baby's bed

Babies need a comfortable environment in which to sleep and rest. For the first two months, the baby's bed may be a large basket or bassinet that has been lined and fitted with a comfortable mattress. After this, the baby will need more space and a crib is an appropriate choice. The mattress in the crib should be firm and protected with a waterproof sheet. Babies do not require a pillow (Figure 4.38).

Sleeping position

The position in which the baby is put to sleep is important, both for the baby to rest properly and to reduce the risk of cot death. Until babies are about three to four months old, they cannot move their bodies and therefore remain in one position until moved. To reduce the risk of cot death, babies should be placed to sleep on their back rather than face down.

Figure 4.38 The baby's bed does not require a pillow.

FEEDING

Newborn babies need adequate nourishment to grow and stay healthy. A mother's milk is considered the best choice for a young baby (Figure 4.39). However, some mothers are unable to breast-feed babies for several reasons.

- They do not produce enough breast milk.
- They are pregnant again.
- They have to go out to work at a workplace far away from home.

Some mothers are embarrassed to breast-feed in public, but they can do this quite easily by covering the exposed breast with a clean towel or rag, being very careful not to cover the baby's face. Many public places today provide facilities for mothers to breast-feed in comfort.

Breast-feeding

There are many advantages of breast-feeding babies.

- Breast milk contains all the nutrients a baby needs for the first few months of life.
- Breast milk protects the baby from several diseases.
- Breast milk is at the right temperature for the baby and needs no heating or cooling.
- Breast milk is always ready when the baby needs it, and is not costly.
- Babies feel loved and very secure when they are held close to mothers' breasts during breast-feeding.
- Breast-feeding is far safer than bottle-feeding since the chance of babies getting gastroenteritis is reduced.

Figure 4.39 A mother's milk is considered the best choice for a young baby.

Bottle-feeding

Bottle-feeding is more costly and time-consuming. Regular supplies of baby formula must be purchased. You also need plenty of bottles and must take special care of all feeding equipment. Bottles should be washed thoroughly, sterilised daily and stored properly. To ensure healthy babies, all feeding bottles must be kept very clean.

Care of bottles and feeding equipment. It is very important that all feeding equipment is kept scrupulously clean by thorough washing and sterilising (Figure 4.40). Here are some guidelines to follow.

- Wash the bottles and teats (rubber nipples of the baby's feeding bottles) in hot soapy water. Use a bottle brush to get into the corners. The brush must be used only for the baby's feeding equipment and should be kept clean after each use.
- Rinse bottles and teats under cold running water or in several changes of fresh, clean water until all traces of soap have been removed.
- Rub teats inside and out with salt until no stickiness remains.
- Rinse teats thoroughly. Squirt water through the hole to ensure it is not clogged.
- Soak bottles and teats in a clean container of boiling water for at least 10 minutes, or soak in a sterilising solution for three hours.
- A large, deep stainless-steel pot with a lid may be used for sterilising baby's feeding bottles but should be used only for baby's feeding equipment.

Preparing a bottle-feed. When mixing feeds for bottle-feeding babies, remember to:

- Follow the manufacturer's instructions on the tin or packet exactly – do not reduce the proportion of milk recommended, otherwise the baby will not get enough nourishment.
- Keep all equipment sterile and use only equipment that has been sterilised.
- Wash your hands thoroughly before and after preparing feeds.
- If using cow's milk, boil it, then allow it to cool in a safe place. Keep it covered from dust and germs.

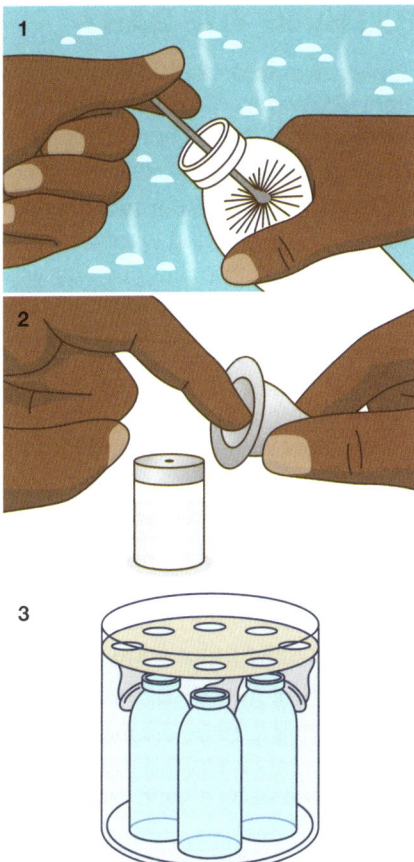

Figure 4.40 Three stages in sterilising bottles

Weaning

At about the age of 4–6 months, or when the baby weighs about 7.2 kg (16 lb), semi-solid foods, along with milk, should be gradually introduced. The transition from breast-feeding or liquid bottled milk to eating a regular well-balanced meal of solid food is commonly called **weaning**.

- In the Caribbean, the first semi-solid food to be introduced is porridge. This should be thick in consistency and should always be fed with a spoon, never in a bottle. Fruit juices and soft, crushed fruit can also be given.
- Between the ages of 6 months and one year, new foods should be introduced, one at a time. These should be finely mashed, minced or chopped, as the baby is still too young to chew adult food.
- By the time the baby is 18 months old, food prepared for the rest of the family may be given in small portions. The baby's portion should be removed from the pot before salt, pepper and other spices are added.

BATHING THE BABY

Babies should be kept clean and comfortable throughout the day and night. They may have a daily bath in the morning or evening, whichever fits in better with the routine. Having a bath is an important part of a baby's daily routine, and fathers can learn to enjoy this task (Figure 4.41).

During the first week or two of life, the umbilical cord that was cut at birth will shrivel up, leaving what we call the navel. Take great care to keep it clean and free from infection by wiping it regularly and keeping it dry. Here are some guidelines to follow when bathing babies.

- Collect everything needed to bath the baby.
- Fill a small tub with water, putting in cold water first, then enough hot water to make the bath pleasantly warm. Do not overfill the tub as it will overflow when the baby is put into it.
- Test the temperature of the water with your elbow to make sure that it feels pleasantly warm, but not hot.
- Undress the baby and wrap in a big towel, then clean the child's eyes, nose and mouth by wiping with damp cotton wool or a face cloth. Use a separate piece of cotton wool for each eye, and wipe from the inside towards the outer edge once, in order not to introduce infection.
- Clean the outside of the ears and the nostrils very gently.
- If the hair is to be washed, hold the baby firmly in your lap, then wet the baby's head and rub the scalp and hair with soap or baby shampoo. Hold the baby's head over the tub and rinse hair well. Dry gently.
- Unwrap the baby and soap the body all over (except the face). Pay special attention to the underarms, folds of the legs and genital area.
- Hold the baby firmly and gently lower into the tub. Make sure the baby's head and shoulders are well supported with one hand. Rinse off all the soap with the other hand.
- If the baby wants to play in the water, encourage this. Then lift the child out of the bath water, dry the body gently and thoroughly. Pay special attention to underarms, folds of the legs and between the toes.
- Powder, oil or body lotion may then be applied before putting clean, fresh clothing on the baby.

Figure 4.41 Having a bath is an important part of a baby's daily routine.

BABY'S CLOTHING

Baby's clothes must be warm, soft, light in weight, smooth, comfortable and roomy. They should be simple in style, loose enough to allow movement, easy to put on and take off, and easy to wash and iron.

Babies need to be kept warm because they are not able to regulate their own body temperature during the first few months of life. However, in the Caribbean it tends to get very hot, so clothes made of cotton fabrics are best for babies. Other fabrics tend to babies too hot and uncomfortable, causing them to cry.

CRYING

Crying is quite natural for babies. It is the only way in which they can indicate their needs and attract your attention. Whenever a baby cries, therefore, it may mean that the child is:

- hungry or thirsty
- lonely or bored
- having wind pains or tummyache
- too hot, too cold, wet or just uncomfortable
- feeling sick and unwell.

Parents usually learn from experience what is wrong with a baby that is crying. For example, if the baby starts crying soon after being well fed, it is hardly likely that hunger is the problem. Sometimes a crying baby just needs to be picked up and cuddled. Never leave a baby to cry (Figure 4.42). If the baby cries a lot or behaves as if unwell, always consult a doctor.

Figure 4.42 Never leave a baby to cry.

TOILET TRAINING

Of all the muscles in the body, those controlling the bowels and bladder are the slowest to mature. Most children, therefore, do not develop physical control until about 1½ to 2½ years old. Appropriate timing, proper equipment and patience will help parents deal with toilet training satisfactorily.

Proper equipment gives the best results. Chairs for toilet training are very useful. If a toilet chair is too expensive, however, a potty will do. A potty is necessary because the regular toilet bowl will be too high and large for the child to sit on.

Toilet training should only begin when the parents think the child is ready. Any attempts before the child is ready will only result in tantrums, tears, failure and frustration. Toilet training should be a happy and relaxed part of a child's development (Figure 4.43).

Guidelines for toilet training

- Remove the baby's diaper (nappy) and encourage the child to sit on the potty before and after meals.
- If the child cries and is not responding favourably, this simply indicates that the child is not yet ready. Try again later.
- Give the child some toys to play with while sitting on the potty. This will make the child more comfortable. Do not be disappointed if nothing happens.
- Do not scold or punish the child for any accidents of the bowel or bladder. This will only make the child upset and delay learning.
- Be patient. There will be times when the child will lapse, for example, when the child is tired, excited or occupied with an activity.

Figure 4.43 Toilet training should be a happy and relaxed part of a child's development.

Immunisation

Children can be affected quite easily by certain diseases, such as poliomyelitis, whooping cough, diphtheria and tetanus. It is very important that babies and small children are protected against these and other childhood diseases. **Immunisation** is the process of making people immune to disease. This is done by having children inoculated or vaccinated. Vaccinations give children immunity against particular diseases.

Vaccinations are given in the form of an injection or a drink, and at different ages. Parents are responsible for taking babies to health clinics to be vaccinated. The doctor or nurse will explain the schedule of visits and will usually record the details of all immunisations on an immunisation record card. Parents should also keep their own immunisation record, listing the date and type of vaccine the child received.

ACTIVITIES

1. Visit the health centre in your area and find out from the nurse
   a. what diseases children in the Caribbean must be vaccinated against
   b. the ages at which children should receive the different vaccinations. Draw up your findings in a table and report to your class.
2. Find out from your parents about their experiences with toilet training their children. Talk with another parent in your community and compare your findings. Report to your class on what parents can do to make toilet training a success.

Design project

According to the World Health Organization (2020) more than 80% of the world's adolescent population is insufficiently physically active. This may be attributed to their sedentary lifestyles and poorly developed eating habits as result of globalisation, their environment and the shift to online school as a result of the COVID-19 pandemic. Potential problems associated with a sedentary lifestyle include increased risk of developing non-communicable diseases such as obesity, diabetes and hypertension and reduced sleep duration, which can impact quality of life and academic performance.

Work with a team to find solutions for students in your year group.

Career corner

Child life specialist

A child life specialist is a healthcare worker who is often employed in the pediatric department of a hospital, among other venues. They work with children under 18 years of age (although patients are often younger children) and their families to make hospital visits more comfortable, as well as to educate children on health issues and topics.

If you're interested in working as a child life specialist, the following are some of the steps you may have to take:

- Study Food and Nutrition, Chemistry and Biology for CSEC and CAPE.
- Gain a bachelor's degree at an accredited school in a relevant field such as Bachelor of Arts in Human Development and Family Studies or Psychology (either in person or through online courses). Some areas of focus should be family law, child and adolescent psychology and guidance and counselling.
- Enter an internship or other supervised professional training program, unless one was included in your degree requirements.
- Earn the Certified Child Life Specialist (CCLS) credential.
- Determine whether it's necessary to earn a state/country license or other special credential in your state/country in order to start your career.

What have I learnt?

Short answer questions

1. Fill in the blanks using the words provided:

   _____ provide us with acquired immunity. [Immunisations, Ancestors]

   A family that is travelling from your country to one that has a polio epidemic _____ be given polio vaccines before travelling. [should, should not]

   A healthy diet _____ protect us against all diseases. [can, cannot]

   Pathogens cause an _____ and parasites cause _____. [infestations, infection]

   A _____ knee increases a person's chances of getting an infection. [bruised, dry]

2. Discuss two aspects of the care that babies need to stay in good health.

3. Discuss any two ways in which babies may be made as comfortable as possible.

4. Explain the meaning of immunisation and name any two vaccinations that babies must receive.

5. Discuss (a) the importance of breast-feeding and (b) the precautions that should be taken for bottle-feeding babies.

6. Outline the procedure for cleaning the rubber nipples/teats of babies' feeding bottles.

7. Explain the meaning of weaning and indicate the age at which weaning should usually start.

8. Explain the meaning of the following: conception, pregnancy, embryo.

9. Discuss the changes that take place in a baby's body proportions during growth.

10. Explain some of the major changes that take place during the first year of a baby's life.

Immunisation

Section 3 Food and nutrition

Chapter 5:   Nutrition

Chapter 6:   Food preparation and service

Food and proper nutrition are important parts of our lives as individuals and families. We plan many of our activities and celebrations around food. As you go through this section, you will explore how to use the design process to solve problems related to nutrition.

Chapter 5 Nutrition

Figure 5.1 A balanced diet is important for good nutrition.

You may ask why these questions are important:
- When deciding on your meals do you think about the taste or how your body will be nourished?
- Do you know the effects of nutrient deficiencies?

In Book 1, you learnt that food provides the body with six different categories of nutrients and that these nutrients have three basic functions. However, there is much more that you should know about these nutrients. In this book, you will learn to classify nutrients as macro-nutrients and micro-nutrients.

In this chapter, you will:
* describe the functions, sources and deficiency diseases for each micro-nutrient
* explain the multi-mix principle
* write menus using the multi-mix principle
* describe the factors that should be considered when planning meals for the family
* describe the factors that affect meal planning
* plan and prepare a suitable packed lunch.

The Kwevanna Community

The Kwevanna community is a rural community where 60% of the people in the village are under 35 years old. Community leaders recently started a health promotion programme to encourage healthy lifestyle practices, with a focus on good nutrition. Many young pregnant women are enrolled in the antenatal clinic, and the health promotion programme aims to help them and their families to adopt healthier habits. Your school board chairman, who was born in the Kwevanna community, has asked your class to create materials for the promotion programme. In this chapter, you will be asked to develop promotional activities to promote better nutrition in the Kwevanna community.

Macro-nutrients

Carbohydrates, fats and proteins are considered **macro-nutrients** because they are essential to the body and are needed in large quantities in order for the body to function at its best.

MORE ABOUT CARBOHYDRATES

Consider this

Carbohydrates are an essential part of a person's diet. In addition to energy, they prevent proteins from being used as energy and also provide the material for the glycogen reserves of the liver and muscles.

Carbohydrates are complex substances that are made up of carbon, hydrogen and oxygen atoms. You get approximately 70% of your energy from them. Besides being valuable energy givers, carbohydrates have two other useful roles in the diet. Carbohydrates are mainly plant-based and are formed through a chemical reaction called photosynthesis.

Carbohydrates contribute to the **glycogen** reserves in the liver and muscles.

There are three main categories of carbohydrates. These are:
- sugars
- starches
- dietary fibre (also referred to as cellulose and roughage).

Did you know?
Carbohydrates serve as protein-sparers, meaning that they prevent proteins from being used for energy production, allowing them to perform their primary function of building and repairing the body's tissues.

Figure 5.2 Some natural sources of sugar

Sugars

Most people think of sugar as the granules that are used to sweeten beverages. They are not wrong. In nutrition, however, the term 'sugar' also refers to the sweet substances that occur naturally in foods (Figure 5.2). In fact, sugar as you know it, comes from two of these very foods. Can you identify them?

Sugars can be classified into two groups – **monosaccharides** and **disaccharides**.

Monosaccharides are simple, single-molecule sugars. The most common monosaccharides are:

- **glucose**, which can be found in ripe fruits, vegetables and honey. It is a common additive to certain high-energy drinks such as *glucosade* and *lucosade*. It is sold in its isolated form and is added to many baby foods.
- **fructose**, which can be found mainly in ripe fruits, vegetables and honey
- **galactose**, which is only present in milk.

Disaccharides are double sugars. They are made up of two monosaccharides joined together. The disaccharides are:

- **sucrose**, which consists of 1-unit glucose + 1-unit fructose and is found in fruits and vegetables
- **lactose**, which consists of 1-unit glucose + 1-unit galactose and is found in milk
- **maltose**, which consists of 2 units of glucose and is formed during the digestion of starch and the germination of seeds. It is commonly present in malted beverages.

Did you know?
Sugar from the cane is mostly produced in tropical regions, whereas sugar from beets is mostly produced in Europe and the USA.

Consider this
Most plant-based foods have sugars in one form or another.

Consider this
Although some sugars are more complex than others, they all have similar characteristics.

ACTIVITIES

To find out what the characteristics of sugars are, complete the following activities and make a note of your findings in your journal.

1. Suck a few grains of table sugar. What does it taste like?
2. Place a spoonful of sugar in a glass of water and stir for a few minutes. What happens to the sugar?
3. Visit the library and do some research to find the name of the substance that is formed when sugar is exposed to dry heat. Note the colour of this substance.
4. Sugars take many forms. Identify five substances in your kitchen cupboard that consist mainly of sugars.

Starch

Starch is more complex than sugar. It belongs to a group of carbohydrates called **polysaccharides** meaning many sugars.

Starch is composed of several units of sugar, so it is a source of energy, but it differs from sugars in many ways. Unlike sugar, starch:

- is not sweet
- does not dissolve in cold water
- becomes clear and thick when it is cooked in water – the next time you make porridge look out for this change

- is changed to **dextrin** when exposed to dry heat. Dextrin is the brown substance that is formed each time you toast bread. It is also formed when flour or other starchy substances are parched (cooked dry by roasting).

When you were introduced to carbohydrates in Book 1, you met sugars and starches, but there is a third type of carbohydrate – dietary fibre.

Did you know?
Sugars and starches provide 4 kilocalories of energy per gram.

ACTIVITIES

Match the foods listed in Column A with the main carbohydrate that it contains in Column B.

COLUMN A (FOOD)	COLUMN B (TYPE OF CARBOHYDRATE)
Brown rice	Lactose
Pasta	Starch
Oranges	Fructose
Milk	Sucrose
Table sugar	Glucose

Dietary fibre

There are two types of dietary fibre.

- **Crude or insoluble fibre** is the cellulose parts of fruits and vegetables, for example, the skin, outer coat of seeds, bran of cereals and the cell walls of fruits and vegetables (Figure 5.3).
- **Soluble fibres**, for example, pectin and gum are the substances that dissolve and thicken during the preparation of jams and jellies. Peas, beans, oats, carrots, okra, pawpaw, citrus fruits and most ground provisions also contain soluble fibres (Figure 5.3).

The substances that are classified as dietary fibre are polysaccharides. But we cannot digest and absorb them, so they do not provide us with energy. However, soluble fibres have other useful functions. They help to:

- reduce the level of cholesterol in your blood (cholesterol is a fat that is associated with heart problems)
- keep your blood sugar level normal
- prevent constipation (hardening of stool) by attracting water to the bowels.

Insoluble fibre:

- stimulates movement in your intestines so that food and waste matter are moved along the digestive tract; it therefore helps to prevent constipation and other bowel disorders
- acts like a broom, sweeping away undigested food and dead cells from your intestines
- adds 'bite' or texture to meals and adds bulk to your diet, thereby giving you a sense of fullness. Therefore, people trying to lose weight are encouraged to eat lots of high-fibre foods.

Figure 5.3 Good sources of soluble and insoluble fibre

Deficiency and excess

If your diet does not have enough carbohydrates, protein is used to provide energy. This means that there may not be enough protein for the growth and repair of tissues. In extreme cases, this results in a disease called energy-protein malnutrition (see Book 3). If your diet does not include enough starch, your body also has difficulty converting fat into energy.

When the body receives more carbohydrates than is needed, the excess is converted to fat, which can build up to produce obesity. See Book 3 for more on obesity.

Eating too many sweets has been associated with dental caries (rotten teeth). If the teeth are not brushed after consuming these foods, acids are formed, which can erode the dental enamel.

> **Did you know?**
> Constipation and bowel disorders are common complaints in people who do not consume enough carbohydrates, but the carbohydrate that is deficient in this case is fibre.

ACTIVITIES

In your notebook, create a table that lists the following categories of carbohydrates and includes two examples of foods that are good sources of each type of carbohydrate:
- Starch
- Pectin
- Cellulose
- Lactose

Fats

Fats are composed of the same elements as carbohydrates – carbon, hydrogen and oxygen (C, H, O).

As you know, fats are also a source of energy. Chemically they are lipids. On average, fats provide 9 kilocalories per gram. Apart from providing energy they also:

- transport fat-soluble vitamins
- provide the body with fatty acids – substances that are essential for the proper functioning of body cells
- protect internal organs from injury by forming a protective layer around them
- insulate our bodies against cold by forming a protective layer under the skin

Fats in our foods add to the satiety (feeling full) value of foods.

> **Did you know?**
> Fats provide the most concentrated source of energy.

Consider this

Not all fats are burned for energy. Excess fat is stored under the skin and around the internal organs. Too much of this fat in the body can lead to various health complications.

In Book 1, you learnt that fats may be visible, or they may be hidden in foods. Fats also come in different states. They may be solid, semi-solid or liquid. Liquid fats (oils) are called unsaturated fats. Solid and semi-solid fats are called saturated fats. Most liquid fats (oils) are of plant origin and most solid and semi-solid fats come from animals. But in recent times, food manufacturers have been changing the state of plant oils from liquid to solid or semi-solid by a process called **hydrogenation**. Margarine and shortening are examples of vegetable fats that have been hydrogenated.

Although fats occur in different states, they have many common characteristics. They:

- do not mix well with water
- have plastic properties, for example, they will change shape easily
- melt when heated
- form soap when mixed with alkalis.

Deficiency and excess

A diet that is low in fat is not a big problem, but a totally fat-free diet could result in a deficiency of fat-soluble vitamins. You will meet these when you study vitamins (page 121). Too much fat in the diet contributes to a variety of diseases, including obesity and heart disease.

ACTIVITIES

With two of your classmates, create a short video (no more than 3 minutes) that illustrates the various forms that fats can take in cooking. In the video, discuss how fats are used in the kitchen and provide some examples of how they can be used in recipes.

Proteins

The basic elements that make up a unit of protein are carbon, hydrogen, oxygen, and nitrogen (C, H, O, N). However, depending on the source, proteins may also contain sulfur (S), iron (Fe), or phosphorus (P). Food sources of protein can be either plant- or animal-based. With the exception of gelatin, animal-based protein sources are considered to have high biological value, while plant-based protein sources, with the exception of soy protein from soybeans, are considered to have low biological value. Fortunately, as shown in Figure 5.5 and Figure 5.6, combining different types of protein-rich plant foods can help to overcome this difference in value.

Although plant and animal proteins differ in value, they are similar in every other way.

- Their elements are arranged into tiny units called **amino acids**.
- They coagulate or thicken when exposed to heat, acid, enzymes and mechanical action.

They carry out the same functions in our bodies. In addition to muscle building and energy production, they are also an important component in body fluids such as enzymes, hormones and blood.

Amino acids

There are 23 known amino acids, 10 of which are essential for growth in children and are therefore called **essential amino acids** (Figure 5.4). Adults can survive on eight essential amino acids. While the body can produce most amino acids, it cannot synthesise the essential ones, which must be obtained through the diet. Proteins that provide all of the essential amino acids are considered to be of high biological value.

The essential amino acids needed by both children and adults are:

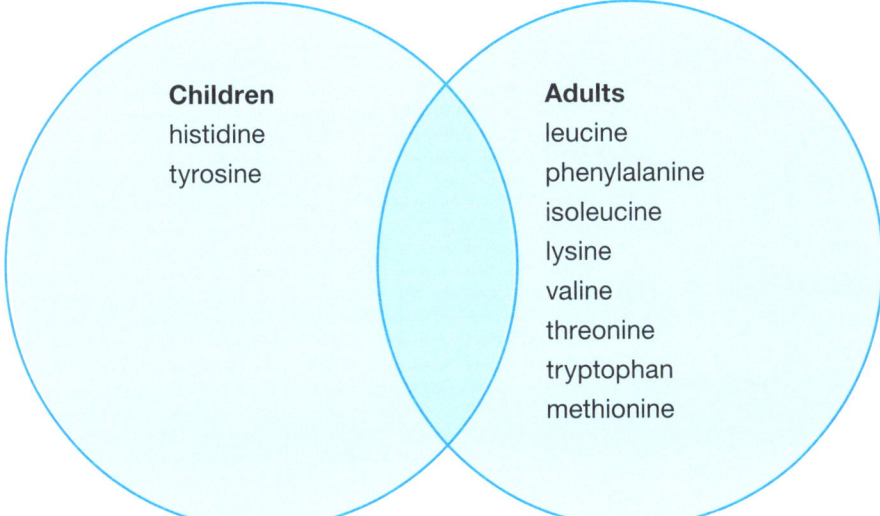

Children
histidine
tyrosine

Adults
leucine
phenylalanine
isoleucine
lysine
valine
threonine
tryptophan
methionine

Consider this

Breast milk contains the optimum (ideal) amount of amino acids needed for an infant's growth and development.

Figure 5.4 Essential amino acids

Proteins of low biological value often lack one or two of the essential amino acids. **Complementary proteins** are combinations of protein-rich foods that provide all of the essential amino acids. Incomplete proteins, on the other hand, are lacking in one or more of the essential amino acids and are therefore of low biological value. Rice, for example, is an incomplete protein because it lacks lysine, which is known as the limiting amino acid. The limiting amino acids in pulses are methionine and tryptophan.

When we cook peas and rice, we get complementary protein. Other examples of complementary proteins are:

- split peas loaf (peas and cereal)
- peanut cookies (nuts and cereal)
- peanut butter and bread (nuts and cereal)
- doubles (a Trinidadian dish that has chickpeas and the bara where wheaten flour is a main ingredient).

Figure 5.5 Improve the quality of the protein in your diet – combine two protein-rich plant foods.

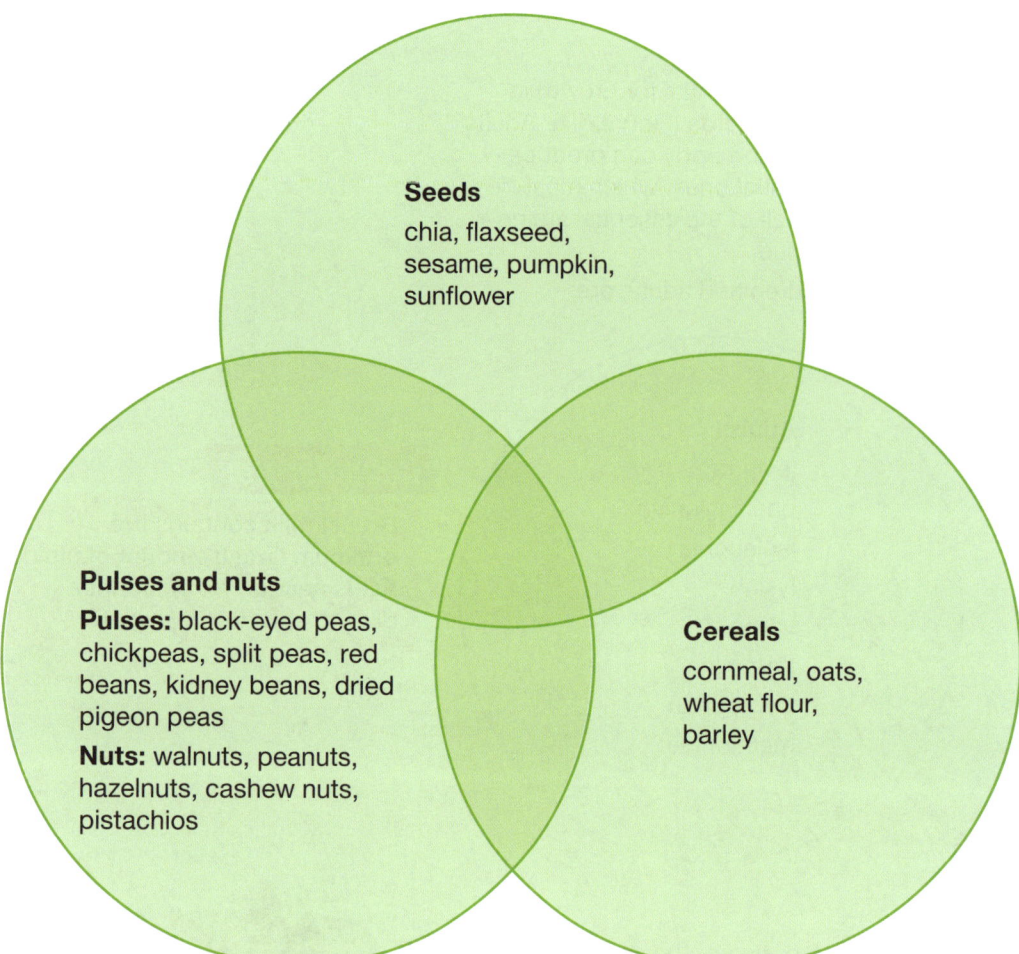

Figure 5.6 Complementary protein chart for strict vegetarians or vegans.

ACTIVITIES

1. For each of the food items listed below, state which of the following categories of ingredients are included (there should be at least two ingredients for each item): **Pulses, Seeds, Cereals, Nuts.**
   - Doubles (made with bara and stewed chickpeas)
   - Banana nut loaf
   - Sesame bread rolls
   - Multigrain loaf with flaxseeds
   - Nutty granola bars
   - Corn tortilla wraps with mixed bean filling
   - Split pea soup with peanut dumplings
   - Potato salad with sunflower seeds and peanut topping
2. Using Figure 5.6, create a poster that shows examples of protein foods, which the mainly vegetarian community of Kwevanna can benefit from.

Deficiency and excess

Consuming a diet with too little protein can contribute to energy-protein malnutrition (see Chapter 5 in Book 3). Surplus protein is converted to energy. If the energy is not used it is stored as body fat. Excess fat in the body leads to obesity and the possibility of chronic diseases occurring.

> **ACTIVITIES**
>
> 1. Visit the market or supermarket nearest to your home and list at least 10 foods with proteins of low biological value.
>
> 2. Use these foods to suggest at least five combinations, which would provide complete proteins.

Micro-nutrients

Micro-nutrients are nutrients that are needed in relatively small amounts. They are vitamins and minerals.

VITAMINS

Vitamins are a group of nutrients that are essential for the body to function properly. They are usually named by letters, which correspond to the order in which they were discovered. Like other nutrients, vitamins are composed of carbon, hydrogen and oxygen, and they are only needed in small amounts. However, they play important roles in the body, and none of the other nutrients can function without them. For example, vitamins are like the matches needed to start a fire or the nails used by a carpenter to build a house – they may be small, but they are essential for many processes. Some studies have also suggested that the antioxidant vitamins A and C may help to reduce the rate of cell deterioration in the body.

There are two groups of vitamins:
- *fat-soluble vitamins*
- *water-soluble vitamins.*

Table 5.1 shows their differences.

Table 5.1 How water- and fat-soluble vitamins differ

FAT-SOLUBLE VITAMINS	WATER-SOLUBLE VITAMINS
Vitamins A, D, E, K	Vitamins B complex, C
Soluble in fat	Not soluble in fat
Not soluble in water	Soluble in water
Fairly stable in heat	Easily destroyed by heat
Excreted through bile	Excreted in the urine
Deficiency appears slowly	Deficiency appears faster
Stored by the body	Not stored by the body

While all vitamins are essential for good health, only vitamins A, B, C and D will be discussed in detail in this chapter.

Vitamin A (retinol)

Vitamin A exists in two forms: retinol and beta-carotene. Retinol is found only in animal-based foods, while beta-carotene is found only in plant-based foods. Beta-carotene is not a true vitamin, but rather a pro-vitamin, meaning that it is a substance that the body can convert into vitamin A. The body can convert 6 units of beta-carotene into 1 unit of retinol.

Good sources of retinol include whole milk, cheese, butter, egg yolk, oily fish, fortified margarine, and liver and kidney meat. Beta-carotene can be found in yellow and orange fruits and vegetables, such as pumpkin, carrots, mangoes and pawpaw. The colour of these foods is due to the presence of beta-carotene, which is a deep yellow-orange substance. Beta-carotene is also present in dark green leafy vegetables and Chinese cabbage although the chlorophyll in these foods masks its colour.

Why vitamin A is necessary

Vitamin A is necessary:
- for growth, especially of bones and teeth
- for night vision
- to keep the skin and lining of body cavities (for example mouth and nose) healthy, so that they can resist infection.
- to regulate fat metabolism.

Deficiency and excess of vitamin A

Vitamin A deficiency can result in:
- night blindness and, eventually, a disorder called xerophthalmia
- keratinisation of the skin, resulting in a dry, scaly layer of skin
- faulty bone growth.
- *Too much vitamin A* causes liver damage, bone deformity, dry, itchy skin and abortions in pregnant women.

ACTIVITIES

1. Ask your Agricultural Science teacher to offer some guidance in planting at least two vegetables that are rich in carotene for a home kitchen garden.
2. Write a report on what you chose and how you planted them.

Consider this

Vegetarians can get their vitamin A from eating carotene rich foods daily.

Vitamin D (cholecalciferol)

Like vitamin A, vitamin D exists in two main forms. One of these is produced when ultraviolet rays from the sun come into contact with a pro-vitamin under our skin. As a result, vitamin D is sometimes called the 'sunshine vitamin'. People who live in the tropics and enjoy an abundance of sunshine rarely suffer from vitamin D deficiency. However, as shown in Figure 5.7, there are some situations that can prevent ultraviolet rays from entering the body. These include spending a lot of time indoors, living in areas with tall buildings that block the sun and experiencing heavy cloud cover.

Consider this

Babies born during the winter months in countries with cold climates are often given vitamin D supplements.

Some good food sources of vitamin D in foods are liver, oily fish, eggs and fortified margarine.

Figure 5.7 How ultraviolet rays can be blocked out

Why vitamin D is necessary

Vitamin D is necessary:

- for the absorption and laying down of calcium and phosphorus in our bones and teeth.
- as it helps to maintain blood calcium and phosphorus levels.

Deficiency and excess of vitamin D

Lack of sunshine or foods that supply this vitamin can cause rickets in children and osteomalacia in adults. One sign of this deficiency in children is deformed bones, especially bandy (bowed) legs. In adults there tends to be severe lower back pain and tenderness in other parts of the body.

Excessive intake may result from overuse of various supplements. Overuse of these supplements may result in high blood calcium levels, kidney damage and growth retardation.

Vitamin B complex

This is a group of vitamins with quite a few qualities in common. One of these is their involvement in the release of energy from nutrients (Figure 5.8). The B vitamins are also widely distributed in foods. Some common food sources are milk, meats (especially offals and pork), fruits and vegetables, legumes, whole-grain cereals and fortified flour.

Why vitamin B_1 (thiamine) is necessary

Vitamin B1 (thiamine) is necessary:

- to release energy from carbohydrates
- to stimulate the appetite and to improve the digestion of food
- to assist the growth process
- for healthy nerves.

Figure 5.8 Vitamin B is essential for the release of energy from energy-giving nutrients.

Micro-nutrients

Deficiency of vitamin B_1

Lack of thiamine causes a disease of the nervous system called *beriberi*. It is common in chronic alcoholics, pregnant women who vomit a lot and poor people who live largely on polished (white) rice. Common signs and symptoms include:

- loss of appetite
- leg cramps
- edema
- vomiting
- mental depression
- weight loss.

Why vitamin B_2 (riboflavin) is necessary

Vitamin B_2 (riboflavin) is necessary:

- to release energy from fats, carbohydrates and proteins
- to maintain healthy skin, especially around the nose and mouth
- to maintain a healthy cornea (the transparent skin over the front of the eyes)
- to produce enzymes and other body fluids.

Deficiency of vitamin B_2

This is uncommon in the Caribbean but when it occurs it causes:

- sore, swollen or cracked skin, especially in the area near or surrounding the eye, mouth-corners, eyeball, tongue, and chin
- nervous depression
- weakness
- poor growth.

Why vitamin B_3 (niacin or nicotinic acid) is necessary

Vitamin B_3 (niacin or nicotinic acid) is necessary:

- to release energy from energy-giving nutrients
- to keep the skin and digestive tract healthy
- to build body protein for growth and repair.

In addition to the foods listed earlier as good sources of vitamin B, some niacin is manufactured within the body from an amino acid called tryptophan. Yeast and yeast products are also excellent sources of niacin.

Deficiency and excess of vitamin B_3

Insufficient niacin in the diet results in a disease called *pellagra*. This disease is also known as the 3 'Ds' because it causes *diarrhoea*, *dermatitis* (rough, dark scaly skin and sore tongue) and *dementia* (severe confusion and shaking). An excess of vitamin B_3 results in flushing, burning and tingling around the neck, face and hands.

Why vitamin B_{12} (cobalamin) is essential

Vitamin B_{12} (cobalamin) is essential:

- for the formation of blood
- for the proper functioning of the digestive tract and nervous tissue
- for healthy nerve tissue; this vitamin usually works along with folate (folic acid), another B vitamin.

Deficiency of vitamin B_{12}

People on strict vegetarian diets tend to suffer from a vitamin B_{12} deficiency, as this vitamin is not found in vegetables. The only plant known to have the same quantity as liver when cooked, is a little-known sea vegetable (sea moss). Vitamin B_{12} deficiency is also seen in breast-fed babies of strict vegetarian mothers and people who cannot produce a special substance that permits the body to absorb this vitamin. The deficiency that results is what is called *pernicious anaemia*.

> **Consider this**
> Wheat flour is often fortified with thiamine and riboflavin.

ACTIVITIES

Describe how the following words are used in public health to prevent or address micro-nutrient deficiencies.
a   food fortification
b   food supplement
c   enrichment
d   deficiency

Vitamin C (ascorbic acid)

Vitamin C is found in many fruits and vegetables but of all the vitamins it is probably the one that is most easily destroyed. Rich fruit sources are West Indian cherries, guavas, cashews, and citrus fruits such as oranges and tangerines. Some rich vegetable sources are tomatoes, sweet peppers, cabbage and dark green leafy vegetables (Figure 5.9).

Vitamin C is necessary

Vitamin C is necessary because it:
- helps to hold body cells together
- helps the body to absorb and utilise iron
- promotes resistance to infections
- assists in the healing of wounds.

Vitamin C deficiency

Vitamin C deficiency results in:
- scurvy, a disease that causes a breakdown of cells
- the most obvious sign is swollen, bleeding gums
- slow healing of wounds
- frequent infections, especially in children.

Meeting vitamin needs

Figure 5.9 Rich sources of vitamin C

Did you know?
Most vitamin deficiencies are reversible.

Consider this
It is essential that you get your vitamins in adequate amounts but overdosing on expensive pills is wasteful and can be dangerous. The following is a questionnaire that you can give to the women in the antenatal clinic in Kwevanna.

Before purchasing your next set of pills, ask yourself the following questions.

- Am I currently in good health?
- Do I eat a variety of foods?
- Do I habitually use drugs that may interfere with the action of vitamins? For example, antacids, alcohol, mineral oils (as a purgative).
- Am I a strict vegetarian?
- Do I have a special need, for example, pregnancy?
- Has my doctor prescribed vitamin pills?
- If you answer 'Yes' for the first two questions and 'No' for the last four, you are probably getting all the vitamins that you need from your diet.

ACTIVITIES

1. Collect the food labels of 10 food items that are available in your community.
2. Make a list of the VITAMINS shown on each label.
3. What are four ways of making sure that you reduce the loss of water-soluble vitamins in vegetables when you are preparing them?
4. In your notebook, match the deficiency diseases with the vitamin that will help to correct this problem.

Deficiency disease	Vitamin
Bleeding gums	Vitamin B_2
Dermatitis	Vitamin C
Night blindness	Vitamin B_1
Edema	Vitamin A
Lesions around the mouth	Vitamin D
Tooth decay	

MINERALS

Did you know?
Your body needs about 19 different minerals for good health.

When you hear the word 'mineral' do you think of metals? If so, you are on the right track. However, some minerals are described as metals and others as non-metals. Compared to other micro-nutrients, calcium, phosphorus, and potassium are needed in relatively large quantities. Together these form close to 4% of your body weight. The other minerals are needed in very small quantities, and only make up a small part of your body weight. As a result, they are often called **trace elements**. This does not mean that they are less important than the other minerals.

As shown in Table 5.2, minerals have several very important functions, but these can be summarised into two broad functions:

1. They are major components in body fluids and hard and soft body tissue.
2. They help to regulate body functions such as muscle contraction and the beating of the heart.

Table 5.2 Some important minerals

MINERALS	SOURCES	SUMMARY OF FUNCTIONS	DEFICIENCY SYMPTOMS
Calcium	Milk and milk products; fish that can be eaten with their bones; cereals; dark green, leafy vegetables; dried beans and peas; drinking water from limestone areas	• Bone and tooth formation • Blood clotting • Muscle contraction and relaxation	• Children – rickets; adults – osteoporosis • Signs include malformed bones and teeth
Phosphorus	Meat; poultry; fish; eggs; dried beans and peas; milk and milk products	• Bone and tooth formation • Helps the body to use carbohydrates	• Weakness • Loss of appetite • Bone pain
Potassium	Orange juice; bananas; dried fruit; meats; peanut butter; dried peas and beans	• Helps the body to use proteins and carbohydrates • Maintains water balance in the body • Muscle contraction • Helps to regulate blood pressure	• Unusual heartbeat • Weakened muscles • Tiredness • Kidney and lung breakdown
TRACE MINERALS	**SOURCES**	**FUNCTION**	**DEFICIENCY SYMPTOMS**
Iron	Liver; red meats; egg yolks; green leafy vegetables; dried fruits; dried beans and peas; potatoes; enriched and whole-grain cereals	• Formation of red blood cells (haemoglobin) • Helps build stronger muscle tissue (myoglobin) • Part of several enzymes and proteins	• Anaemia (tiredness, paleness and shortness of breath)
Iodine	Seafood; iodised salt; water that passes through soil that has large amounts of iodine; vegetables grown in these soils	• Aids normal growth and development • Helps with the formation of the hormone, thyroxine, which controls the release of energy in the body • Helps in the development of the nervous system of the foetus	• Goitre (enlarged thyroid gland) • In newborns – retarded growth and cretinism
Fluorine	Fluoridated water; foods grown with or cooked in fluoridated water; fish; gelatine; fluoride added to toothpaste also reduces tooth decay	• Protects against tooth decay • Helps to keep bones strong	• Extreme tooth decay

ACTIVITIES

1. List four symptoms, which were frequently observed in the children in the Kwevanna community, that may prompt you to ask the visiting physician whether a multi-vitamin and mineral supplement would be appropriate.
2. Some of the children are showing signs of anaemia. Plan four multi-mix snack items along with beverages, to give to these children as a nutritious mid-morning snack during their upcoming summer camp.

The importance of water

Water does not have nutritive value in the sense that other nutrients have, but it is extremely important for good health. It fulfils the following functions as a:

- *carrier* – moving food, nutrients, blood cells and other substances around the body
- *cooling agent* – keeping the body temperature under control (stable)
- *builder* – adding bulk to cells; 70% of the body is made up of water
- *lubricant* – as the basis of the fluid that surrounds joints, it prevents them from rubbing sore as you move
- *moisturiser* – making part of saliva and other body fluids, it prevents your mouth, nostrils and other openings becoming dry and inflamed
- *facilitator* – as the only medium in which some substances can exist.

HOW MUCH WATER DO WE NEED?

No one can tell you exactly how much water you need, but six to eight glasses are recommended per day. Whether it is six or eight depends on several factors:

- the weather
- the amount of activity you do during the day
- the type of food you eat.

Hot, dry weather and strenuous activity cause your water needs to increase. Why do you think this is so? Salty, sweet, and dry foods also increase your body's need for water. Generally, your thirst is a good indication of how much water you need. The only problem is that we often ignore it.

You can boost your water intake by drinking milk, beverages and soups, and by eating more juicy fruit and vegetables. Water is also produced in your body when proteins, carbohydrates and fats are broken down to produce energy.

WHAT HAPPENS TO ALL THAT WATER?

The water that does not become a part of your body is excreted in stool, urine, sweat and the water vapour that you breathe out. One of these waste products helps to cool your body. Which one is it? From your Science classes, you would have noted that sweat or perspiration cools the body.

> **Did you know?**
> You can live without food for two to three weeks. But you cannot live more than a few days without water. Next to air, your body's greatest need is water.

Some people claim that drinking water with meals is harmful because it dilutes digestive juices. For healthy people this is not true, but water should not replace thorough chewing. To reduce the risk of indigestion, food needs to be chewed well and mixed with saliva.

Deficiency of water

There is very little risk associated with drinking too much water, but you can become dehydrated if you do not consume enough water.

How important is energy?

The truth is, we cannot live without **energy**. We need it for the following reasons:

- To carry out the basic body processes, for example, taking a breath, moving blood along the veins and even growing. You will notice that these are all involuntary processes that we are quite often unaware of.
- To maintain normal body temperature. Your body cannot exist without warmth. Most of your body warmth is generated when energy is used to carry out other body functions.
- For all types of physical activity. Energy is needed to help you carry out every physical activity that you can think of – walking, running, bowling or even moving your eyes and head to read. The more strenuous the activity, the greater your need for energy (Figure. 5.10).

Now that you are aware of the many functions of energy let us look at a definition for this word.

Energy is the power or ability to do work (voluntary and involuntary).

The amount of energy a person needs, measured in kilocalories, is based on their individual needs and can vary, depending on factors such as their activity level and basal metabolism. People who are more active, like athletes and swimmers, tend to have higher energy needs because they burn more calories during their daily activites. Basal metabolism refers to the energy required to maintain basic body functions at rest, and it can vary from person to person. In addition to activity level and basal metabolism, the body also uses energy to digest, absorb and transport nutrients from the food we eat.

Did you know?

Dehydration results from a lack of water in the cells. Its symptoms: dry lips, thirst, dry skin, darkness under the eyes.

Consider this

If someone tells you that their main reason for eating is to get energy, would you think that they are crazy? You would be correct to question this claim, as growth and protection from disease are also important functions of food.

Figure 5.10 Strenuous activities require more energy.

> **ACTIVITIES**
>
> 1. Discuss four activities that you engage in everyday, which utilise the highest amount of energy.
> 2. List two high-energy foods that you really like.

HOW HAS NATURE PROVIDED FOR OUR ENERGY NEEDS?

Vitamins and minerals do not produce energy, but the three macro-nutrients do. These are fats, carbohydrates and proteins. This energy has its origin in the sun. The leaves of green plants, which contain chlorophyll, use the sun's energy to make carbohydrates. The carbohydrates are then transported to other parts of the plants to be stored. When animals eat these plant parts, the carbohydrates are used to make energy, and some are converted to fats and proteins.

HOW MUCH ENERGY DO YOU NEED?

Your energy needs depend on your **basal metabolic rate (BMR)** and your activity level. Your BMR is the amount of energy your body needs to carry out involuntary activities such as breathing while it is at rest. These involuntary activities include: breathing, heart rate and pulse, digestion of food, production of urine and elimination of waste. Women usually have a lower BMR than men, and young people have a higher BMR than older people.

Activity level varies from person to person. People who are very active require more energy than those who lead a sedentary (inactive) life.

HOW IS ENERGY MEASURED?

The standard units for measuring energy are joules (metric) and calories (imperial). Because food contains large amounts of energy, the actual unit used is usually kilojoule (kJ) or kilocalorie (kcal), meaning 1000 joules or 1000 calories.

One kcal is equivalent to 4.1 kJ. A **kilocalorie** is the amount of energy that is required to raise the temperature of one kilogram of water by 1 °C.

Although a kilocalorie is 1000 calories, some authors have kept on using the word calorie when they really mean kilocalorie. Others use a big 'C' to pinpoint the difference, so keep this in mind when reading other books.

Each of the three energy-giving nutrients has a different energy value. Of the three, fat has the highest energy value.

> **Did you know?**
>
> 1 gram of fat produces approximately 9 kilocalories.
> 1 gram of carbohydrate produces approximately 4 kilocalories.
> 1 gram of protein produces approximately 4 kilocalories.

The amount of energy contained in foods may be calculated once we know the amount of carbohydrate, fat and protein present in the food.

For example, one tablespoon of vegetable oil contains 15 g fat. That is therefore equal to 45 kcal. Since 15 g fat × 9 kcal = 45 kcal

1 tsp honey is 5 g and contains 20 kcal (5 g honey × 4 kcal= 20 kcal).

ACTIVITIES

1. Compare the energy requirements of two sporting activities that a young person may engage in.
2. What are the three differences between animal fats and vegetable oils? Use two examples of each.
3. Calculate the number of kilocalories in a drumstick of chicken that contains 20 g fat, 15 g protein and 12 g carbohydrate.

Meal planning

In Book 1, you read about planning balanced meals and breakfasts. In this section you will read about the multi-mix principle and other aspects of meal planning. Meal planning is important to ensure that we consume all the right nutrients. There are several tools that are used to plan meals. The multi-mix principle is one such tool.

THE MULTI-MIX PRINCIPLE

Not everyone has access to balanced meals on a daily basis due to factors such as location or income. However, there is a simple way to ensure that your meals are always balanced: follow the multi-mix principle of meal planning.

This is a principle that teaches you to combine foods from the Caribbean food groups to make nutritionally balanced meals. The simplest way of balancing meals is to choose a variety of foods from the six food groups. A meal that contains foods from all six food groups is the most nourishing, but such lavishness is not always possible nor is it always necessary.

Only four of the Caribbean food groups are used in combination when planning the meals. They are:

- staples
- food from animals
- legumes and nuts
- vegetables.

One rule that must always be followed when using the multi-mix principle is to start with the staple food group and combine it with the other food groups.

There are three multi-mix types: two-mix (double), three-mix (triple) and four-mix (quad-mix).

When you are not using foods from all the groups, always begin by selecting your staple that provides the energy. Then add foods from as many of the groups as you can afford.

Add to your staple (cereal), a legume.

Figure 5.11 Typical Caribbean staples

Let's consider our legumes.

Figure 5.12 Legumes

Some examples of this type of two-mix may be bara, dhal puri, doubles and Chinese cakes. A lot of these foods are popular in Guyana and in Trinidad and Tobago.

You can also add to your staple, a food from an animal source.

Foods from animals

Figure 5.13 Foods from animals

> **Consider this**
>
> What are three snacks that are popular in your territory, which are combinations with this type of two-mix?

Table 5.3 Two-mix combinations

STAPLES AND FOOD FROM ANIMALS	COMBINATION
Macaroni cheese	Macaroni + cheese
Sausage roll	Wheat flour pastry + beef sausage
Curried chicken and roti	Wheat flour roti + chicken
Mashed potato and chicken nuggets	Potato + chicken
VEGETARIAN: CEREAL AND LEGUME	
Doubles	Bara (wheat flour) + stewed chickpeas
Pholourie	Wheat flour + ground split peas
Chinese cakes	Wheat flour + black-eyed peas
Dhal puri	Wheat flour + split peas
STAPLE (STARCHY ROOT, FRUIT OR TUBER) + FOOD FROM ANIMALS	
Plantain and salt egg	Plantain and egg
Cassava and beef stew	Cassava and beef
Creamed yam pie	Yam and cheese
Sweet potato fish fritters	Sweet potato and salt fish

The fourth group used in the two-mix or multi-mix combination is coloured vegetables.

Coloured vegetables

Remember:

- To plan meals using four or five food groups, plan a good three-mix, then add foods from one or two of the groups that you have not used so far.
- Sometimes, people can only afford to eat foods from two food groups. These meals are not as nutritious as meals containing foods from three or more food groups, but they can get a good rating if they are selected wisely. Where foods from only two food groups are used it is best to make the staple a cereal, as these have a higher food value than starchy roots and tubers.

Add to the staple, a food from an animal source OR a food from the legume group. If a starchy root, fruit or tuber must be used, always combine it with a food from an animal source.

Figure 5.14 Some vegetables used in Caribbean cuisine

Meal planning

Three-mix or triple mix

A three-mix is combined by adding a vegetable or legume to the two-mix.
Table 5.4 shows some combinations:

Table 5.4 Three-mix or triple mix combinations with examples

THREE-MIX COMBINATIONS	EXAMPLE
Staple (cereal) + legume + vegetable	Saffron rice + kidney bean stew + cucumber slices Red bean pasta casserole + green salad Tortilla wrap with chickpeas and vegetable salad
Staple (starchy vegetable) + food from animal + vegetable	Breadfruit croquettes + frizzled saltfish/codfish + tomato wedges
Staple (cereal) + food from animal + vegetable	Pelau/Jollof rice/Risotto/Jambalaya/Cook-up rice Lamb Stew with broccoli rice Chow mein with chicken and vegetables
Staple + food from animal + legume	Rice + chicken + pigeon peas Dumplings + chicken + split peas

ACTIVITIES

Plan two lunch menus for a pregnant woman who is a strict vegetarian, using the first type of three-mix (cereal + legume + vegetable).

Did you know?

The main difference between shepherd pie and cottage pie is in the meat; shepherd pie contains lamb, whereas cottage pie contains beef.

Quadri-mix

The quadri-mix is the most nutritious of the multi-mix approach since it uses all four of the foundation food groups – staple, legume, food from animals and vegetables.

Consider this

Variety is a very important factor in meal planning and promotes optimum nutrition.

Table 5.5 Quadri-mix or four-mix combinations with examples

FOUR-MIX COMBINATIONS	EXAMPLE
Staple (cereal) + legume + food from animal + vegetable	Paella/dhalpurri roti + curried chicken + pumpkin choka
Staple (starchy) + legume + food from animal + vegetable	Creamed yam + lemon pepper peas + fried fish + steamed carrots

Consider this

When choosing the combination, you must always consider the age of the person the meal is being prepared for. For example, if the three-mix meal is being planned for a young child it is best to make the third food a green leafy vegetable, as these add to the iron content of the meal. Another good three-mix combination, which can be used for all age groups, is a meal that contains: a staple + food from animals + legumes.

Factors to be considered when planning meals for the family.

I	The skills of the cook
	It is best to plan meals that the cook knows how to prepare. Planning new recipes that the cook is unfamiliar with, may lead to wastage and failure.
II	The foods that are readily available to the family
	Foods that are in season should be fully utilised, since these will be more economical, fresher and of better quality.
III	Time available to the cook
	Working persons have to consider the time they have available for cooking; lots of pre-preparation may be necessary, such as cutting vegetables on the weekend and storing in airtight bags for freezing.
IV	The occasion one is preparing for and the time of day
	There are special occasions such as birthdays and anniversaries, as well as holidays, which necessitate special foods.
V	Financial resources
	The amount of money available to purchase food must be carefully considered. Where there are limited funds, one should consider supplementing with a kitchen garden or buying in bulk.
VI	Having a variety of foods according to the multi-mix principle
	Utilising a variety of coloured fruits and vegetables will provide a wide spread of micro-nutrients.
VII	Cooking facilities available
	This includes space, type of cooking equipment and tools, and whether a refrigerator and freezer are available.

Apart from considering the seven factors above, there are some things that the household will be affected by:
Factors that affect meal planning

I	Personal preferences or likes and dislikes
	Each individual will have foods that they like and appreciate and others that they prefer not to have.
II	Religion, tradition and customs
	At times such as Christmas and holidays there are specialty foods. Some persons will only think of specialty foods and not balance it with other nutritious foods.
III	Economy
	The state of the economy may affect availability and distribution of food supplies. The household then has to use what is available.
IV	Food fads and fallacies
	Persons have beliefs about foods that may affect their choices. Some foods are thought to have magical powers, while others are thought to be of little or no value.
V	Geographical location and climate
	The location and climate of the place where we live will determine availability of foods and the seasons of various foods.
VI	Knowledge of nutrition
	A person's educational level and their willingness to learn about healthy eating affects their choice.
VII	Satiety value (some persons will choose high-calorie foods because they are more filling and satisfying)
	In the Caribbean we love high-calorie dishes and cakes because they are so filling.

ACTIVITIES

Jill had just learnt that she got all As in her exam. She called her Dad and said, 'We have to celebrate. This is a big deal. Please buy some things to celebrate with tonight.' Her father was overjoyed and asked her what she wanted. Her list included:
- French fries
- Chicken nuggets
- Cheesecake
- Doughnuts
- Chocolates
- Non-alcoholic champagne

Discuss at least two factors that are influencing her choice.

Career corner

Community nutrition officer

> My name is Dane. I am a community nutrition officer. I love my work. My responsibilities include educating people in the community about their eating habits, foods, and the effect of foods on health.

> I assist with preparing nutrition education materials, pretesting them in the community and then distributing those materials.

> Part of my work also involves collecting data, which is used to identify deficiencies accurately and come up with a plan to address them.

Do you want to become a community nutrition officer?

Education: BSc in Nutrition and Dietetics or Public Health and Nutrition
Work opportunities: NGOs such as UNICEF, WHO, PAHO
Average salary: USD 50,000–59,000 per annum

In Book 1, you read about the different meals that are eaten during the day. It is not always possible for people to eat all their meals at home. When you go to school, you usually eat your lunch and snacks during the day while you are at school. Some children leave home so early in the morning that they must also take their breakfast with them. Adults who are away from home must also take meals with them.

Such meals are called **packed meals**, as they must be prepared, packed in suitable containers and taken outside the home. Careful planning is needed to ensure that adequate nourishment is provided.

PACKED MEALS

Many people use packed meals because of the convenience. Packed meals may be used by:

- children who take meals to school
- workers who carry meals to be eaten at their place of employment
- children and adults who take food on picnics and hikes
- persons whose work takes them into the field.

Whatever the occasion, all meals should be carefully prepared and attractively served. Like other meals, packed meals require a great deal of thought and care in the planning and preparation.

Aspects to consider

The following aspects should be considered when planning and preparing packed meals.

Who is going to eat the meal? The age, state of health, level of activity of the person who will eat the meal must be taken into account. Young children and teenage girls, for example, may require a lighter meal than teenage boys. Why do you think this is so? Manual workers will need heavier meals than sedentary workers.

How is the meal to be transported? The type of food will be determined by the mode of transport. Packed meals for people who have to walk, ride a bike or take a bus or taxi should be light enough to carry, easy to pack and satisfying when eaten. They should never appear bulky and clumsy.

Is the meal to be taken to school in a lunch kit by a small child? If so, the lunch kit must be sturdy enough to withstand rough treatment from young children. Lunch kits for children should be made of heavy, durable plastic or metal. The containers used should be well sealed to prevent leakage or spillage but must also be easily opened by the child.

Where and how is the meal to be eaten? Are tables and chairs available? Is there a special lunch room? Is the meal to be eaten in the open air? At school, meals may be eaten under a tree in the schoolyard, in the classroom where there may be a desk, or in the cafeteria or dining hall. If the meal is to be eaten by an adult at the office, there may be adequate space for a place setting, therefore a more elaborate meal may be prepared.

Suitable foods for packed meals

Consider this

Not all types of foods can be effectively packaged.

Did you know?
Packed meals are becoming more and more popular.

ACTIVITIES

1. List at least six foods that you loved to have in your lunch kit as a child.
2. List six nutritious snacks suitable for school aged children.

A variety of foods and prepared items, both cooked and raw, may be included in packed meals. You may choose from:

- sandwiches, rolls or pastry, with a protein filling, such as eggs, meat, fish or cheese; avoid tomatoes – they will make sandwiches soggy
- boiled eggs with bread, bake or other breadstuff
- chicken parts, baked, fried, grilled and so on
- salads with protein foods, such as chicken and eggs; these salads can be used as main dishes if served with suitable starchy vegetables
- green vegetables; tomatoes (whole, sliced or wedged); carrots (sticks or slices); cucumber (slices); lettuce and shredded cabbage
- fresh fruits, for example, mangoes, oranges and plums
- canned fruits can be used as a dessert
- cupcakes, slices of cake, Swiss/jelly roll, doughnuts, sweet rolls, sweet bread, cookies or biscuits can all be chosen for dessert
- beverages – fruit drinks are very satisfying for children; adults may enjoy iced tea, hot tea, coffee or cocoa, but special vacuum flasks are needed to transport hot beverages safely
- soups, particularly main dish soups with meat and vegetables; special vacuum containers that will keep the soup hot are needed.

Suitable containers for packed meals

To ensure that the food retains its quality until it is ready to be eaten, the containers used are very important. The choice of container also depends on the type of meal (solid or liquid foods; hot or cold items), the form of transportation and the accommodation (storage until ready to be eaten).

A range of containers in which to pack and carry meals are available on the market. These include:

- plastic boxes with covers
- plastic bottles with lids
- stainless steel containers with covers
- vacuum flasks in various sizes
- paper bags, plastic bags, greaseproof paper, aluminium foil and plastic wrap
- cardboard boxes with covers.

Always make sure that the containers you choose are easy to clean and secure, so that food can be transported in them safely.

Consider this

Select your containers carefully. Some materials may release toxins into hot foods.

Guidelines for packing meals:
- Wrap foods carefully to prevent air from getting in and making them dry. Use plastic wrap or waxed paper so that it will be easy to identify the wrapped item.
- Cover all bottles and vacuum containers tightly.
- Avoid the use of mayonnaise dressing and other foods that spoil quickly in heat.
- Pack salads without any dressing, as the dressing will cause the leafy greens to wilt.
- Do not include too many starchy and sweet foods such as buns, bread, cakes, cookies. One sweet item for dessert is quite enough.
- Make sure that you do not spoil a nutritious light meal by filling up the lunch box with candies.

SNACKS

Snacks are light refreshments that are eaten between meals. They are not intended to take the place of meals. They are generally eaten to delay the feeling of hunger until regular mealtimes and should not be eaten too close to a meal, as this will interfere with your appetite. Sometimes we eat snacks when we are bored.

Snacks should be nutritious and should supply the body with at least one important nutrient. A variety of very tempting items, hot and cold or sweet and savoury, can be provided as snacks.

Suitable foods for snacks
- Sandwiches: meat, cheese, eggs, vegetable.
- Biscuits: sweet and savoury.
- Cookies: plain or decorated.
- Cakes: scones, muffins, pastries, rolls.
- Fresh fruits such as carambola, mangoes, oranges, pawpaw.
- Dried fruits such as prunes, raisins, cherries.
- Cold drinks: milk, fruit juices, punches.
- Preserved fruits, such as pickled mangoes and cherries, salted plums, stewed tamarind, tamarind balls and so on are very tasty and popular with children. They also provide energy.
- Nuts such as roasted peanuts, walnuts, almond nuts, pecan. These can be used alone or in combination with dried fruits.
- Chips, fries or crisps made from starchy vegetables such as plantains, breadfruit, or potatoes. This may be served with a dip, sauce or salsa.
- Dishes made with peas and beans such as bara, doubles, pakooras or pholourie.
- Small chunks of meat such as chicken nuggets, fish fingers and meat balls.

ACTIVITIES

The children from the Champion Children's Home are going on a day trip to visit several agricultural processing sights.

1. Plan a mid-morning snack consisting of:
    a. a savory sandwich
    b. a sweet item
    c. fresh fruits
2. A light lunch, suitable for packing, should consist of:
   a three-mix
   a fruit beverage

General guidelines to consider when planning snacks:
- variety in textures
- variety of flavours
- variety in colour
- nutritious
- appropriate portion sizes
- satisfying enough to delay until the next meal
- tasty and eye appealing.

LIGHT MEALS AT HOME

Light meals are useful for all members of the family. Light meals at home can be eaten at noon or in the evening, depending on the time of day at which the heaviest meal is eaten. Light meals must be:
- nutritionally well balanced
- satisfying
- attractive and appealing to the eye
- varied in colour, texture and flavour
- easy to prepare
- easy to eat.

> **Consider this**
>
> When planning, preparing, and serving light meals, the same guidelines should be followed as for the heavier meals.

ACTIVITY

Discuss with your classmates, two activities at home or at a workplace that may warrant having a light meal.

Foods suitable for light meals:
- Sandwiches and salads containing meat, fish, cheese, poultry.
- Soups containing meat, fish, beans, peas, vegetables.
- Chicken with french fries.
- Stir fries such as fried rice or chicken and vegetable chow mein or lo mein.
- Casserole dishes such as shepherd's pie or macaroni casserole
- Fruit juices, fruit drinks, milk, milk drinks, fruit punches, milk punches; tea, coffee, cocoa, other beverages.
- Desserts – chilled, frozen, jellied, baked sweet items.

Subject link

As a part of your design project, you will be required to include your knowledge from English Language A, Visual Arts, Human and Social Biology and Integrated Science. Let these subject teachers know very promptly that you will be checking in with them to ensure that your project is of a high standard.

Design project

Kwevanna Community Council has identified the following nutrition concerns:
- iron deficiency anaemia
- instances of iodine deficiency including cretinism
- pockets of energy-protein malnutrition among young children
- dental caries prevalent among school-aged children.

1 The head of the Kwevanna Community Council has opted to engage your secondary school to participate in the *poster competition* aspect of its health promotion activities among teenagers and pregnant women. It is compulsory to prepare a poster showing a three-mix combination.

2 Do some ideas storming with your classmates, several topics from this chapter that you can explore for your posters and document these.

3 Plan a five-day cycle menu for the school children, which includes: one snack item (three-mix and a fruit beverage, and prepare a poster to show that information).

4 Select three topics for the posters that you would like to create.

5 Plan and conduct your own internal poster competition with the help of your teachers.

6 Display two posters for each of your three selected topics for your classmates, teachers and school administration to view.

7 Prepare a report on your activities.

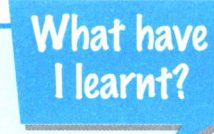

Multiple choice questions

1. Which description best suits cellulose as a carbohydrate?
   A Digestible
   B Non-digestible
   C Disaccharide
   D Monosaccharide

2. A protein sparer is _____
   A a carbohydrate.
   B a food that is rich in protein.
   C a food that allows protein to be used for body building and not energy.
   D a food that has the most concentrated form of energy for the body.

3. Fats are composed of the following elements:
   A Carbon, hydrogen and oxygen
   B Carbon, hydrogen, oxygen and nutrition
   C Fatty acids and sulfur
   D Water, fatty acids and sulfur

4   Which of the following has the largest amount of protein?
    A   Split peas soup with dumplings
    B   Fruit scones
    C   Chocolates
    D   Honey and oats granola bars

5   The multi-mix principle in the Caribbean uses the following four groups.
    A   Fats, carbohydrates, vitamins and minerals
    B   Fruits, vegetables, legumes and nuts
    C   Legumes, starchy vegetables, dairy products and meats
    D   Staples, food from animals, legumes and coloured vegetables

6   The following is the best example of a healthy two-mix.
    A   Potato and spinach pie
    B   Stuffed eggs
    C   Peanut butter sandwich
    D   Squash pie

7   A strict vegetarian mum wants to make a sweet bread that follows the multi-mix principle. Which combination of ingredients can be added to ensure that this is done?
    A   Raisins and grated coconut
    B   Sunflower seeds and cashew nuts
    C   Cornstarch and pumpkin flour
    D   Ginger powder and cinnamon

8   Which factor is the least important when planning meals?
    A   The cooking facility
    B   Available ingredients
    C   Rainy season
    D   Skills of the cook

9   Which meal is best suited for a packed lunch for a farm worker?
    A   Vegetable soup and bread
    B   Pelau and fried plantain
    C   Chicken salad and croissants
    D   Cheese sandwich and cupcakes

10 Which factor does NOT affect food availability in a community?
    A   Type of supermarket
    B   Soil type
    C   Economy
    D   Weather pattern

Short answer questions

1   Name the major elements that make up carbohydrates.
2   What are the types of carbohydrates that will prevent the following health problems:
    a   constipation
    b   energy-protein malnutrition.

3   Suggest three snacks that young mothers can make for their children, to ensure that they have enough protein.

4   A few of your classmates who buy sodas every day complained that when they brush their teeth, they notice that they are spitting blood.

   a   What nutrient may be lacking in their diet?

   b   Suggest a replacement for the sodas in their midday meal.

5   Give two examples of a complementary protein.

6   Why is vitamin D called the sunshine vitamin? Name three other sources of this vitamin.

7   Using the multi-mix principle, plan two four-mix meals that are suitable for a staff lunch.

8   You have been given two pints of bottled water and the following selection of foods to take along on a half-day nature walk: watermelon, salted nuts, roasted peanuts, oatmeal biscuits, oranges, fruit drink, chocolates. Which of them would you (a) avoid, (b) use freely to avoid dehydration? Give reasons for your decision.

9   Give two reasons why having a balanced diet is important.

10 Identify two activities that you engaged in during the week, which can be considered as high-energy activities.

11 Plan a picnic basket for three classmates who are going on a day tour. The group will leave the school at 7.00 a.m. and return at 5.00 p.m. (include two snacks).

Chapter 6 Food preparation and service

Figure 6.1 Good food handling practices help to protect people from foodborne illnesses.

- Have you or anyone you know ever suffered from food poisoning?
- What are the ways in which foodborne illnesses can be prevented?

In the Caribbean culture, food plays a key role in the family's goal of healthy living. Families get together for at least one meal of the day. Here, it is important to enjoy healthy, nutritious and safe food served in a pleasant atmosphere. This contributes to the family's enjoyment of one another.

In this chapter, you will:

* define the term **food safety**
* explain the importance of promoting food safety
* describe the conditions and practices that promote safe food handling
* demonstrate safe food handling practices during the preparation, storage and service of food
* examine the guidelines to follow when shopping for and storing food
* identify foodborne illnesses
* discuss foodborne illness as a health issue for individuals and families
* identify the key components of a recipe
* interpret and use a basic recipe
* evaluate a basic recipe for its accuracy
* classify the methods of cooking
* recognise the role of fish in the diet
* identify the uses of fats and oil in food preparation
* prepare a variety of cakes
* develop skills in table setting.

Rose is an experienced cook who works at the Champion Children's Home. She has been tasked with training the newly employed kitchen staff on food safety during storage, preparation, cooking and service. She has sought your assistance in helping her to put together some training material, since she thinks you may have some great ideas. As you go through this chapter, you will acquire valuable skills that may help a cook to do a more effective job at preparing nutritionally balanced attractive meals.

ACTIVITIES

1. Do some ideas storming for some of the questions and ideas that must be discussed before you can start your task.
2. Discuss the first idea that you considered.

Food safety

Family members who prepare and serve nutritious and tasty meals provide the foundations for good health. They also contribute to the happiness of the whole family. One of the goals of meal planning is to provide nutritious meals from locally grown foods that will not only keep bodies healthy and satisfy hunger, but will give a feeling of contentment and the desire to live good-quality lives.

Two important aspects of food preparation include preparing and serving safe food and the selection and storage of foods. The foods you choose depend on your social and cultural background. Food customs and eating patterns play an important role in the selection, preparation and service of food for the family.

This chapter deals with shopping for and storing food at home for family meals; two additional methods that can be used for cooking foods; food from animals – fish; foods from the food groups of fruits and vegetables and fats and oils. It will also cover cake-making; beverages; table setting and service; planning packed meals, snacks and light meals at home.

> Planning meals ahead of time will assist with budgeting, proper purchasing and ensuring that one has adequate storage space.

Over the years, there have been many advances in food technology, which have improved the safety of foods.

WHAT IS FOOD SAFETY?

The term **food safety** refers to the practices used to ensure that food is kept safe at each stage of preparation. In the home, food safety means making sure that food is handled, prepared and stored properly to prevent foodborne illness and injury.

The importance of food safety

- Food safety is an important aspect of food production and handling, as it ensures the health and safety of consumers by protecting them from any food-related issues such as physical, chemical and biological hazards that can occur in the food cycle.
- When food becomes contaminated, it must be disposed of, which results in the food being a waste. Practising correct food safety reduces food waste. This also has an impact on the cost of the food, as it will need to be replaced.
- The risk of nutritional deficiencies is reduced.
- The risk of diseases and deaths caused by unsafe foods is reduced.
- The risk of non-communicable diseases caused by unhealthy food is reduced.

Did you know?
More than 200 diseases are spread through food.
The '5-second rule' isn't true – bacteria can attach to food as soon as it touches the floor.

Fun fact
The same pathogens that cause food poisoning can cause arthritis, kidney failure and meningitis.

Consider this
Millions of people fall ill every year and many die because of eating unsafe food. To improve food safety, many professionals are working together, making use of the best available science and technologies. Additionally, different governmental departments and agencies, encompassing public health, agriculture, education and trade, are collaborating and communicating with each other and civil society, including consumer groups.

Access to sufficient amounts of safe and nutritious food is key to sustaining life and promoting good health. Everyone can contribute to making food safe.

What are some of the ways that consumers, policy makers and food handlers can make the food safe?

Here are some examples of effective actions that can be taken:
- Build and maintain adequate food systems and infrastructures.
- Foster multi-sectoral collaboration among all sectors of the economy.
- Integrate food safety into broader food policies and programmes.
- Think globally and act locally to ensure that food that has been produced domestically remains safe when exported internationally.
- Read labels to make informed choices.
- Handle and prepare food safely.

ACTIVITY

Technology-based activity

Can you list some of the food protection agencies involved in food safety? Categorise them as local, regional and international.

Create a mind map, which highlights some of the food protection agencies and their roles in food safety.

Conditions and practices that promote safe food handling

When food is handled properly, it can be kept safe for consumption by reducing food spoilage and food contamination. To ensure that this occurs, food handlers must:

- be educated on hygiene and safety
- obtain a health certificate
- practise proper personal, food and kitchen hygiene
- identify hazards that can occur during the food production process
- monitor and evaluate the food production process
- display relevant signage to promote good practices
- document standards and protocols.

DEMONSTRATING SAFE FOOD HANDLING PRACTICES DURING THE PURCHASE, STORAGE, PREPARATION, SERVICE AND CONSUMPTION OF FOOD

Food safety occurs at four levels – buying, storing, cooking/serving and consuming.

Buying and storing food

With high prices and food shortages, the family must plan meals carefully and shop wisely in order to get the best value for their money. Here are a few guidelines to follow when shopping for food.

Figure 6.2 Food safety principles

- Plan meals as far ahead as possible to reduce your number of shopping trips.
- Check the contents of cupboards and the refrigerator to find out what you need to buy.
- Make a list of the items you need to buy.
- Make sure that you have enough money to buy what you need.
- Buy foods from shops, groceries, supermarkets and market vendors that display high standards of sanitation.
- Buy from shops where there is a rapid turnover to avoid buying stale food.
- Buy fruits and vegetables in season, when they are cheaper, and richer in food value.
- Buy staples such as rice, flour and sugar in large amounts if storage space is available.
- Read labels carefully before buying. Do not be fooled by packaging; check the cost and the weight.
- Buy only what you need. Do not be misled by advertisements.
- Check ingredients of prepared foods carefully before buying to cater for any special dietary needs of family members.
- Avoid 'junk foods'. These are foods with very little nutritional value, for example, soft drinks (carbonated sweet drinks), potato chips and frozen, flavoured drinks made from powders.

> **Did you know?**
> Meal planning saves time, money, energy and results in better health.

Consider this

What about setting up a master shopping list in the following categories:
- Meats, fish and eggs
- Dairy
- Legumes
- Fruits
- Vegetables
- Dry goods
- Cleaning agents and toiletries

> **Problem-solving tips**
> Prepare a spreadsheet for a master shopping list and list all the major items that your family can buy every month. Seek the help of others in your home to finalise your list. When you are done, seek your teacher's assistance to improve its format and content.

Storage of food

Store the food you have bought in conditions that will ensure that the quality is maintained until the food is needed. In the home, food storage may be of two types: dry storage and refrigerator or freezer storage. Dry storage is used for non-perishable foods and refrigerator storage for perishable food items.

Guidelines for storing food

- Food should be stored in cool, clean places that are free from insects, pests or vermin.
- Cupboards should always be clean, dry, tidy and free from dust. To ensure this, storage cupboards should be checked monthly, containers washed and dried and shelves dusted and sprayed with insecticide. Make sure that all the food is removed from the cupboard first and protected from dust and insecticide.

- Perishable foods, such as fish and meat, should be wrapped carefully and placed in the deep freeze or coldest part of the refrigerator. Perishable foods cannot remain at room temperature for very long and must be cooked as soon as possible.
- Evaporated and sterilised milk can be stored for long periods in the cans and packages in which they have been manufactured. Once they have been opened, they must be refrigerated. Condensed milk will keep in a clean bottle for about five days without refrigeration. The sugar acts as a preservative.
- Butter, margarine and shortening should be kept in the refrigerator. If there is no refrigerator, they can be stored in a covered container in the coolest part of the kitchen or in a food safe.
- Cheese should be placed in a covered dish and stored in a refrigerator, icebox or the coolest part of the kitchen.
- Fruit can be kept at room temperature if it is under-ripe. Ripe fruits (except bananas) should be stored in the refrigerator or a cool part of the kitchen.
- Green vegetables should be put into plastic bags and stored at the bottom of the refrigerator or in a crisper. If there is no refrigerator, they should be placed in a vegetable rack or basket and used as soon as possible after buying, as storage destroys vitamin C. To prevent drying out, place stems in water and cover with a damp cloth.
- Root vegetables should be stored in a wire rack or basket in a well ventilated place. Any vegetable that shows signs of decay should be removed at once.
- Bread can be kept in a ventilated bin. Biscuits and cakes should be stored separately in airtight containers, as they make bread become soggy.
- Canned and packaged foods should be clearly labelled. Keep a supply of these for emergencies.
- Be sure to place earlier supplies of food towards the front of the cupboard so that they are used before newer supplies. The first set of foods bought should be used up first.

Figure 6.3 Root vegetables stored in a wire basket

Remember the following
- Foods must be stored according to type: perishable, semi-perishable and non-perishable.
- Use food in rotation by having an appropriate management system – Last In First Out (LIFO), First In First Out (FIFO).
- Use appropriate packaging materials.
- Clean storage conditions frequently with non-toxic cleaners.
- Follow storage instructions on packaging.
- Check areas of storage to ensure that they are at the correct temperature, for example, the refrigerator should be at 4 °C or below.
- Keep foods out of the danger zone, 4 °C to 40 °C.

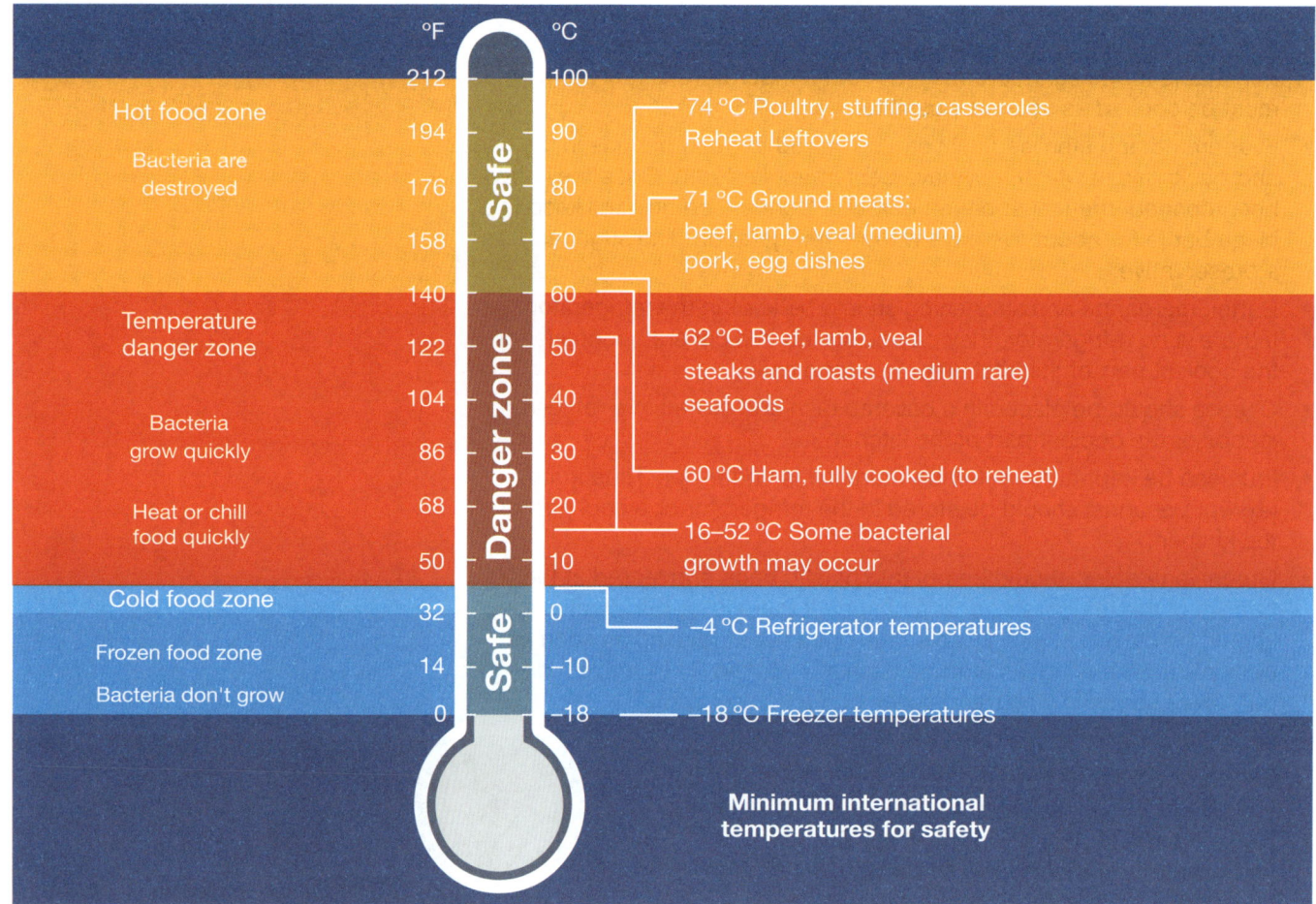

Figure 6.4 The temperature danger zone

ACTIVITIES

You have just completed shopping at the local market. You have to prepare the items for storage. Draw the following table in your notebook and complete the table.

- eggs
- canned beans
- whole chicken
- cheese
- ice cream
- parsley
- yoghurt
- bread rolls
- pak choi
- packaged flour
- minced beef
- apples
- tomatoes
- bell peppers
- whole fish
- large tin of crackers
- packaged milk powder
- rice
- pasteurised milk
- dry cereals
- pasta
- cupcakes iced with butter cream
- bottled orange juice

ITEM	PREPARATION, IF ANY	STORAGE AREA
		crisper
		freezing compartment
		kitchen cupboards
		refrigerator compartment
		securely covered container

How to pack the refrigerator

In Chapter 2, you read about using the refrigerator. This section will deal with storing food in the various storage areas of a refrigerator, namely:

- the freezing compartment or freezer
- the chiller trays
- the refrigerator compartment
- the door
- the crisper.

Each of these areas is suited for storing different types of food. Figure 6.5 shows how to pack a refrigerator as outlined below.

The freezing compartment. In double-door refrigerator-freezers, this is the area in which all frozen foods should be stored. These include those bought ready-frozen and those that must be home-frozen, for example, meat, fish, poultry, game, ice cream.

In single-door refrigerators, use the ice-making section, which has an interior door.

Store all frozen foods here.

Store already frozen foods in their original wrappings or containers.

For home-frozen foods, wrap in freezer paper, plastic wrap, clean used plastic bags, freezer bags or place in covered plastic containers.

Label and date packages carefully.

> **Did you know?**
> The refrigerator has its own micro-climate. Though the internal temperature should be below 4.5 °C, some parts will be colder than other parts.

The chiller tray. In single-door refrigerators, this is positioned below the freezing compartment. In more modern models, this has been replaced by a container with or without a cover, similar to the crisper.

- Store all small cuts of meat, fish and poultry that are to be used within a day or two.
- Store cold cuts, such as cured and smoked meat, sliced cooked ham and sausages.
- Store foods in their original wrappings or wrap in plastic wrap or aluminum foil.

The refrigerator compartment. This is the main section of the refrigerator with several shelves that are adjustable. They can be moved up and down to accommodate items of different heights. Most foods that need to be stored at a low temperature to prevent contamination are stored here, namely:

- milk dishes, such as custards and puddings in covered containers to prevent evaporation
- stocks, soups, prepared dishes and some leftover foods
- large cuts of meat, fish, poultry and game, for safe thawing
- marinated meat or fish before cooking.

> **Consider this**
> The temperature in a refrigerator should be below 4.5 °C (40 °F). This will ensure that perishable foods will remain safe without freezing.

Figure 6.5 How to store food in a refrigerator

> **Did you know?**
> You should cool hot foods such as soups and stews before storing them in the refrigerator. This is because the heat from them will cause a rise in the overall temperature of the refrigerator.

All these foods should be kept in covered containers or wrapped in plastic wrap to prevent transfer of odours. Never store raw meat or poultry above cooked meat, as the blood can drip onto the cooked meat and contaminate it.

The door. The door of the refrigerator is fitted with racks, special shelves and small containers.

- Store eggs, cheese, cream, butter, margarine and other solid fats in the special sections provided. Most of these sections may be labelled.
- Milk bottles, bottled drinks and water that need to be chilled, opened cans or packages of milk, fruit and vegetable juices are all stored here.
- Condiments, jams, jellies and other preserves can also be stored in the door.

The crisper. In most refrigerators, this section fits under a glass or plastic cover at the bottom of the main compartment. More modern refrigerators may have two bins for high humidity and low humidity storage. Do not put heavy items on the lid as it may crack.

- Store all green, leafy vegetables such as watercress, lettuce, cabbage, celery, parsley. Before storing, wash them in cold water, then drain well and trim.
- Store green vegetables with skins, such as sweet peppers, cucumbers and string beans. Before storing, wash and dry them and place in clean plastic bags.
- Wash and dry most fruits and store them here. However, some fruits such as cherries, plums and other soft fruits, keep better if they are not washed before storing.
- If the crisper is not large enough to accommodate all the vegetables and fruits for the family, items such as lettuce and watercress can be stored in tightly wrapped plastic bags and placed on the lowest shelf of the main compartment.

> **Did you know?**
> Proper storage of foods ensures their safety for a longer time.

ACTIVITIES

Rose sometimes goes to the market to buy vegetables and fruits without a shopping list.

1. Outline two ways that Rose can benefit from shopping with a list.
2. What are two types of information that can be found on food labels and why should we read them?
3. Rose told her fellow workers always to clean the refrigerator and food storage cupboards before doing major shopping. What are two reasons for why you think she does this?

Checklist: Preparation of food

✔ Wear appropriate clothing such as a hairnet and apron.
✔ Wash all fruits and vegetables.
✔ Separate cooked and raw foods.
✔ Wash hands properly with soap before, during and after the preparation of food.
✔ Use separate cutting boards for raw and cooked foods.
✔ Thaw frozen meat, poultry and fish at the bottom of the refrigerator.
✔ Cook food thoroughly at sufficient temperature or to the appropriate doneness.
✔ Use gloves when preparing uncooked foods that are to be served.
✔ Keep foods covered.
✔ Avoid cross-contamination of food.

Checklist: Serving and consuming food

✔ Follow the 2-Hour rule – The absolute maximum time for leaving prepared foods at room temperature is 2 hours.
✔ Discard any perishable foods that have been left at room temperature for longer than 2 hours. If you are eating outdoors at a picnic or barbecue on a hot day, discard foods after 1 hour.
✔ To serve hot foods later, divide into small portions, place in shallow containers, and refrigerate or freeze. Remove stuffing from whole cooked poultry and refrigerate separately.
✔ Keep hot foods at 60 °C or warmer by using chafing dishes, slow cookers and warming trays.
✔ Keep cold foods at 60 °C or colder by placing them in an ice bath. You may also use small serving trays and replace them often.
✔ Make sure there are separate serving utensils for each dish to prohibit the mixing of foods from different dishes.
✔ Be sure to provide a serving spoon and plates for dips and salsas. Placing chips and dips at opposite ends of the buffet table may also help to discourage 'double-dipping'.
✔ Use clean plates and cutlery.
✔ Ensure that foods do not have a foul odour.
✔ Wash and sanitise hands before consuming a meal.

4 STEPS TO FOOD SAFETY

CLEAN

SEPARATE

COOK

CHILL

Figure 6.6 Four simple steps to food safety

Conditions and practices that promote safe food handling

ACTIVITIES

Technology-based activity

* Research practices that should be utilised to decrease microbial contamination when growing food crops.
* Share the information gathered using any type of presentation software.
* Create a video, which showcases the practices that should be utilised **when preparing, storing and handling food**.

Foodborne illness

Everyday around the world, people become sick from the food they eat. This sickness is known as a foodborne illness. It is disease that results from eating foods that are contaminated with harmful bacteria and/or other microorganisms.

Preventing microbial contamination is the best way to prevent disease and improve your health and that of your family and community.

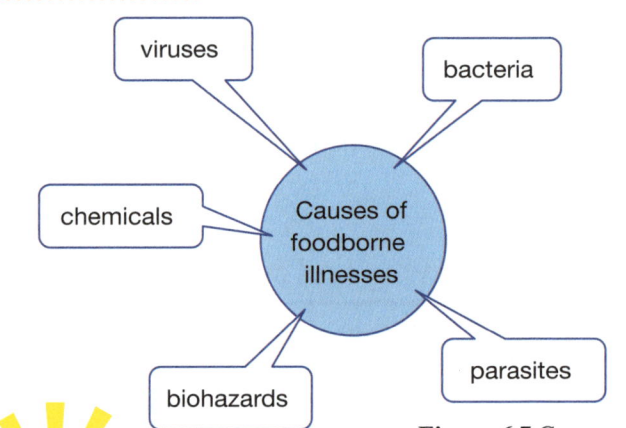

Figure 6.7 Causes of foodborne illnesses

ACTIVITIES

Figure 6.7 shows the causes of foodborne illnesses. Create a brochure of some of the common foodborne illnesses from each cause. Your brochure should include:

* organism
* name of illness
* incubation period
* signs and symptoms
* duration
* food sources.

FOODBORNE ILLNESS AS A HEALTH ISSUE FOR INDIVIDUALS AND FAMILIES

Foodborne illnesses are preventable. These illnesses are a burden on public health and increase the cost of healthcare. Foodborne illnesses caused by the consumption of unsafe food can cause a cycle of disease and malnutrition, which affect infants, young children, older people and the sick. If unsafe food is consumed at home there is the possibility of several members of the family being sick. Although any family member can get a foodborne illness, young children and the older people are at greater risk because of their reduced immunity.

Foodborne illnesses can also affect the financial stability of the family and community by straining healthcare systems, harming national economies, tourism and trade, because it reduces earning and the amount of public funds available to spend on other social needs.

Did you know?

You cannot see, taste or smell the food poisoning organisms in the food.

Career corner

Food safety and quality assurance supervisor

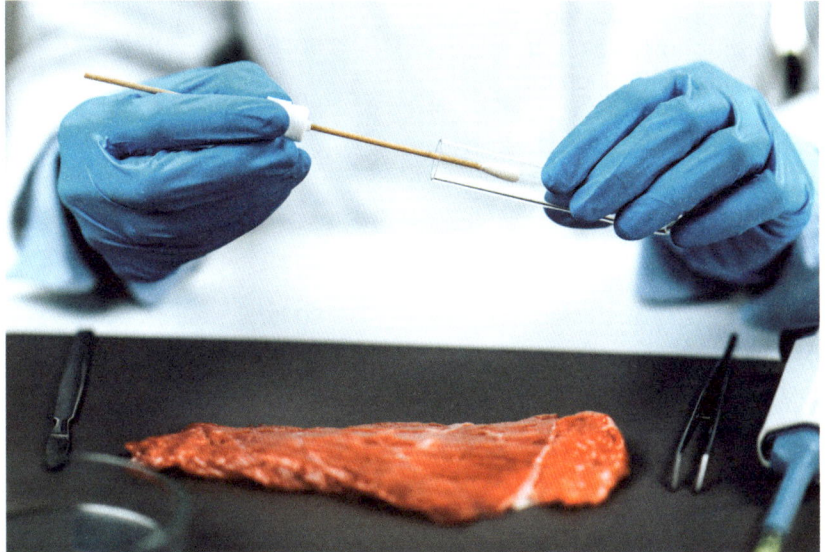

Figure 6.8 Food safety

Key responsibilities
- Assist in overseeing quality and food safety programmes including implementation, staff training and documentation.
- Work with consumer safety inspectors, protection agencies and health inspectors; assist in obtaining environmental and product testing samples as needed.
- Assist with the audit programme for quality and food safety plans.
- Conduct daily sensory evaluation of foods being produced and packaged.
- Use all required safety equipment and consistently follow all food-related sanitation and operating safety guidelines; ensure that food production staff does the same.

Qualifications
- Bachelor's degree in Food Technology, Food Safety, Food Science or Regulatory Compliance or equivalent from a recognised tertiary institution.
- Training in the implementation and maintenance of quality systems such as International Organisation of Standardisation (ISO), Food Safety System Certification (FSSC), Safe Quality Food (SQF) and so on.
- Training in Hazard Analysis Critical Control Points (HACCP).

Salary
- Approximately USD 59,000 per annum

Subject link
Food safety can be linked to Biology, Chemistry and Agricultural Science. Can you list one subtopic in food safety that overlaps with the subjects identified?

ACTIVITY

The danger zone

Instructions:

The danger zone, where bacterial growth can occur, is indicated on the thermometer. Copy the statements into your notebook and put a 'Y' next to the ones that are true for the foods that will be in the danger zone and 'N' next to those that are not.

1. Letitia cooked her chicken to an internal temperature of 75 °C. _____
2. Lorraine did not want to throw away the remains of her beef shanks, even though it had been in the refrigerator for more than a week. _____
3. Stanley went to the supermarket early in the morning where he bought a pack of marlin. He continued his day by running errands and only reached home at midday. _____
4. When everyone had had enough of their Sunday lunch, Evelyn portioned the food, allowed it to cool, then placed it in the refrigerator. _____
5. Jason left the turkey to thaw out on the counter overnight. _____
6. Sarai reheated her lunch in the microwave, ensuring that she stirred it occasionally. _____

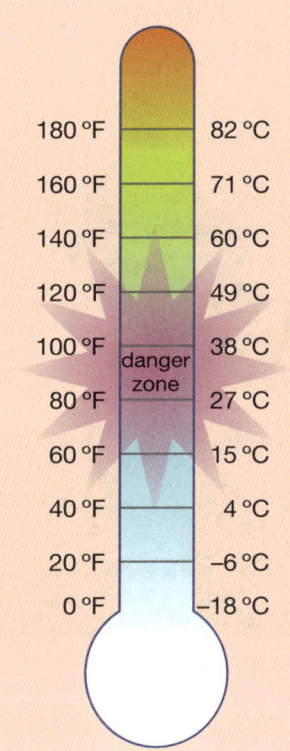

Components of a recipe

Recipe 1

Cassava bakes ← Title or name of recipe

Ingredients

1¼ cup cassava flour
1¼ cup flour
4 tsp sugar
1 tsp baking powder
1 tsp nutmeg
1 tsp cinnamon
½ tsp salt
1 cup of water
½ tsp vanilla essence
oil for frying

← Ingredients with quantities required

Figure 6.9 Cassava bakes

Method ← Preparation method

- Place all dry ingredients in a bowl.
- Gradually add the water (and the vanilla essence) and stir until all ingredients are combined. The mixture should be soft but not runny.
- Heat oil in a shallow or deep skillet and fry spoonfuls of the mixture until golden brown.

Chapter 6 Food preparation and service

Recipes may also contain
- Time for preparation and cooking of the dish
- Temperature required to cook the dish
- Recipe yield
- Variations (optional)
- Nutritional analysis.

Checklist: Guidelines for writing recipes

✔ Indicate the measurements clearly using the same mode of measurement – metric (grams) or imperial (lbs and ozs).

✔ List the ingredients in the order that they appear in the recipe.

✔ List every ingredient that is used in the preparation section.

✔ Indicate the type of ingredients, for example, 1 cup finely chopped nuts.

✔ Organise the ingredients using headings when different types of processes are used to complete a dish. For example, if you are making a meat pie, list the heading and give the ingredients for the pastry, and then do the same for the meat filling.

✔ Indicate any advance preparation that must be done ahead of time.

INTERPRET AND USE A BASIC RECIPE

A well-written recipe is designed to make the cooking process as simple as possible. Therefore, it is important to understand how to use a basic recipe so that you can achieve successful results and make the process as uncomplicated as possible.

The following steps should be taken to use a recipe correctly:

- Thoroughly read the recipe before beginning the preparation of the dish.
- Ensure that you understand the ingredients list.
- Check for division in the recipe, as ingredients may need to be divided or are repeating in sections.
- Prepare various cuts of the ingredients identified in the recipe after weighing and measuring. For example, 1 cup of halved tomatoes.
- Research substitutions before beginning the dish.
- Gather and accurately weigh and measure the ingredients. (Read Chapter 5 Book 1).
- Have the correct utensils and equipment on hand.
- Follow the preparation method carefully and look for keywords. For example, simmer, al dente, cream, baste.
- Test for doneness using the time given or the description provided of a good-quality product.

EVALUATE A BASIC RECIPE FOR ITS ACCURACY

To evaluate a basic recipe for its accuracy, check:

1. If the correct quantities of ingredients, terms, time, temperature and yield were given.
2. The product's sensory characteristics. This can assist with deciding on a measured description of all the sensory attributes that can be identified, or the ranges in criteria. For instance, the following sensory characteristics such as taste, texture and or consistency, appearance and aroma can be utilised to make a rubric for analysis.

ACTIVITIES

1. Research the following food sensory characteristics – taste, texture/consistency, aroma and appearance
2. Work with a group and report how each aspect of the sensory evaluation is conducted.

How to evaluate
- Place samples of the food in clean containers to identify each sample clearly.
- Provide a sample for each evaluator.
- Provide water to rinse mouth between each sample to clean the palate.
- Give the evaluators time to record findings before moving to the next sample.
- When evaluating the finished bake product, a rubric (Table 6.1) or a scorecard can be used.

Name of product: Vanilla cupcakes

Please select the criteria that best describes the cake.

Table 6.1 Rubric for assessing a cake by the creaming method

QUALITIES	DELICIOUS	GOOD	NEEDS IMPROVEMENT	POOR
TEXTURE	Fine, even crumbs	Chewy	Crispy	Dense
SHAPE	Well risen	Uneven top	Peaked	Sunken or cracked
COLOUR	Correct/golden brown colour	Irregularities in colour	Pale colour	Burnt
FLAVOUR	Rich creamy flavour	Medium fat flavour	Low to non-fat richness	Dry, no flavour

Figure 6.10 Vanilla cupcakes

Standards scorecard: Rubbing-in cakes				

Recipe prepared: _____

Standards scorecard: Rubbing-in cakes

Directions: Rate the finished product in each of the following areas by circling the appropriate number on the scorecard.

	EXCELLENT	GOOD	FAIR	POOR
EXTERIOR				
Uniform shape with slightly round top; no peaks or cracks	4	3	2	1
Uniform size; light in weight in proportion to size.	4	3	2	1
Uniform golden brown colour (colour, however, may be affected by flavouring such as spices or chocolate)	4	3	2	1
Tender, smooth crust	4	3	2	1
INTERIOR				
Uniform colour, characteristic of type of cake	4	3	2	1
Fine, even grain, free of tunnels	4	3	2	1
Velvety, moist and tender texture	4	3	2	1
Not soggy or too dry	4	3	2	1
Pleasing flavour, well blended and characteristic of the kind of cake	4	3	2	1
Total score				

Figure 6.11 Standards scorecard

ACTIVITIES

1. Using the basic information required to construct a recipe, develop a recipe for the following:
   - a cold beverage using local fruit
   - a carbohydrate dish using an indigenous staple.
2. Create a rubric or a standards scorecard to evaluate your item.
3. Clip a recipe from a magazine, newspaper or from another source. Stick it in your notebook. Use the recipe to answer the following questions.
   a. Is the format correct?
   b. Do the ingredients have quantities?
   c. Are the instructions clear and logical?
   d. Is the cooking time and the temperature clearly stated?
   e. What extra information does the recipe provide?

Methods of cooking

Foods are cooked for many reasons:
- to kill harmful bacteria and make food safe to eat, for example, fish, pork
- to soften and make them easy to digest, for example, potatoes, rice
- to preserve them so that they can last longer, for example, vegetables, fruits
- to bring out the full flavour of the food, for example, meat
- to add variety to meals, for example, roasted meat, fried fish, stewed meat
- to make foods tastier, for example, meat and poultry.

Cooking in specific ways allows for cultural identity to various national dishes.

What does the word 'cooking' mean? Cooking is the preparation of food for eating by applying heat. Food is cooked in a number of different methods (ways). Some methods are simpler than others. Different methods are suitable for different foods. In general, there are eight basic methods of cooking food, which can be categorised into three broad groups:

Moist-heat methods. These include grilling/broiling, steaming, stewing and braising.

Dry-heat methods. These include baking, roasting, grilling/broiling.

Frying is a method of cooking that makes use of hot fat rather than moist or dry heat.

Did you know?
Cooking adds great variety to the number of dishes that we can prepare from one food.

Consider this
Steaming, grilling and sautéing are among the methods of cooking that preserve the most nutrients.

MOIST METHODS OF COOKING

Boiling

This is a quick, easy method of cooking (Figure 6.12). It is done by cooking food in a liquid at 100 °C (212 °F). Boiling is done in a covered pot. This prevents the steam from escaping, so that the steam will cook the food. When boiling jellies, jams and syrups, the pot should be uncovered.

During boiling, the food is completely covered by the boiling liquid. It is not necessary for the liquid to bubble rapidly during the entire cooking period. If the liquid bubbles briskly, the food may break up. The heat should be lowered so that the liquid simmers rather than bubbles vigorously. Water and milk are usually used, but some food may be cooked in wine or stock.

Figure 6.12 Green beans boiling in water

ADVANTAGES OF BOILING	DISADVANTAGES OF BOILING
- It is a very simple method that requires little attention. - It is suitable for softening tough foods, for example, some cuts of meat and starchy root vegetables. - A number of different foods can be cooked in the same pot, for example, plantains, carrots and potatoes. - It is suitable for a variety of foods, for example, starchy foods, vegetables, meat, poultry and eggs. - It can be used to make stocks that are used as the base for soups and sauces. Stock is the liquid in which meat, fish, bones or non-starchy vegetables have been boiled.	- If the temperature is not controlled, food may break up by over-boiling. - Some vitamins and minerals are lost in the cooking liquid, which is usually thrown away. - Some foods may lose their flavour and be very bland.

Foods suitable for boiling

Lots of different foods are suitable for boiling. These include:
- root vegetables
- whole eggs
- pasta (macaroni, spaghetti, vermicelli, etc.)
- tough parts of meat such as cow heel, trotters, neck, tripe and salted/pickled meat
- starchy foods (ground provisions).

Guidelines

Place the food in either cold water or boiling water. Use cold water to start cooking bones and meats for soups, whole eggs, soaked legumes. Use boiling water for vegetables, starchy grains and meat in which the flavour should be retained.

Reduce the heat and allow the food to simmer rather than boil rapidly.

Cover the cooking pot/pan to prevent steam from escaping, except when boiling jellies and syrups.

Keep the cooking temperature steady at all times. Keep foods the same size as much as possible, but if some pieces are larger than others, place the smaller pieces on top of the larger ones.

> **Consider this**
>
> Water is the most common liquid used for boiling foods. Other liquids such as stocks, broth and coconut milk can be used.

ACTIVITIES

1. What is the best way to cook ground provisions?
   - **A** Peel and cut 1 lb potatoes into batonettes (6 cm × 1 cm × 1 cm).
   - **B** Cook in three different ways (boil, fry in deep oil, and steam using a perforated vessel).
2. Draw a similar table in your notebook and fill out the information as your findings.

RATE EACH CRITERION ON A SCALE OF 1 TO 3; 3 BEING THE HIGHEST AND 1 BEING THE LOWEST.					
Potatoes	Starch cooked	Attractive appearance	Time taken to cook	Conserve energy	General comment
Fried					
Boiled					
Steamed					

Steaming

Steaming is cooking food in the steam that rises from a boiling liquid (Figure 6.13). There are different ways of steaming food (Figure 6.14):
- between two plates over a pot of boiling water
- in a double boiler
- in a covered vessel in a pot of boiling water
- in a perforated vessel in or over a pot of boiling water
- directly on top of cooking food, for example, steaming vegetables or dumplings on top of boiling root vegetables or rice.

Figure 6.13 A steamer cooking food

Methods of cooking

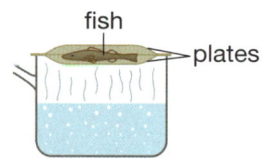  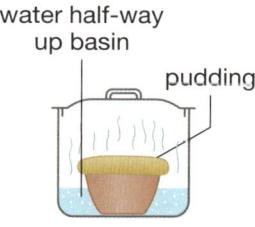 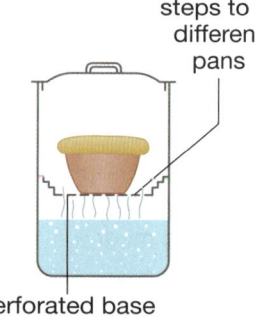

a Steaming fish between two plates   **b** Double boiler   **c** Steaming in a saucepan   **d** Stepped/graduated steamer

Figure 6.14 Different ways of steaming food

Foods suitable for steaming
- Small portions of poultry, such as breasts and wings
- Fish: whole, slices, cutlets, fillets
- Fruits and green vegetables
- Root vegetables
- Tender cuts of meat
- Rice
- Puddings and custards
- Dumplings.

ADVANTAGES OF STEAMING	DISADVANTAGES OF STEAMING
• Steamed food remains moist and is easily digested. It is therefore ideal for young children and convalescents. • Food is not overcooked. • Cold food can be heated through easily. • More than one food can be cooked at the same time, saving fuel and washing-up.	• Needs constant attention to make sure that water does not boil away. Water may need replenishing. • It is a long, slow method of cooking for some types of food, such as puddings. • Foods may lack bite if not well seasoned.

Rules for steaming
- Always keep a kettle or pot of boiling water handy to replace water that has evaporated.
- A steamer must never boil dry.
- Food should never come into contact with the water.
- Cover puddings with aluminum foil or heavy waxed paper to prevent them becoming soggy from condensed steam.
- Cut pieces of food thinly so that the steam can penetrate easily.

ACTIVITY

Practise steaming food between two plates over boiling water or in a double boiler. Use Recipe 2 on page 163.

Recipe 2

Steamed fish. Serves 4

Ingredients

500 g (1 lb 2 oz) fish, thin slices or fillets

lime or vinegar water

5 ml (1 tsp) salt

2 ml ($\frac{1}{2}$ tsp) black or white pepper

45 ml (3 tbsp) lime or lemon juice

15 ml (1 tbsp) tomato sauce/ketchup

2 ml ($\frac{1}{2}$ tsp) soy sauce or Worcestershire sauce

25 g (1 oz) margarine

Figure 6.15 Steamed fish

Method

- Wash fish pieces with lime or vinegar and water.
- Mix salt, pepper, lime/lemon juice, tomato sauce and soy sauce together, then spread over fish.
- Put dots of margarine on the fish slices and place between two plates over a pot of boiling water or double boiler. Steam for 10–15 minutes. Serve hot with green vegetables and boiled root vegetables or dumplings.
- Garnish with onion rings, bell peppers and parsley.

Recipe 3

Patriotic pudding. Serves 4

Ingredients

170 g (6 oz) flour

5 ml (1 tsp) baking powder

2 ml ($\frac{1}{2}$ tsp) ground cinnamon spice

75 g (3 oz) butter

75 g (3 oz) white sugar

5 ml (1 tsp) lemon zest

1 egg

$\frac{1}{2}$ cup reconstituted milk

1 tsp vanilla essence

$\frac{1}{4}$ cup jam (strawberry, raspberry or guava)

Figure 6.16 Patriotic pudding

Method

- Prepare a large pot or steamer by filling it with water up to one-third high. Put water to boil. Place perforated base in the pot.
- Grease a six-ounce pudding mould or Bundt pan. Place the jam at the bottom of the pudding mould or Bundt pan. It must fit into the pot on a perforated base.
- In a medium mixing bowl, sift flour, baking powder and spice.
- Add the butter and cut it into the flour with a spatula.
- Rub in the mixture with the tips of the fingers until it resembles fine breadcrumbs.
- Mix in the sugar and lemon zest.
- Beat the egg in a separate bowl and add the milk and essence.
- Make a well in the centre and pour in the egg mixture.

- Mix until all the dry ingredients are just moistened.
- Add to the pudding mould and secure tightly with the lid. If using a Bundt pan, secure tightly with heavy duty foil.
- Lower the pudding mould onto the perforated base with the help of a pot spoon.
- Leave to steam for 35 minutes or until well cooked. When cooked, the pudding will begin to leave the sides of the mould and a skewer inserted in the middle will come out clean.
- Leave for about 10 minutes before attempting to unmould the pudding.
- Serve as a dessert.

ACTIVITY

Reflect on the dishes that are prepared by steaming. Consider two ways to make each one more attractive and appetising.

Consider this

Both roasting and baking are usually done at high temperatures. Compare baking meats with roasting them, looking at two similarities and two differences.

Baking and roasting

Baking is cooking food in the heated air that is trapped inside an oven (Figure 6.17). The aim of baking and roasting is to cook the food to a pleasing brown colour, and until starch grains, cellulose and meat tissues are softened or mixtures set.

Roasting is cooking food in hot fat in an oven or on a roasting spit over or under an open fire.

ADVANTAGES OF BAKING AND ROASTING	DISADVANTAGES OF BAKING AND ROASTING
• The food requires little attention. • More than one type of food may be cooked in the same oven at the same time, for example, baked chicken, green banana pie. • Foods do not become greasy and soggy. • Foods retain most of their nutrients. • Foods are very digestible.	• Foods tend to dry out if not basted occasionally during roasting, or when temperatures are not controlled. • There is some wastage of fuel, as ovens must be pre-heated for use. • It is also an uneconomical method if only one dish is placed in the oven. • Only good-quality foods are suitable, particularly for roasting, therefore it is an expensive method. • Foods that are suitable for baking or roasting contain enough moisture and/or fat to help them to be palatable and enjoyable after they are cooked. • Foods that are suitable for baking include: bread, cakes, buns, cookies, biscuits, pies, custards, puddings, eggs, whole fish, fillets and cutlets, juicy vegetables, meat, steaks and joints, poultry. • Foods that are suitable for roasting include: tender meat joints, poultry and game, fish and vegetables such as potatoes and onions.

Did you know?
Fresh vegetables can be roasted.

Figure 6.17 Baking fish in an oven

ACTIVITIES

The next time your mum is roasting chicken or other meat, cut up a selection of various coloured vegetables using different shapes. Place them in an oiled roasting pan, sprinkle with some black pepper and salt and add a sprinkling of vinegar. Cover with aluminum foil and place them in the hot oven. Cook for 20 minutes.

Do some reflections on the outcome, write these in your journal, and share with your teacher.

1. Which vegetables did you choose?
2. Were the vegetables tender after 20 minutes?
3. Were they too tender or just right?
4. Assess these qualities: retention of colour, texture, mouthfeel, taste.
5. What would you add or do differently?

Guidelines

- Make sure that the oven is clean before preheating it.
- Place oven shelves in their correct places before preheating the oven.
- Grease baking and roasting pans to prevent food from sticking to them.
- Set the oven to the required temperature (Table 6.2).
- Do not crowd the oven. Arrange baking dishes on racks to allow air to circulate. Remember that hot air rises, therefore the top shelf is the hottest shelf in the oven. The lower shelves are a few degrees cooler than the top shelf.
- Open and close the door gently. Do not slam it as this may disturb the flame or the food.

Table 6.2 Oven temperatures

DESCRIPTION	°F	°C	GAS MARK	TYPE OF USAGE
Very slow or cool	250–275	130–140	$\frac{1}{2}$–1	Slow cooking of meats, drying meringues, dried fruit
Slow or cool	300–325	150–170	2–3	Very rich fruit cakes, parching nuts
Moderate	350	180	4	Rubbed in mixtures Creamed cakes
Moderately hot	375	190	5	Short pastries, biscuits, scones, breads
Hot	400–425	200–220	6–7	Reheating foods, roasting meats and vegetables
Very hot	450–475	230–240	8–9	Quick browning

- Avoid opening the door unnecessarily. Do not allow heat to escape once the food is in the oven.
- Make full use of the oven when it is on. This helps to save on fuel.
- Clean up spills when the oven is cool. Hot ovens can burn you.
- Use oven gloves when removing hot dishes from the oven. Be careful not to touch hot parts. Do not use damp towels.
- If foods become brown too quickly, lower the temperature or reposition dishes so that their contents can be cooked right through.

Methods of cooking

- Turn off the oven immediately when food is cooked. But remember that the oven retains heat for a long time. If the food is not removed, it will continue to cook.
- If the oven has a drop-down glass door, do not rest baking dishes on it, or allow wet or cold items to come in contact with it while it is still hot. Doing these things may cause the glass to crack.
- When roasting, baste the food with hot fat or dripping to keep them from drying out.

ACTIVITY

Use Recipe 4, fish broth, to practise cooking food by boiling. Serve the broth for yourself and your best friend.

Recipe 4

Fish broth. Serves 4

Ingredients

450 g (1 lb) fish (1 small whole fish) such as snapper or carite (mackerel)

1 lime or 5 ml (1 tsp) vinegar

salt and pepper

1 medium onion, peeled

1 medium tomato

2 springs Spanish thyme

2 blades chives or scallion

1 clove garlic, peeled

15 g ($\frac{1}{2}$ oz) margarine

500 ml (1 pint) water

salt and pepper to taste

Method

- Clean, wash with lime juice or vinegar and season fish with salt and pepper.
- Chop seasonings (onion, tomato, thyme, chives). Crush garlic.
- Melt margarine and sauté (lightly fry) seasonings.
- Add fish and water and bring to the boil. Let the mixture simmer for about 10–15 minutes.
- Remove fish from broth and remove skin and bones.
- Strain the broth. Return fish flesh to broth.
- Season with salt and pepper to taste, reheat and serve.

Figure 6.18 Fish broth

Frying

Frying is cooking food in hot fat or oil until the outside is crisp or sealed and the inside is cooked. It is a quick method of cooking and fried foods are usually quite delicious and well flavoured. Frying is usually done in a skillet on a burner (Figure 6.19).

Figure 6.19 Bacon frying in a skillet

Types of frying

There are three main types of frying, depending on the amount of fat that is used (Figure 6.20).

Dry frying. No fat is used. The foods already contain a quantity of fat, for example, bacon and sausages.

Shallow-fat frying. Just enough fat is used to cover the bottom of the skillet or saucepan. This is suitable for fried eggs, omelettes, fried fish and liver.

Deep-fat frying. This uses a large quantity of fat. The food is completely covered by the fat. This is suitable for chicken parts, plantain chips, doughnuts, French fries, salt-fish cakes, accra/fritters and meatballs.

Figure 6.20 The main types of frying

Did you know?
Frying is one of the fastest methods of cooking and adds satiety to foods.

Foods suitable for frying

- Small portions of poultry, such as chicken thighs, wings, drumsticks, breasts and legs.
- Thin slices of vegetables, such as melange, breadfruit, plantain and potatoes.
- Fillet of fish, fish steaks/slices, small whole fish, fish cakes.
- Tender cuts of meat and small meat items such as meatballs and patties.
- Bakes, doughnuts, roti.

ADVANTAGES OF FRYING	DISADVANTAGES OF FRYING
• Frying is a quick and easy method. • It is suitable for small pieces of food. • Little preparation is needed for frying. • There is little loss of food value since the hot fat seals the surface of the food and juices do not escape. • Foods are attractive in colour and the flavour is well developed.	• Foods need constant and careful attention, since they must be turned to ensure even cooking and to prevent them from burning. • Fat must always be at the correct temperature so that food does not get soggy. • It is not suitable for large, thick or tough pieces of food. • Expensive method, as fat or oil must be of a good quality. • Some fried foods may be indigestible.

Air frying

What is air frying? Air frying is cooking food in an air fryer (Figure 6.21 on the next page), which uses convection heat to make the food crisp and golden brown. Very little fat is used.

ADVANTAGES OF AIR FRYING	DISADVANTAGES OF AIR FRYING
• There is less fat and fewer calories in the food. • There are fewer harmful compounds. • The cooking time is shorter. • Less energy is use. • Air fryers are portable and convenient to travel with.	• It may cause burns if not properly handled. • An air fryer has a s mall cooking surface in comparison to an oven or a stove-top. • It can be large and bulky for a counter top.

Preparation of food for frying

Before frying, many foods have to be coated. They should be coated to prevent them from:
- absorbing the fat
- sticking to the pan
- breaking up.

Coating also seals in the food juices and prevents them from escaping during cooking. It also makes some foods more attractive.

Types of coating

There are several types of coating for foods. These include:
- batters (see Book 3, Chapter 6)
- egg and breadcrumbs
- milk and seasoned flour
- seasoned flour
- cornmeal.

Rules for frying

Take care when frying foods to ensure that the food is well cooked, looks attractive and appetising. Care is also needed to avoid causing a fire with the hot fat and open flame from the burner. The following rules are essential for successful frying of foods.
- Dry wet foods to remove excessive moisture before coating.
- Use clean fat or oil.
- Use a dry, strong skillet or frying pan or shallow-frying; for deep-fat frying, use a pot that will hold enough oil to cover the food.
- Heat the fat or oil to the correct temperature before use. A faint blue haze should rise from the fat. Test for readiness by placing a tiny cube of bread into the fat. If it becomes crisp and brown in 30 seconds, the fat is ready. If it sinks, the fat is not ready.
- Place food gently into the pan, or use a frying basket for deep-fat frying to prevent splashing.
- Do not attempt to fry too many pieces of food at the same time. This lowers the temperature of the fat and causes the food to absorb the fat.
- Turn food with a fish slice/spatula.
- Avoid piercing food while turning. Piercing causes food juices to escape.
- Keep the heat low enough to maintain the desired temperature and prevent burning.
- Drain fried foods on absorbent paper.
- Cool, strain and store fat after use. Do not use rancid fat.

Figure 6.21 Chicken in an air fryer

ACTIVITIES

1. Rose has invited you to help with some cooking at the home, as they will be frying a large batch of fish fillets. doughnuts and cassava croquettes. Record the following:
   a the types of food fried
   b the type of frying done
   c the rules followed when frying the food
   d the type of fat used on each occasion and the coating used, if any.
2. Practise cooking foods by shallow-fat frying. Prepare pancakes, fried bakes and French toast for breakfast.

RECIPES

Recipe 5

Pancakes. Serves 4

Ingredients

100 g (4 oz) flour
2 ml ($\frac{1}{2}$ tsp) salt
1 egg
250 ml (8 fl oz) milk
30 ml (2 tbsp) oil, for frying
30 ml (2 tbsp) granulated sugar
15 ml (1 tbsp) lime juice

Method

- Sift flour and salt together into a bowl and make a well in the centre.
- Lightly beat the egg with 15 ml (1 tbsp) of the milk.
- Add the beaten egg slowly to the flour, stirring well with a wooden spoon to avoid lumps. Add half of the milk, beating well from the centre and working outwards to the sides of the bowl.
- Add remaining milk and beat until batter is smooth.
- Heat a little of the oil in a shallow frying pan. When it is hot, pour in enough of the batter mixture to coat the bottom of the pan.
- Allow to cook until small bubbles appear on the surface. Turn pancake and cook until golden brown.
- Remove from pan and drain on absorbent paper. Keep warm.
- Repeat frying the pancakes until the batter is used up. Sprinkle a little sugar and lime juice on each pancake and serve while still warm.

Figure 6.22 Pancakes

Recipe 6

Fried bakes. Makes 10

Ingredients

225 g (8 oz) flour
7 ml (1$\frac{1}{2}$ tsp) baking powder
2 ml ($\frac{1}{2}$ tsp) salt
10 ml (2 tsp) sugar
25 g (1 oz) margarine or lard
45 ml (3 tbsp) cold water
30 ml (2 tbsp) oil, for frying

Figure 6.23 Fried bakes

Method

- Sift dry ingredients into a bowl, then add sugar and mix well.
- Add margarine or lard and rub it into the flour until the mixture looks like fine breadcrumbs.
- Add water and stir to make a soft, but not sticky, dough.
- Pinch off about 25 ml (1$\frac{1}{2}$ tbsp) of dough for each bake and shape into balls.
- On a lightly floured board, and using hands or a rolling pin, flatten each ball into a circle about 7.5 cm (3 in) in diameter.
- Heat oil in a large frying pan. When hot, fry the bakes until golden on both sides.
- Drain on absorbent paper and serve hot.

Recipe 7

French toast. Serves 3

Ingredients

1 egg
75 ml (3 fl oz) milk
1 ml ($\frac{1}{4}$ tsp) salt
3 slices bread
15 ml (1 tbsp) oil, for frying
15 ml (1 tbsp) jam, jelly or syrup

Method

- Lightly beat the egg in a shallow bowl, then add milk and salt, and stir well.
- Dip the slices of bread into the egg mixture, coating both sides; then heat the oil in a shallow frying pan.
- When oil is hot, fry bread slices until golden brown on both sides. Serve immediately with jam, jelly or syrup.
- For a savoury mid-morning or mid-afternoon snack, serve with grated cheddar cheese, cooked bacon or sausages instead of jam.

Figure 6.24 French toast

Recipe 8

Pumpkin fritters. Serves 3–4

Ingredients

500 g (1 lb 2 oz) pumpkin, peeled
75 g (3 oz) flour
1 ml ($\frac{1}{4}$ tsp) grated nutmeg
1 ml ($\frac{1}{4}$ tsp) salt
1 egg
5 ml (1 tsp) baking powder
45 ml (3 tbsp) oil, for frying

Method

- De-seed pumpkin, then grate finely and place in a deep bowl.
- Add remaining ingredients except the oil and mix well.
- Heat oil in a large frying pan. When hot, drop spoonfuls of the pumpkin mixture into the hot fat and fry until crisp and brown on both sides.
- Drain fritters on absorbent paper and serve immediately.

Figure 6.25 Pumpkin fritters

Recipe 9

Salted codfish fritters. Serves 4–6

Ingredients

225 g (8 oz) salted codfish

100 g (4 oz) flour

1 ml ($\frac{1}{4}$ tsp) salt

65 ml ($2\frac{1}{2}$ fl oz) water

2 blades chives, finely chopped

15 ml (1 tsp) onion, finely chopped

15 ml (1 tsp) sweet pepper, finely chopped

1 ml ($\frac{1}{4}$ tsp) white pepper

1 egg white

30 ml (2 tbsp) oil, for frying

Figure 6.26 Salted codfish fritters

Method

- Pour boiling water over codfish and let it soak for 10 minutes.
- Drain and repeat or soak overnight in cold water. Remove skin and bones from fish, then flake and put aside.
- Sift flour and salt together into a bowl. Make a well in the centre and mix to a smooth paste with the water. Cover and leave to stand.
- Mix flaked fish with the chives, onions, sweet pepper and seasoning and stir into flour mixture.
- Beat egg white until stiff and fold into fish mixture. Heat oil in a frying pan. When hot, drop spoonfuls of the fish mixture into the oil and fry until golden brown on both sides. Drain on absorbent paper and serve hot.

ACTIVITIES

Think about the dishes you have prepared and write about your experience.

1. How did you feel about frying these items?
2. What would you do differently?
3. How can you present each dish more attractively?

Fish

People who live in the Caribbean are fortunate in having a large variety of freshwater and saltwater fish. A basic knowledge of the different types of fish, the nutritive value of fish in the diet and the choice, preparation and storage of fish will help the family with meal planning and preparation decisions. Let's take a closer look at fish that is used in cooking.

Fish is of great importance in the diet, as it:

- contains protein of high biological value, vitamins A and D, calcium, iron, iodine, fat and water
- can be used instead of meat, poultry or game as the main dish in a meal
- is very easy to digest and is therefore suitable for convalescents and young children

- can be eaten at any meal of the day
- can be prepared in many different ways
- can be purchased in various forms – fresh, frozen, dried and salted, smoked or canned.

TYPES OF FISH

Fish can be classified into three groups (Figure 6.27).

White fish. The fat is stored in the liver, leaving the flesh white, for example, carite, redfish, grouper, trout and snapper.

Oily fish. The fat is distributed throughout the flesh, making it darker in colour and not as easy to digest as white fish, for example, herring, bonita and cavalla, sardine and mackerel.

Shellfish. Read the following text in the speech bubble.

The group of seafood known as shellfish cannot be classified as fish. Animals in this group are either crustaceans (such as shrimp, crab) or molluscs (such as clams, oysters).

Figure 6.27 Types of fish

CHOOSING FISH

When buying fish, it is important to make sure that it is of the best quality. The following points should be remembered.

- There should be a pleasant, fishy smell.
- There should be plenty of scales on scaly fish, and the scales should be firmly attached.
- The eyes should be bright and bulging, and the gills red.
- The flesh should be firm to the touch.
- Any spots should be bright in colour.
- Buy from clean vendors and shops. Ensure that the surroundings are sanitary.

Consider this
Fish is highly perishable, therefore the correct handling and storage is important.

CUTS OF FISH

Fish can be cut into different pieces according to the dish to be prepared.

- Small fish, for example, jacks and small red snapper, can be cooked whole.
- Large fish can be stuffed, baked and served whole.
- Fish can be cut into fillets (bones removed).
- Fish can be cut into cutlets, steaks, head and shoulders and tail piece (Figure 6.28).
- Large whole fish that are bought from seaside vendors may include the roe. Roe is fish eggs and is rich in protein.

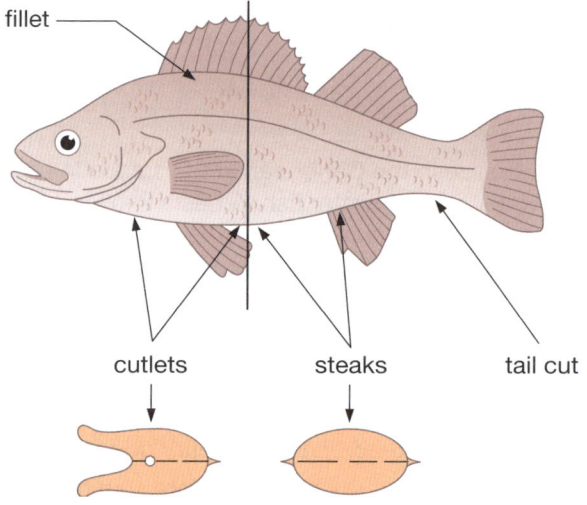

Figure 6.28 The cuts of fish

PREPARATION OF FISH

Fish is usually cleaned by the fishmonger. However, you may sometimes have to dress clean fish. Figure 6.29 shows a simple way of doing this.

1. Cut off the fins with a sharp knife.
2. Remove scales by gripping the fish by the tail and scraping the edge of a knife towards the head. A fish scaler may also be used.
3. Cut the fish open from the head to the tail on the underside, and remove the insides. Lay aside the roe, if any.
4. Remove any dark blood and rinse fish thoroughly in clean water.
5. Drain fish, then dry on absorbent paper. Cut up for cooking as desired.

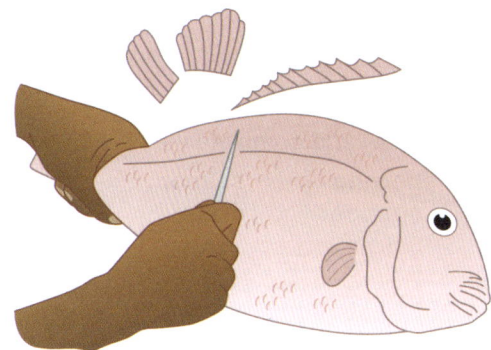

Figure 6.29 How to clean a fish

METHODS OF COOKING FISH

Fish may be cooked by many dry-heat and moist-heat methods, depending on the type and cut of fish (Figure 6.30).

- Boiling: large fish, crabs, head and steaks can be used in soups or for stock.
- Steaming: delicate pieces of white fish.
- Baking: large whole fish, steaks, cutlets, fillets, tail cut.
- Grilling: steaks, cutlets, fillets, medium-sized whole fish.
- Frying: steaks, cutlets, fillets, tail cut, small whole fish, for example, jacks.
- Sautéing: salted codfish, smoked fished, canned tuna flakes or chunks.
- Poaching: steaks, cutlets, fillets of white fish.

STORAGE OF FISH

Fresh fish should be cooked as soon as possible after purchasing. However, with modern refrigeration it may be stored for a few hours or frozen and kept for longer. Here are a few guidelines.

- If fish has to be stored for a few hours it must be cleaned properly, washed thoroughly and sprinkled with salt and lime juice or vinegar.
- The fish should be covered and placed in the refrigerator, or kept in a cool place.
- If fish is to be frozen, it should be washed thoroughly, portioned in quantities needed for cooking and wrapped in plastic wrap or placed in freezer bags.

PRESERVATION OF FISH

There are many ways in which fish is preserved and made available throughout the year.

- **Frozen:** all types of fish; whole, cutlets, fillets, steaks, head, tail.
- **Canned:** sardines, herrings, mackerel, tuna, salmon – available in oil or water to satisfy different needs.
- **Salted:** cod, all types of local fish.
- **Salted and smoked:** herring, salmon, mackerel, all local fish.

A variety of ready-to-cook fish products are now available.

a

b

c

Figure 6.30 (a) fried fish, (b) grilled fish, (c) steamed fish

ACTIVITIES

1. Draw and complete the following table by placing the fish below in the correct category.

   herring   salmon   shrimp   cod   mackerel   sardine   trout
   snapper   crab   hussars   lobsters   flying fish   tilapia

WHITE FISH	OILY FISH	SHELLFISH

2. Apart from steaming and frying, suggest four other methods of cooking fish.
3. 60 lbs of fresh cod fish were donated to the Champion Children's Home where Rose works. Describe one way that Rose can prepare and preserve the cod fish.

Here are some fish dishes that you can try:

Recipe 10

Fish soup. Serves 4–6

Ingredients

½ medium breadfruit, peeled, deveined and diced

2 firm ripe tomatoes

1 onion, peeled and chopped

1 tbsp chopped parsley

2 sprigs fine thyme

500 g (1 lb 2 oz) fish, cleaned, scaled, deboned, cut into fillets and seasoned

Salt and pepper to taste

½ cup tomato sauce/ketchup

15 g (1 tbsp) margarine

Figure 6.31 Fish soup

Method

- Place breadfruit in a saucepan, cover with water and bring to the boil.
- When almost tender, add tomatoes, onion and chopped parsley.
- Add thyme to the mixture.
- Add fish and taste to correct seasoning. Cover and allow to simmer for 30–40 minutes.
- Add tomato sauce, margarine and seasoning to taste. Serve hot.

Recipe 11

Corn-crusted trout fillets. Serves 4–6

Ingredients

500 g (1 lb. 2 oz.) fish fillets
15 ml (1 tbsp) lime juice or lemon juice
2 ml ($\frac{1}{2}$ tsp) black or white pepper
2 ml ($\frac{1}{2}$ tsp) paprika
5 ml (1 tsp) salt
15 ml (1 tbsp) soy sauce
7–8 ml ($\frac{1}{2}$ tbsp) tomato sauce/ketchup
1 egg
50 g (2 oz) corn flakes, crumbed
125 ml (4 fl oz) oil, for frying

Method

- Wipe fish and season with lime juice, pepper, paprika, salt, soy sauce and tomato sauce.
- Lightly beat egg, and coat fish in beaten egg, then cornflake crumbs, covering both sides evenly.
- Heat oil in a frying pan. When hot, fry fish fillets until golden brown on both sides.
- Drain on absorbent paper. Serve at once with fresh, green vegetables.

Figure 6.32 Corn crusted trout fillets

Fats and oils

In Chapter 5, you read about the difference between fats and oils, their chemical composition and sources in the diet. This section will deal with the various uses of fats and oils in food preparation and their importance in the diet.

USES OF FATS AND OILS IN FOOD PREPARATION

Fats and oils are used in various ways, as listed below.

- **Frying all types of food:** fish, meat, poultry, eggs, vegetables, flour mixtures. Various brands of oil are available for frying. Take care that the fat or oil does not become overheated, as this breaks it down and causes fumes, which irritate the nostrils and eyes.
- **Shortening:** fat combined with flour to make cakes, breads and pastries.
- **Creaming:** fat mixes well with sugar and sources in the diet. Air is incorporated during the beating, thereby making mixtures such as cakes light.
- **Foaming emulsion:** oil combines with vinegar and egg to make mayonnaise and other salad dressings.

Figure 6.33 Fats and oils are sold in a variety of forms.

Pastry and cookies produce a flaky or crisp texture once fat is added.

IMPORTANCE OF FATS AND OILS IN THE DIET

Fats and oils are sold in a variety of forms (Figure 6.33). They may be animal and vegetable fats, for example, butter, margarine, ghee, lard, suet, shortening, or vegetable oils (commonly called cooking oils), for example, coconut, olive, soya bean, corn oil. Some other foods such as cheese and peanuts are also high in fats and oil. They are important in the diet because they:

- supply warmth and energy
- have satiety value; fats take longer to digest than other foods, so it takes you longer to feel hungry again after a meal that contains fat
- affect the texture and flavour of prepared dishes; the taste is enhanced in many cases
- ensure the maximum absorption of the fat-soluble vitamins.

Table 6.3 Fats and oils and their uses

FATS AND OILS	USES
Suet: prepared from fat around the kidneys and other internal organs of sheep and cattle.	A part of some pudding mixtures that are to be boiled or steamed. Makes flaky pastries as in Jamaican patties.
Lard: obtained from the fatty tissues surrounding the kidneys and intestines of the pig. It has good shortening properties.	Excellent for frying, as it remains stable. In other words, it does not break down at high temperatures. It is also used in the making of short crust pastry.
Butter: made from the fat of milk	Spread on bread. Cake ingredient. It adds flavour and creams well.
Margarine: made from a mixture of animal oil, and vegetable oils, which are hydrogenated to make them solid. It is usually fortified with vitamins A and D. Colouring and flavouring and added.	A good butter substitute in cake and pastry making.
Vegetable oils: soya bean, corn, coconut, peanut, cottonseed, palm, olive	They form the base of margarines, lard substitutes, and as salad dressings. Excellent for shallow and deep-frying as most oils can reach a temperature of 400°F, before breaking down. Coconut oil and olive oil are exceptions.

ACTIVITIES

1. Prepare a poster for the Champion Children's Home, showing the different types of fat that are sold in the nearby supermarket.
2. List five other foods that are high in fats. For one of the foods listed, provide a recipe for a snack that can be made for the home using the suggested food item.

Cake-making

Cakes are delicious, sweet items that can be served as a snack or dessert after a meal. They are an important item for celebrations such as holidays, weddings, anniversaries or other family occasions.

MAIN INGREDIENTS

The main ingredients used in making cakes are:
- flour: all-purpose, cake or self-raising flour is suitable
- fat: butter, margarine or oil may be used, depending on the method of cake-making
- sugar: granulated, fine brown sugar or caster sugar may be used, depending on the recipe
- eggs: may be whole eggs, yolks only or yolks and whites separately; they add lightness
- raising agent: may be air, water vapour, baking powder or baking soda, depending on the specific recipe.

The ingredients that go into a basic cake are shown in Figure 6.34. Other ingredients for variety and flavouring may be used. Water, milk or fruit juice is used if liquid is needed.

> **Did you know?**
> Once you learn the basic proportions and methods of cake-making, you can make a variety of different kinds of cakes.

Figure 6.34 The ingredients that go into a basic cake

METHODS OF CAKE-MAKING

Different types of cakes are made using different methods. There are five cake-making methods.

Rubbing-in method. The fat is rubbed into the flour until the mixture looks like fine breadcrumbs. Coconut cupcakes and rock buns are made using this method.

Creaming method. The fat and sugar are beaten together until the mixture is smooth, creamy and fluffy. Layer cakes or sandwich cakes are made using this method. It is also the popular method for pound cakes, fruit cakes for weddings and birthdays or plain cakes without fruit.

Melted fat method. The fat is melted and added to the flour mixture. In some cases, oil is used instead of melted fat. Muffins and gingerbread are made using this method.

Whisking method. The eggs or egg whites and sugar are whisked together until light and frothy. This method is used for Swiss/jelly roll and true sponge cakes. They contain no fat.

One-stage or all-in-one method. All the ingredients are put into a bowl, mixed together and stirred well. Liquid is added to bind the dry ingredients and give the batter the desired consistency. Best results are obtained when an electric mixer is used. Buns and coconut cake are made using this method.

Different methods of cake-making require different proportions of fat and sugar to flour (where fat is required). The consistency of the mixture is also different for each method. Different baking temperatures are utilised for different cakes and different types of cakes, depending on how rich the mixture is.

Rubbing-in method

Ingredients: Flour, margarine or butter, sugar, eggs, baking powder, milk, salt, flavourings

Proportions: Half or less fat and sugar to flour

Method

1. Sift flour, salt, baking powder and any other dry ingredients, for example, spices.
2. Rub the fat into the flour until the mixture looks like breadcrumbs.
3. Add sugar and fruit, etc. Stir well.
4. Beat eggs and add to any other liquid to be used, for example, milk.
5. Add liquids to dry ingredients and mix to a sticky dough.
6. Drop spoonfuls onto a greased cookie sheet or put into greased muffin tins.

Consistency: Stiff for buns; soft and dropping for cakes.

Oven temperature

- Buns, 180 °C/350 °F/Gas mark 4
- Cakes, 180–190 °C/350–375 °F/Gas mark 4–5

Recipe 12

Rock Buns. Makes 12

Ingredients

225 g (8 oz) flour
2 ml ($\frac{1}{2}$ tsp) salt
10 ml (2 tsp) baking powder
1 ml ($\frac{1}{4}$ tsp) mixed spice
100 g (4 oz) margarine
100 g (4 oz) granulated sugar
75 g (3 oz) currants
1 egg
125 ml (4 fl oz) milk
2 ml ($\frac{1}{2}$ tsp) vanilla essence

Figure 6.35 Rock buns

Method

- Sift flour, salt, baking powder and spice together in a bowl.
- Rub in the margarine until the mixture resembles fine breadcrumbs.
- Add the sugar and currants, then stir well.
- Beat the egg and add the milk and vanilla essence.
- Make a well in the centre of the flour mixture and add egg-milk liquid.
- Mix well to form a soft dough. Divide dough into 12 pieces and shape each to form a 'rocky' cone.
- Place on greased baking sheet and bake at 190 °C (375 °F), Gas mark 5, for 15–20 minutes. Remove buns from the oven, lift from the baking sheet using a spatula and put on a wire rack to cool.

Prepare coconut cake using the rubbing-in method. Use Recipe 13, as follows.

Recipe 13

Coconut cake. Makes 8-10 slices

Ingredients

225 g (8 oz) flour
2 ml (½ tsp) salt
10 ml (2 tsp) baking powder
75 g (3 oz) margarine
75 g (3 oz) sugar
50 g (2 oz) grated coconut
2 ml (½ tsp) grated lime peel
1 egg
125 ml (4 fl oz) milk
5 ml (1 tsp) vanilla essence

Figure 6.36 Coconut cake

Method

- Sift the dry ingredients into a bowl and rub in the margarine until the mixture resembles fine breadcrumbs.
- Add sugar, coconut and grated lime peel.
- Beat the egg and add most of the milk to it.
- Add the vanilla essence. Make a well in the centre of the flour mixture and add the liquid, then mix well to a stiff consistency, adding more milk if necessary.
- Put mixture into a greased 15 cm (6 in) cake tin and bake at 180 °C (350 °F), Gas mark 4, for 70–90 minutes, until a skewer inserted comes out clean.
- Remove cake from tin and cool on a wire rack.
- Decorate as desired and serve.

Creaming method

Ingredients: Flour, fat, sugar, eggs, baking powder, flavourings

Proportions: Half or more than half fat and sugar to flour.

Method

1. Prepare the cake tins by greasing and lining them or greasing and flouring them.
2. Preheat oven to desired temperature.
3. Sift dry ingredients together and set aside.
4. Have fat at room temperature and beat with a wooden spoon or cake mixer in a deep mixing bowl.
5. Add sugar to the fat and beat.
6. Beat eggs and essence together. Add eggs a little at a time to the creamed mixture. All the sugar crystals must be dissolved.
7. Fold in the dry ingredients, alternately with any liquid used. Blend well after each addition.
8. Pour mixture into prepared cake tins and bake until done.

Consistency: Very soft, dropping.

Oven temperature:

Rich cakes 150 °C/300–325 °F/Gas mark 3

Economical cakes, buns, 180 °C/350 °F/Gas mark 4.

Swiss/jelly rolls 180–190 °C/350–375 °F/Gas mark 4–5.

Test for cooking: Cakes should be evenly browned and shrunk a little away from the sides of the tin. When pierced with a skewer or coconut leaf mid-rib (pointer), it should come out clean.

Recipe 14

Spicy pound cake

Ingredients

250 g (8 oz/1 cup) margarine

250 g (8 oz/1 cup) granulated sugar

250 g (8 oz/ 2 cups) cake flour

5 ml (1 tsp) baking powder

5 ml (1 tsp) mixed spice

4 eggs

5 ml (1 tsp) vanilla essence

50 ml ($\frac{1}{5}$ cup) milk

Optional: $\frac{1}{4}$ cup dried raisins and cherries

Figure 6.37 Spicy pound cake

Method

- Preheat the oven to 350 °F/Gas mark 4/180 °C.
- Grease a 9-inch round or square cake tin. (Use a Bundt tin if you have one.)
- Sift flour, baking powder and mixed spice together and set aside.
- Cream the margarine and sugar together in a deep bowl until pale and fluffy, using a wooden spoon or a cake mixer.
- Beat the eggs and the essence together and gradually add to the creamed mixture.
- Gently fold in half of the flour mixture to the creamed mixture.
- Add the milk, blending it gently, then add the remaining flour, again folding it in gently.
- Pour into the prepared cake tin.
- Bake in the preheated oven until done; a skewer inserted should come out clean.

Melted fat method

Ingredients: Flour, fat, sugar, syrup, eggs, salt, liquid, raising agent, flavourings

Proportions: One-third fat and sugar to flour

Method

1. Sift dry ingredients together.
2. Gently melt fat, add sugar and syrup or molasses.
3. Add melted mixture to dry ingredients and stir with a metal spoon.
4. Add beaten egg and other liquid ingredients.
5. Pour into greased muffin tins or prepared baking pans.

Consistency: Pouring batter; lumpy for muffins.

Oven temperature: 180 °C/350 °F/Gas mark 5

Test for cooking: Firm to the touch. No bubbling sound. Cakes should shrink slightly from sides of the pan.

Recipe 15

Cheesy cornmeal muffins. Makes 12

Ingredients

100 g (4 oz or 1 cup) all-purpose flour

100 g (4 oz or 1 cup) cornmeal

5 ml (1 tsp) parsley flakes

1 cup finely grated cheddar cheese

80 g ($2\frac{1}{2}$ oz or 5 tbsp) margarine

1 egg, beaten

50 ml ($\frac{1}{4}$ cup) milk

5 ml (1 tsp) mustard

Figure 6.38 Cheesy cornmeal muffins

Method

- Preheat the oven to 180 °C/350 °F/Gas mark 5. Grease a 12-hole muffin pan and set aside.
- Measure and sift the dry ingredients in a bowl. Add the parsley flakes and grated cheese and stir.
- Melt the margarine and combine with the beaten egg, milk and mustard.
- Add the melted margarine mixture to the dry ingredients and stir with a metal spoon until all the ingredients are wet.
- Use a quarter cup measure and pour the mixture into each muffin tin.
- Place in the preheated oven and bake for 25–30 minutes are until done.
- Serve as a breakfast dish or snack.

Whisking method

Ingredients: Flour, sugar, eggs, flavouring, pinch of salt

Proportions: 1 egg to each 25 g (1 oz) caster sugar and 1 oz flour

Method

1. Preheat oven and prepare pan by greasing and lining it with baking paper.
2. Sift flour and set aside.
3. Whisk eggs and sugar until soft peaks are formed.
4. Fold in sifted flour.
5. Add any flavouring or liquid that is to be used.
6. Pour into prepared pan.
7. Bake until done.

Consistency: Thick, creamy and pouring consistency.

Oven temperature: 200 °C/400 °F/Gas mark 6

Test for cooking: Cake will have a light brown, even colour. Sides should shrink slightly from the sides of the pan and cake will spring back to the touch.

Recipe 16

Citrus sponge squares. Serves 8–10

Ingredients

75 g (3 oz) flour

3 fresh eggs, separated

75 g (3 oz) sugar

5 ml (1 tsp) vanilla essence

15 ml (1 tbsp) melted butter

15 ml (1 tbsp) orange juice

5 ml (1 tsp) grated lemon zest

Figure 6.39 Citrus sponge squares

Method

- Preheat oven to 180 °C. Grease and line a six by nine-inch Swiss/jelly roll pan.
- Sift flour and set aside.
- Whisk the egg yolks and sugar until pale yellow and fluffy.
- Beat the egg whites in a separate bowl using a clean whisk until soft peaks form.
- Fold the sifted flour into the egg yolks and sugar mixture.
- Then carefully, fold the beaten egg whites into the flour, egg and sugar mixture.
- Gently stir in the essence, melted butter, orange juice and lemon zest.
- Pour into the prepared pan.
- Bake at 180 °C for 15 minutes until done.
- Cool and decorate with butter cream.

Butter cream

Mix together 25 g (1 oz) butter, 100 g (1 cup) icing sugar, 2 ml ($\frac{1}{2}$ tsp) lemon juice and 5 ml (1 tsp) warm water. Beat until smooth and creamy. Add food colouring as desired and pipe or spread onto the cake to decorate.

Recipe 17

True sponge cake. Serves 8

Ingredients

2 eggs
1 ml ($\frac{1}{4}$ tsp) salt
50 g (2 oz) caster sugar
2 ml ($\frac{1}{2}$ tsp) zest from the rind of a lime
5 ml (1 tsp) lime juice
50 g (2 oz) flour

Method

- Line a 17.5 cm (7 in) cake tin with greaseproof paper.
- Preheat oven to 180 °C/350 °F/Gas mark 4.
- Separate eggs, then beat whites with salt in a bowl using a whisk or rotary beater. Beat well until soft peaks are formed.
- Gradually add sugar, beating well after each addition to keep a stiff consistency.
- Add the yolks, one at a time, beating well after each addition.
- Fold in lime zest and juice.
- Sift flour into a bowl and fold in about one-third of the flour to the whisked mixture. Continue folding in the flour gradually.
- Pour the mixture into the prepared tin and bake in the preheated oven for 20 minutes or until a skewer inserted into the centre comes out clean.
- Remove cake from tin and allow to cool on a wire rack.

Figure 6.40 True sponge cake

General guidelines for cake-making

For successful results in cake-making, observe the following guidelines:

- Read the recipe carefully before starting.
- Collect all the utensils and ingredients you need before starting.
- Baking tins should be of the correct size and suitably prepared.
- Weigh and measure ingredients accurately. Never add a little extra for good measure.
- The oven should be at the correct temperature before the cake is put in.
- Make sure that the oven shelves are level and in the correct position.
- Record the time at which you put the cake into the oven and time the baking period.
- Do not open the oven door before the cake has set.

Qualities of a good cake

A well-made cake should have the following qualities:

- **shape** – well risen, even top; not peaked, sunken or cracked
- **colour** – correct colour, depending on ingredients used
- **flavour** – distinctive flavour, depending on ingredients used
- **texture** – fine, even texture, springy to the touch.

> **Consider this**
>
> Consistency refers to how the mixture feels after being mixed and texture refers to the appearance after being baked.

What goes wrong and why

Often, cakes are not successful. It helps to know what goes wrong and why (Figure 6.41). Here are some of the common faults in cake-making and their probable causes.

Table 6.4 Common faults and causes in cake-making

FAULT	CAUSE
Close, heavy texture	• Oven was not hot enough • Not enough raising agent was used • Too much liquid was used • Cake not baked long enough • Beating mixture after adding dry ingredients
Dry texture	• Not enough liquid was used • Cake baked for too long • Too much raising agent used
Sunken in the middle	• Too much raising agent used • Oven was too hot • Cake not baked long enough • Cake exposed to cool air before setting • Too much liquid used
Cracked cake or cake with peaked top	• Baking tin used was too small • Too much raising agent • Oven was too hot • Cake placed too high in the oven
Uneven rising	• Oven shelf was uneven • Oven not heated to the correct temperature before the cake was put in • Cake placed too near source of heat
Large holes in cake	• Raising agent not mixed in properly • Beating while adding dry ingredients
Fruit sunk to the bottom of cake	• Fruit wet when added to mixture • Mixture too thin • Oven not hot enough
Buns spread out on tin	• Oven not hot enough • Too much liquid used • Too much fat used

Figure 6.41 It helps to know what has gone wrong when cake-making is not successful.

Table setting

In Book 1, you read about some of the general rules to observe when setting the table for a meal and some specific rules when setting a cover. In this chapter, you will learn about the linens, napkins, dinnerware, flatware and glassware for table setting and how they should be placed for table service.

Figure 6.42 Table setting for special occasions should be simple but attractive.

TABLE LINEN

The term 'table linen' applies to any table covering, whether the fabric is cotton, linen, rayon, polyester, plastic or lace. Real linen fabric remains the finest material for table coverings, but plastic tablecloths are easily available today at very affordable prices.

Table linen should provide a background for the dishes, cutlery and food. It must never be so brightly coloured or highly decorated as to distract attention from the food. The type of table linen used must also be in harmony with the dishes. This includes napkins and table mats.

TABLE NAPRONS

Napron comes from the word apron. It is a covering for the tablecloth that is attractive, colourful and can act as a silence cloth. The silence cloth is used underneath the tablecloth and is made of flannel or felt. Naprons are often made of cotton, damask, brocade. It may also be called an overlay tablecloth and usually fits in with the overall décor of the room and the colour scheme for special occasions.

Nicely appliquéd or embroidered table runners are sometimes used for decorating the table.

> **Consider this**
>
> Take a look at the colour wheel you would have explored in Visual Arts. What are some neutral colours that you can use for a tablecloth?

TABLE NAPKINS

Napkins are square with dimensions of between 16 inches (40 cm) square to 21 inches (53 cm) square. The more formal the occasion, the larger the napkin. Napkins are used to keep your fingers and lips clean while eating and to protect your clothing from spilled food. Like tablecloths, they can be made from a variety of fabric and may come in matching colours with table coverings. They are also available in different sizes, dinner napkins being larger than regular breakfast and lunch napkins. Paper napkins are a convenience and are quite popular for everyday family meals, snacks, parties, etc., because they can be discarded after a meal.

TABLE MATS

A variety of table mats (also called placemats) are available on the market today. They may be made of fabric, plastic, local straws or crochet designs, and are suitable for place settings. They help to protect the table covering and outline the space allocated for each person to be served at the table.

Specially designed, padded table mats are also available for placing hot dishes on the meal table. These should not be used over plastic table coverings as the heat from the hot dish is likely to penetrate the padded mat and damage the table covering.

If table mats are used, allow 40–50 cm (16–20 in) space at the table for each person. Table mats are usually rectangular, but may also be round, oval or have other shapes.

DISHES/DINNERWARE

Dinnerware is available in a variety of materials and at a range of prices to suit individual tastes and preferences. Fine china, porcelain and pottery are quite popular, but costly. Plasticware is also used a lot because it is relatively inexpensive and durable (lasts a long time).

Convenience and practicality are important. Here are some guidelines:

- A plain pattern, for example, white, cream or yellow with little or no decoration. Pretty patterns on plates detract from the colour of the food placed on the plate.
- A pattern that will continue to be in stock indefinitely so that replacements for damaged dishes can be found. Such stock is called 'open stock'.
- Fireproof glass and pottery serving dishes that are intended for use at table. They can be brought directly from oven to table and placed on suitable heatproof mats or metal stands to protect the table and table covering.

Figure 6.43 Plain pattern dinnerware

FLATWARE

All knives, forks, spoons and serving utensils used at the table for a meal are called **flatware** (Figure 6.44). They can be made of silver and are often called **silverware**. These are very expensive. Most flatware is made from stainless steel.

The type of flatware a family uses is determined by the amount of money they can afford to spend on buying it, the type of meals served and the type of dishes used. As long as it is clean and properly placed, flatware adds to the attractiveness of the table.

Plastic flatware is suitable for outdoor meals, picnics and other informal occasions.

When buying flatware, a desirable quantity is a set of twelve. However, the minimum number of pieces to start with is a set of six. This includes:

- dinner knives
- dinner forks
- teaspoons.

Other pieces that may be added over time include:

- dessert spoons
- soup spoons
- butter spreaders
- salad forks
- fish knives and forks
- steak knives and forks
- serving spoons.

Sets of four knives, forks, teaspoons and dessert spoons are popularly available on the market, many with attractive coloured handles made of plastic. These may be suitable for small families or families who are starting out.

Figure 6.44 Types of flatware

Placement of flatware

Some rules on how to lay a setting were given in Book 1, Chapter 6. Here are some additional rules:

- Place knife, fork and soup spoon 2.5 cm (1 in) from the edge of the table.
- If more than one course is being served, arrange flatware pieces so that what is to be used first is placed furthest from the plate.
- Place the fork to the right if it is the only flatware to be used during the meal. If a spoon is also used, place the fork to the left and the spoon to the right of the plate.
- Place the butter spreader or butter knife across the top of the bread-and-butter plate. It may also be placed on the rim of the bread-and-butter plate, parallel to the other flatware.

GLASSWARE

The drinking glasses, goblets, tumblers and glass serving dishes that are used at the table for a meal are referred to as **glassware**. They come in various sizes, shapes and colours for different purposes. Fine glassware is called **crystal** and is very expensive.

Clear, colourless glass is fine for ordinary use. The less etching or pattern on the glass, the easier it is to clean. Special glasses are designed for serving water, fruit drinks, milk, wine, champagne, liqueur and other alcoholic drinks served as appetisers (see Appendix 5, page 232). Plastic 'glasses' are suitable for outdoor activities.

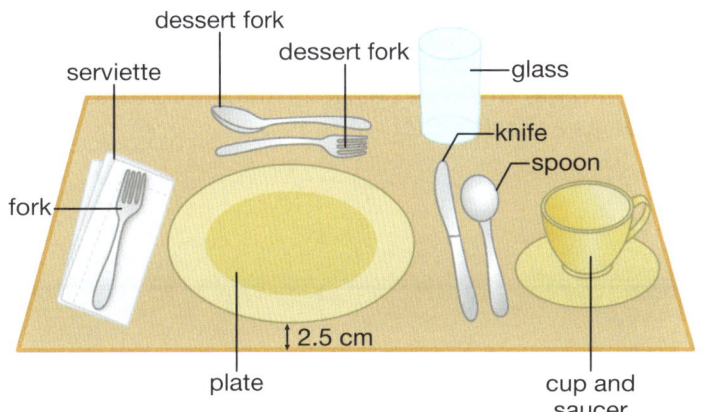

Figure 6.45 Placement of dinnerware, flatware and glassware for a simple lunch cover

Placement of glassware

Look at Figure 6.45. Place the water glass at the tip of the dinner knife.

Place the milk or juice glass slightly to the right of the water glass.

ACTIVITIES

Prepare a place setting for one person for a **two-course meal**, to demonstrate your skills in the placement of dinnerware, flatware and glassware.

Include a napkin and table mat in the place setting.

Ask a classmate to check your effort by rating it according to the rules outlined in this chapter.

Career corner

On the way to becoming a professional chef

My name is Rose. I work in a children's home as a cook. I really enjoy my work because the children in the home love my cooking. With my training in food and nutrition, I prepare nutritious meals and snacks for the children and staff. Aside from meal preparation, I use my training from culinary school everyday to properly manage the purchasing and storing of the food.

When my work contract ends in a few months, I plan to work as a sous chef in a restaurant. With my Bachelor of Science in Culinary Arts, at the end of three years, I'll be a certified sous chef. I'll probably travel and cook in different restaurants around the world as I earn certifications as an executive chef and then as a master chef.

Figure 6.46 A professional chef

Design project

Your school is planning to host a health fair in observance of World Home Economics Day. Your class has been requested to focus on preparing and serving a variety of dishes to sell.

1. Outline all the aspects that must be considered to produce the food items safely.
2. Generate ideas about possible items that can be offered for people to buy.
3. Examine the pros and cons of each and reach consensus regarding the dishes that will be sold.
4. Prepare a budget and seek approval for the activity.
5. Write a plan of how you will execute your event. Explain who else will be involved and how they can each help.
6. Plan and execute a trial run by preparing and selling the items that were selected.
7. Conduct a survey to evaluate the trial run sale.
8. Complete your report and present it to your teacher and peers.

Subject link

Your insights from English Language A, Visual Arts, Sociology and Agricultural Science will be extremely useful as you complete the project in this chapter.

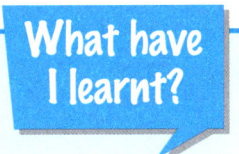
What have I learnt?

Multiple choice questions

Instruction: Answer the questions by circling the letter that corresponds with your response.

1. Which of the following does not promote safe handling of food?
   A Hazards that can occur along the food production process are identified.
   B Documentation of standards and protocols are not completed.
   C The food production process is monitored and evaluated.
   D Relevant signage is displayed to promote good practices.

2. Which of the following is not an advantage of planning your shopping list?
   A It helps you to store food properly.
   B It helps to save time.
   C It helps you with budgeting.
   D It helps with menu planning.

3. Which group of foods should be refrigerated immediately after opening?
   A Soya sauce, tomato sauce/ketchup, mustard
   B Dehydrated soup mixes, seasoning salts
   C Canned beans, canned sweetcorn
   D Sliced bread, muffins

4. LIFO and FIFO is a system used for
   A Computing electronics
   B Employment, where workers move from one location of employment to another
   C Inventory management
   D Queuing

For questions 5 to 12, write T next to the statement that is True and F next to the statement that is false.

5. Steaming is a dry method of cooking.
6. Frying is suitable for tough cuts of meat.
7. Deep-fat frying uses a large quantity of fat.
8. Coating foods helps to prevent them from breaking up in the pan.
9. Fish for cooking can either be in the category of white fish, oily fish or shellfish.
10. Fruit and vegetable salads are a good source of protein and fat.
11. The rubbing-in method of cake-making is often used to make buns and sweet breads.
12. Flatware refers to tumblers, drinking glasses and glass serving dishes.

Short answer questions

1. Explain five components of a recipe.
2. Name two different methods of frying.
3. Outline four rules to follow when frying, especially for the cooks in a children's home.
4. The cook in the children's home has the following vegetables to prepare as an accompaniment to the main meal after being told that the meal is not colourful or nutritious enough (green beans, bell peppers, cabbage). Would you select steaming or frying? State two reasons for this choice.

Table setting

5 Select the most appropriate method of steaming for each food in the table below by using matching arrows.

FOOD
Steamed custard
Steamed dumplings
Fish fillets
Okra and spinach

METHOD OF STEAMING
Directly on top of boiling food
Between two plates
Double boiler
Pudding mould in a pot of boiling water

6 What is one important function of fat used in each of the following food items?
   a Shortcrust pastry
   b Pan-fried fish
   c Fruit cake
   d Creamed potatoes

Fill in the blanks in each sentence.

7 The _____ method of cake-making is most times used to make rock buns.

8 Four of the major ingredients used in cakes made by the creaming method are butter, _____, _____ and flour.

9 The proportions of fat and sugar to flour in the melted fat method is _____ to one.

10 The correct consistency for mixtures made by the whisking method is creamy, thick and _____

11 Aphia made a raisin cake and the raisins all sank to the bottom of the cake. Explain two reasons why that may have happened.

12 Name two types of linen used in table settings.

13 Your cousin is getting married and you are assisting her with shopping for tableware.
Write a shopping list for 10 items, which includes flatware, glassware and dinnerware.

Section 4 Clothing and textiles

Chapter 7: Clothing and textiles

Clothing and textiles play a valuable role in shaping a person's image and environment. It is one of the areas that allows people to be creative and innovative, whether they are working with new materials or recycled material. It is also a major global industry, which provides employment opportunities.

As you work through this section, you will use the design process to create a product for household use using available fabric.

Chapter 7 Clothing and textiles

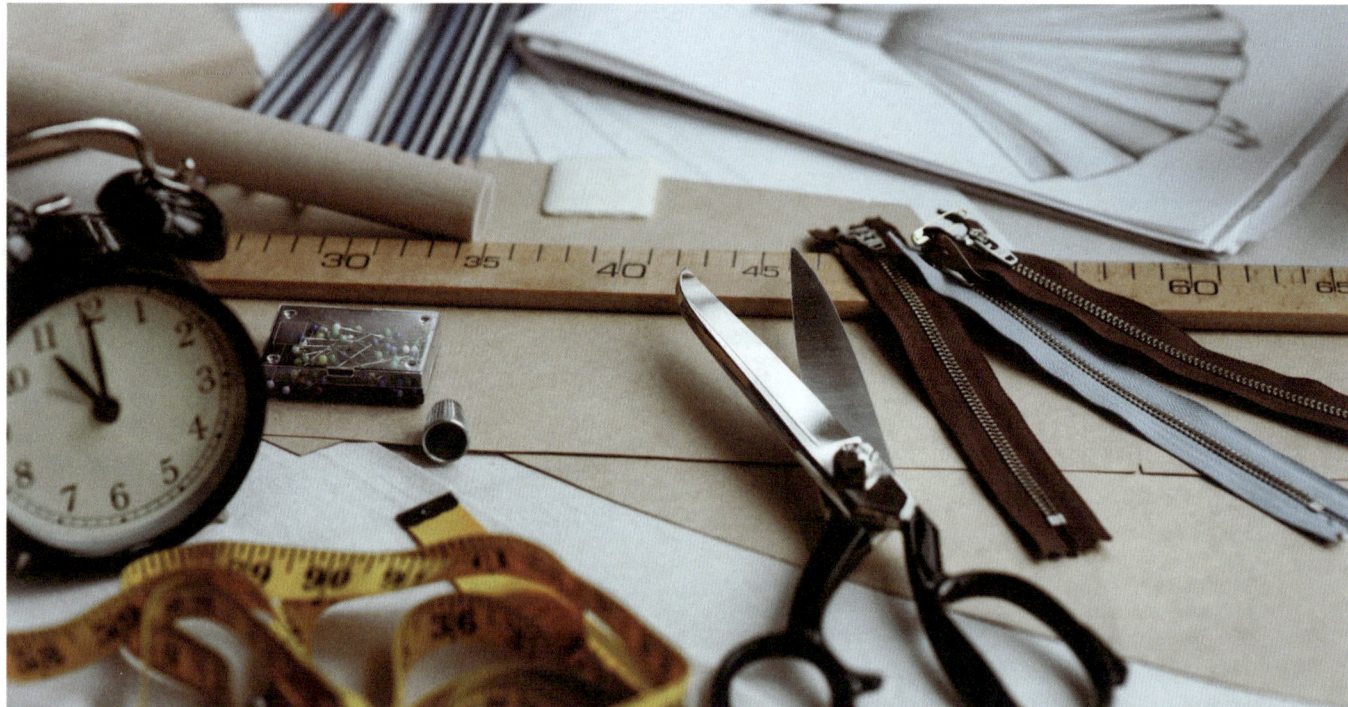

Figure 7.1 Some of the tools and equipment needed for sewing projects

The first thing anyone you meet notices is what you are wearing, as clothing is entirely a reflection of who you are. In this chapter, you will be introduced to clothing decisions and how it affects personal appearance. You will explore reasons for wearing clothes, how to take body measurements and determine figure types, evaluate and plan a wardrobe, shop for clothes, and practise basic clothing care.

- Observe three persons that you have met and describe what they were wearing.
- Describe your impression of them based on what they were wearing.

In this chapter, you will:

* explore the main reasons for wearing clothes
* determine how messages are communicated through apparel (clothes) and overall personal appearance
* analyse and plan a wardrobe for an individual or group
* examine the factors to consider when purchasing clothing
* evaluate a project against an established project rubric
* explore the relationship between body measurement and figure types and sketch the main figure types
* gain more knowledge of the elements and principles of design, and pattern and colour in design.

Apparel decision and personal appearance

Figure 7.2 Comfortable clothing makes a good impression.

Consider this

People assess you the moment they see you. What you look like is the first impression people get about you. How you are dressed, your general appearance, your body language, your demeanor and your mannerisms influence a person's opinion about you. While first impressions are often defined by several factors, it is the person's choice of clothes and manner of styling that set the tone. Therefore, the right clothes can make the difference, dress neat, smart, confident and comfortable if you want to make an excellent first impression.

Clothing decisions

If you think about your daily life, you will realise that you have different kinds of clothes that you wear for different purposes. For example, you wear your school uniform for school and school events, and you wear them every day, as long as you are going to school. When you get home after school, you change clothes and put on the clothes you wear at home. These are different from the clothes you wear to school.

If you play games and sports, you probably have different clothes for those activities, too. When you get ready to sleep at night, you change from play clothes to night clothes for sleeping. If you go to religious worship, you probably have special clothes to wear. If you go to the beach or for a swim in a pool, you will also need to wear special clothes. When people are invited to special functions, such as weddings and other formal occasions, they usually wear special outfits, such as suits and long dresses.

As you take the time to observe the people you meet every day, you will notice that, in your community and country, people wear a lot of different kinds of clothes. But have you ever wondered why people wear clothes?

Figure 7.3 Deciding on what to wear is not always that easy.

REASONS FOR WEARING CLOTHES

Clothing is one of our basic needs. People all over the world, and in various cultures, wear clothes for various reasons. These may include the following.

Protection

The most important reason for wearing clothes is to protect the body from direct exposure to the natural elements (sunshine, heat, cold, wind) which may otherwise harm the body or make you sick. It absorbs perspiration, prevents sudden chills, and acts as a buffer between your body and accidental burns, scratches and rough surfaces. The right garments can insulate your body against extremely hot or extremely cold temperatures.

Figure 7.4 Clothes are worn for protection.

Safety

Some jobs are very hazardous and require wearing special clothing that offers safety while working. This clothing is termed 'safety' to identify it from regular clothing. Firemen wear asbestos clothing in hazardous situations. Police officers wear bulletproof vests. Road workers wear fluorescent orange vests so that drivers can see them easily and prevent accidents.

Figure 7.5 Safety clothing worn while working

Self-expression

In many cultures, people use clothing to express themselves. For this reason, many teenagers like to choose their own style of clothing. As they develop into adulthood, their choice of clothing will still be a way of expressing themselves and their personality. You may find that while your parents are excited about a pair of jeans that they have purchased for you, you do not share in their excitement because the garment is not as trendy and stylish as you would like. You would prefer to choose clothes that you think will suit you and depict the image that you want people to have of you.

Figure 7.6 Teenagers like to choose their own style of clothing.

Decoration

Clothing improves the physical appearance of people. It is a way of adorning the human body and enhancing physical attraction. When you choose clothing for a special occasion, such as a wedding ceremony, you will probably try to be as glamorous as possible by selecting garments that are very stylish, eye-catching, attractive and will highlight your appearance when worn. In many cases, clothing attracts the attention of friends, loved ones and members of the opposite sex.

Ceremonies

Ceremonial dress is part of the cultural heritage of people. In the Caribbean, people delight in dressing appropriately for special occasions and functions. Babies wear special outfits for christenings. Many students wear special formal clothes for their graduation ceremonies. People wear elaborate and expensive outfits to weddings that are normally quite different from the types of attire worn at other religious ceremonies. In some religions, priests and clergy wear special clothes when conducting religious ceremonies. It is becoming quite common to see people attired in traditional ceremonial wear for national ceremonies.

Figure 7.7 A graduate with her relatives

Status

Clothing may be worn to indicate the rank or status one holds in society. For example, lawyers and magistrates wear robes while in court; police officers indicate their rank by the special stripes and colours of the uniforms they wear; nursing staff in healthcare facilities also indicate their rank by the colour and special features of the uniforms they wear. In a business organisation, managers are usually dressed differently from the machine operators and clerical employees. In these ways, clothing is worn as a status symbol.

Figure 7.8 Clothing indicating rank or status

Group identity

If you take a look at the schools in your town or community, you will notice that the children who attend the different schools wear different uniforms. This makes it easy to identify the children from each school, even without knowing their names or where they live. People in some professions, such as nursing, the army, navy and police service, are easily identified by the uniforms they wear. Persons who are members of youth organisations, such as Boy Scouts, Girl Guides and the Red Cross, usually wear special uniforms that identify them as being part of the group. It is common in today's society for banks, insurance companies and other businesses to provide clothing for their employees. In these ways, people wear clothing to identify them as belonging to a specific group.

Figure 7.9 People wear uniforms according to their professions.

ACTIVITIES

1. Visit a busy shopping area in your community and observe the different types of clothing that people wear. Look around your community on a day when people go to church and other places of worship and observe the types of clothing they wear. Draw sketches to show some of the different types of clothing you saw people wearing.

2. Observe the types of clothing that people in your community wear for formal occasions, such as weddings, and the different national festivals. Ask your parents and any other two people in your community to explain why these clothes are worn on such occasions.

CLOTHING SELECTION

Did you know?
Your need for a wide range of clothing will increase gradually as you grow older and your daily activities expand beyond those of school. Teenage children are usually given the opportunity to select their own clothing, however, this requires careful decision-making and wardrobe planning.

Figure 7.10 Teenage children are given the opportunity to select their own clothing.

Factors to consider when selecting clothing

There are several factors to consider when selecting clothing. These include:
- personal likes and dislikes, about colour, fabric, design features, etc.
- personal comfort
- figure type
- the climate
- the available budget
- religious beliefs
- knowledge of styles and fabrics
- suitability for the occasion
- cultural background
- age of the wearer.

Figure 7.11 There are many factors to consider when selecting clothing.

Figure 7.12 Select clothing that is suitable for the occasion.

Clothing decisions 197

Guidelines for selecting clothing

Here are a few guidelines to follow when selecting clothing.
- Choose colours that are suitable for your personality, complexion and body size.
- Buy colours that will harmonise with many other colours, and will match with what you already have in your wardrobe.
- Choose clothing that fits comfortably. It should allow enough room for you to move about (sit, bend and stretch/reach) comfortably.
- Choose fabric and style features that are suited to the climate in which the clothing will be worn. In the Caribbean, cotton and linen fabrics are suitable for the hot weather. Synthetic fabrics will make you hotter.
- Choose styles and fabrics that are suited to the occasion for which the garment will be worn.
- Buy clothes you can afford.
- Purchase clothing that will be useful to you.

Figure 7.13 Buy clothes that will be useful to you.

INTERPRETING CLOTHING MESSAGES

> **Did you know?**
>
> Non-verbal communication can be just as powerful as verbal communication. Our clothing choices are constantly communicating and making a statement about how we want to be perceived each day. It is therefore important to ensure that your choice of clothing sends the correct message. So, take a look in the mirror, what are you wearing today? Is your outfit communicating what you want it to?

If you are told that there is a man walking down the corridor in your school in a white lab coat, what would you say his profession is? Probably a laboratory technician. You know that because clothing communicates. Your clothing style can communicate an occasion, your occupation, culture, mood, level of confidence, interests, age, authority, values, religion and sexual identity.

Consider how clothing style might send a negative message. A sloppy appearance sends the message, 'I don't care', whereas appropriate attire demonstrates the importance of the occasion. Shorts and a T-shirt might appear attractive but will not convey the right message at a public speaking event.

Figure 7.14 Clothing always sends a message.

DRESSING FOR THE OCCASION

One should try not be overdressed or underdressed for an occasion, however formal or casual it may be.

When dressing, particularly for special occasions, be sure to find out beforehand the type of dress that is required, whether formal, semi-formal or informal wear. Clothing for special occasions requires more consideration than clothing for work, school and sporting activities.

Clothing for special occasions

Here are some of the guidelines that could assist you in dressing suitably for a special occasion.

- For women, accessories such as hats, bags, shoes and gloves should be of the same colour. For men wearing a suit, shoes and belts should be of the same colour.
- Men should not wear caps and other hats while indoors.
- White shoes are not appropriate for evening wear.
- Tuxedos or black suits should be worn for formal occasions.
- Ties should be worn 2.5 cm (1 in) above the belt.
- Do not wear too much jewellery. Glittering jewellery should be avoided with daywear.
- Perfumes should be worn sparingly and worn in the evenings and at night. Eau de toilettes and colognes are suitable for daytime wear.
- Make-up should be well applied, and should not be overpowering.
- Nails should be clean and well shaped, and nail polish should not be chipped.
- Hairstyles should be appropriate for the occasion, and not be gaudy (over the top).
- Chewing gum is in poor taste and should be avoided.

Formal occasions

Formal occasions usually take place in the evenings and at night, but can be held during the day. Formal occasions include functions such as weddings, graduation ceremonies and balls, military ceremonies, and formal luncheon and dinner parties. It is customary to wear outfits such as suits, tuxedos, evening gowns and military uniforms for formal occasions. Clothing is dark in colour and accessories are usually rich and luxurious (Figure 7.15).

Figure 7.15 Dress for formal occasions

Semi-formal occasions

These are parties, dances and church functions. Unlike formal occasions, the dress lengths are shorter and men are not required to wear tuxedos. A simpler suit or a blazer can be worn instead of a more formal jacket. Clothes are not as fancy as for formal occasions, but neither are they casual (Figure 7.16).

Figure 7.16 Dress for semi-formal occasions

Informal occasions

These occasions include sports, picnics, shopping, or even working around the home (Figure 7.17). Informal clothes are designed for a more relaxed atmosphere and for freedom of movement. Such casual wear is not suited for work. Clothing for work should suit the type of job and the work environment. For example, while denim overalls would be suitable for maintenance workers, they are unsuitable for clerical workers in an office. Some jobs require uniforms and some businesses operate with a dress code or acceptable standard for employees' dress. It is good practice to obey the dress codes for work.

Figure 7.17 Dress for informal wear

WARDROBE PLANNING

Wardrobe planning is an ongoing process that involves selecting clothes that are basic in style but classic. This ensures that the clothes have longevity, as they are appropriate for the present and will still be stylish in the future. A carefully planned wardrobe should fit your lifestyle, be of good quality, be versatile and include articles for various occasions. A well-maintained wardrobe is evaluated and updated either seasonally or annually to ensure that it suits your changing needs. As a result, your wardrobe will include the clothes, shoes and accessories that work for your environment, lifestyle, personal preferences and needs.

A wardrobe should include both basic garments and wardrobe extenders. Basic garments are the essential pieces present in a wardrobe, which are worn regularly. Extenders are the items that are added to enhance or alter the basic garments or as needed by the occasion.

Figure 7.18 New avatar technology allows you to try on clothes to see how they will look on you. You can even see the different colours and textures of the clothing.

Importance of wardrobe planning

Wardrobe planning helps you to decide on the items you need versus those you want, to evaluate what you already have, and to identify the missing pieces in your wardrobe.

Key benefits of wardrobe planning:

- less time spent searching for, purchasing, or returning items
- easy to dress for any occasion because wardrobe items are easily coordinated into appropriate outfits
- saves money and avoids duplication or the inclusion of incompatible items, as you know what you want to buy when you go shopping
- fewer items but more options
- focus on quality garments, which will last longer and eventually save money
- promotes sustainability and avoids the pitfalls of fast fashion because you buy less and keep your clothes for longer.

Did you know?
A person can create 75 outfits from five basic suits and white, tan and powder blue shirts. What colours do you think the basic suits need to be to accomplish this? Do a quick search of the internet to confirm your answers.

Factors that influence wardrobe planning

Many elements determine the clothes that you select for your wardrobe.

Aesthetics
Fashion influence
Item quality and appearance

Economics
Occupation and income
Price
Ease of care

Factors that determine wardrobe

Psychological
Personal taste

Sociological/environmental
Age
Gender
Social environment
Climate
Lifestyle and activities
Health

Did you know?
A functional wardrobe is one that contains the right type of clothes for you to go about your day-to-day life.

Figure 7.19 Factors that determine your wardrobe

Clothing decisions 201

Planning your wardrobe – a 10-step programme

Figure 7.20 shows the 10 steps that can be used to plan a wardrobe that is functional, versatile and stylish for all occasions.

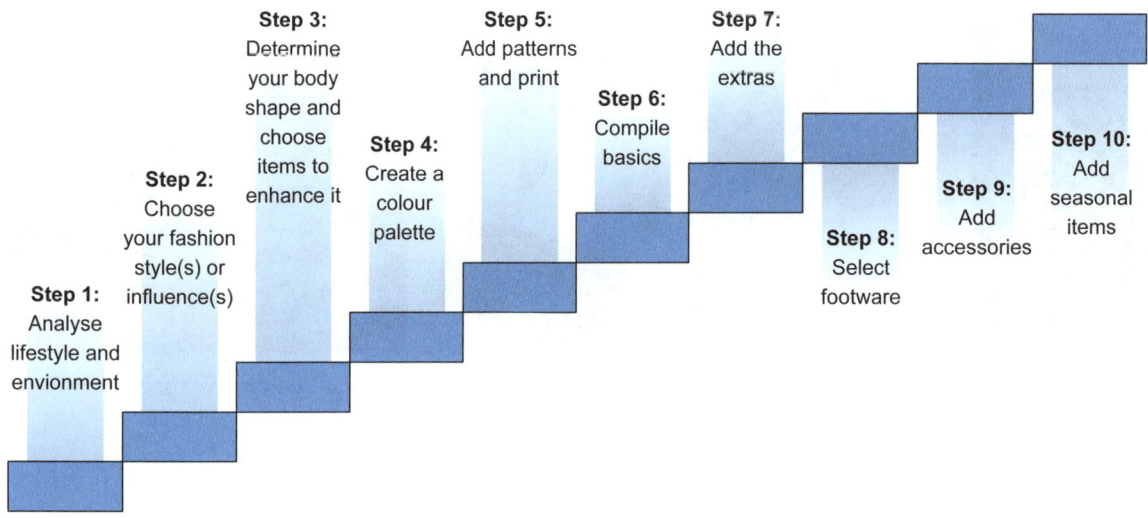

Figure 7.20 Steps to plan a wardrobe

ACTIVITIES

1. Use the internet to find more details about the step assigned to your group.
2. Imagine that you are a personal stylist and you create a basic questionnaire that you will use to ask new clients – both male and female – to ensure that you have the information necessary to plan a wardrobe.
3. Use role play with your classmates, where they pretend to be people from different professions and with different lifestyles to test whether the answers to the questions supply the information you need.

WARDROBE INVENTORY

This is a necessary maintenance practice and involves a periodic assessment of all the clothes, accessories and shoes that make up your wardrobe. This assessment reveals the items that need to be replaced or removed because they are worn out or unused. Once the inventory is complete, you can refresh your wardrobe with the confidence that new purchases do not include pieces that you already have.

Figure 7.21 gives some guidelines to follow for a wardrobe inventory.

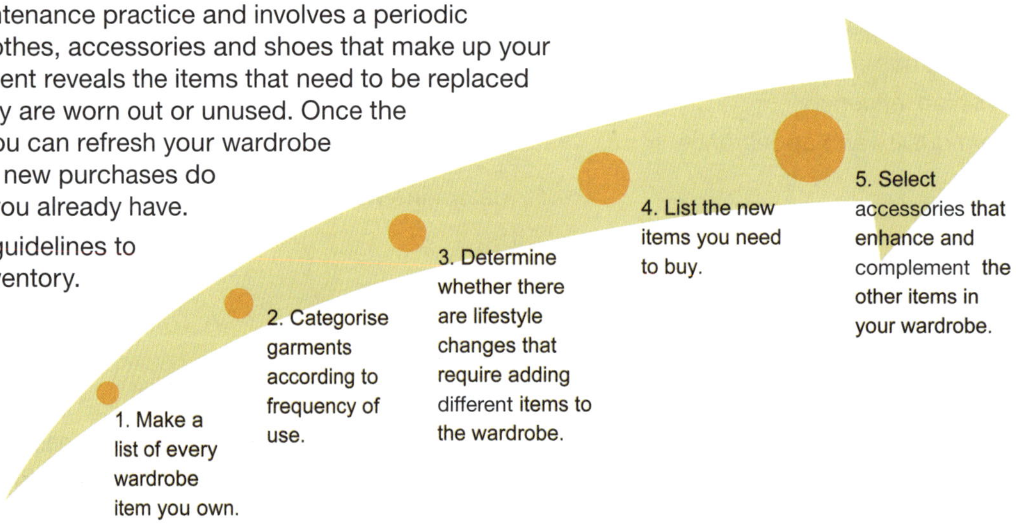

Figure 7.21 Guidelines for a wardrobe inventory

1. Make a list of every wardrobe item you own.
2. Categorise garments according to frequency of use.
3. Determine whether there are lifestyle changes that require adding different items to the wardrobe.
4. List the new items you need to buy.
5. Select accessories that enhance and complement the other items in your wardrobe.

Chapter 7 Clothing and textiles

> **ACTIVITIES**
>
> Use the internet to find a wardrobe decluttering flowchart that you can modify and use to maintain your family's wardrobes.

Did you know?
Accessories can be decorative or functional, as well as essential or optional. Can you think of examples that would fall into each category?

PURCHASING CLOTHES

Purchasing clothes is necessary whether you are planning or maintaining a wardrobe. There are several things to consider to ensure that your wardrobe is stylish, as well as suitable for your lifestyle and economic situation.

Choice of clothing

When choosing clothes, design, colour and quality of construction are some of the important factors to consider.

Design

It is natural for teenagers to want to wear fashionable clothing, but styles should not be chosen just because they are fashionable.

- Select styles to suit the figure type and personality of the wearer.
- Styles should flatter the figure and not detract from it. For example, a short, plump girl should avoid miniskirts even though they are quite fashionable. Likewise, a tall skinny boy would want to avoid wearing a pair of big baggy cargo pants.

Figure 7.22 Select the style that suits your figure

Colour

The choice of colour for clothing usually depends on what the wearer is comfortable with. There are also some other important considerations.

- Colour chosen should be suited to the personality and complexion of the wearer. Draping some fabric over the shoulders, close to the face can help to determine what colour is suitable.
- Sometimes colours are chosen according to the occasion to which the garment is to be worn. In the Caribbean, colours such as black and purple are associated with attending funerals.
- Colour may also be chosen according to the mood of the wearer. A person who is in a cheerful and happy mood may choose to wear bright colours rather than dull colours such as black or brown.

Figure 7.23 Colour enhances your personality.

Quality of construction

Some people may claim that the way a garment looks on the inside is not important as the side of the garment that is not seen. But a good finish on the wrong side is as important as the appearance on the right side. When choosing clothing, be sure to select items that are well finished, both on the wrong and right sides. Rough seams, sagging hems, torn fastenings and missing buttons all detract from the appearance of the clothing. They contribute to an untidy appearance on both the wrong and the right side and could be very embarrassing.

Figure 7.24 The quality of construction is important.

ACCESSORIES

Accessories are an important part of dressing (Figure 7.25). They should complement the clothing. When carefully chosen, they contribute to the total look. Belts, ties, handbags, socks, stockings, shoes, jewellery and even umbrellas are called accessories. The clever use of accessories can turn a casual outfit into one that is suitable for a special occasion.

After dressing, make it a habit to stand in front of the mirror and take a good look at yourself. Assess the overall effect of the accessories you have chosen. They should suit your personality. The colours should also suit the colour scheme of the outfit, so that there is evidence of harmony in colour.

Figure 7.25 Fashion accessories

CARE OF CLOTHING

It is necessary to care for clothing in order to prolong its life and to ensure that clothes are in good condition and ready for wearing. The clothing you choose can tell a lot about you and so can the condition of that clothing. When the clothing you wear is well maintained, this contributes to the total look. Clothing care includes laundering, pressing, repairing, storing and other tasks needed to keep clothes looking good.

Guidelines for caring for clothing

- Air clothes after taking them off and before placing them in the laundry basket.
- Clothing that has been worn should also be aired before storing for future use.
- Hang clothes on clean, rust-free hangers and not on nails, since nails may be rusty, which can damage clothing. Where clean, rust-free hangers are not available, you can use garment bags, as well as suitcases or chests. Lined boxes can also be used, but take care to store them in dry places.
- Large plastic bags and laundry bags can be made into storage bags by cutting a small hole in the bottom and inserting a hanger. They will protect clothing from dust.
- Repair torn sections, split seams and damaged hems; replace buttons and other faulty fastenings before laundering.
- Clean clothing often to keep it free from dirt, perspiration marks and body odours.
- Launder clothing according to the type of fabric and follow the manufacturer's instructions.
- Whatever the method of storage, laundered clothing must be put away immediately.
- Do not store clothes that are soiled. Remove stains immediately.
- Store clothing in clean, dry areas that are free from dust, cooking odours and moisture. The more popular choices for storage are wardrobes, closets, and drawers.
- Keep the storage area for your clothing well organised. Keep a special place for each type of clothing. This helps with the organisation of the storage space, especially if the space is shared with another family member.
- If the storage area is tidied regularly, it will save time and effort.
- Use closet sprays and mothballs to help keep your clothing fresh smelling.
- Press garments to remove creases, folds and wrinkles before wearing them.

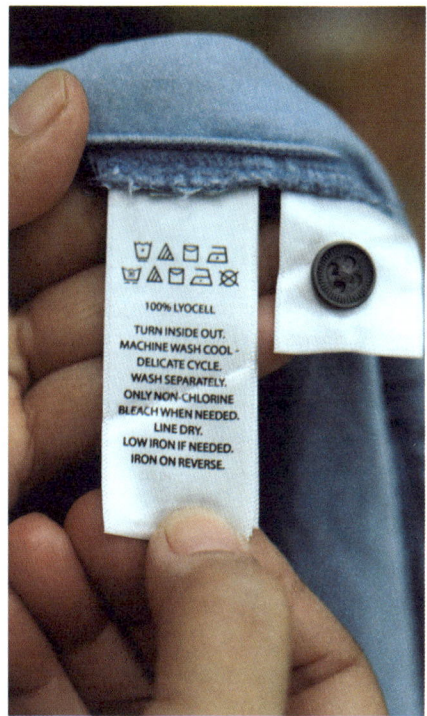

Figure 7.26 Proper care for clothing is indicated on the label.

Figure 7.27 Fold and store laundry correctly.

Figure 7.28 Protect clothes from dust during storage.

Figure 7.29 Store clothes in the correct storage space.

Figure 7.30 Launder clothes according to the manufacturer's instructions.

Clothing decisions

> **ACTIVITIES**
>
> Collect pictures or drawings and compile a folder of outfits that illustrate the total look for formal, semi-formal and casual occasions. Name the occasions for which the outfits are suitable.

READY-TO-WEAR CLOTHING

The industry for the production and marketing of ready-to-wear garments has expanded greatly over the years. Some people find it more convenient to purchase a ready-to-wear garment rather than making one themselves, or getting one made. This may be due to one or more of the following reasons:

- an emergency
- lack of knowledge and skills in garment construction
- lack of desire or time to make one's own clothing
- a wider range of clothes from which to choose
- the prestige of wearing ready-to-wear garments
- uniqueness in fabrics and trimmings used for making high-quality ready-to-wear garments
- the high cost of custom-made garments. Some readymade garments are even cheaper than custom-made ones.

There is a wide range of well-finished ready-to-wear clothing from which to choose, if you do not want to use a tailor or dressmaker for custom-made clothing.

Whether you choose custom-made or ready-to-wear clothing will depend entirely on your circumstances and your skills in clothing construction, fashion designing or tailoring. However, if you are able to produce well-constructed garments for yourself, you will not only save some money, but also gain great personal satisfaction from your efforts.

Figure 7.31 A variety of ready-to wear clothing

Guidelines for purchasing ready-to-wear

Take care when deciding to purchase ready-to-wear purchases. Be guided by the following tips.

- Do not buy when you are in a hurry. Take time to check construction details, fit, colour, suitability for the occasion, and suitability for your complexion.
- Check the quality of the construction, including the stitching. The least expensive garments are not necessarily well constructed. Less expensive garments tend to have seams that rip easily or may not hold their shape.
- Check seams, linings, pockets, trimmings and other details to make sure that they are properly constructed. Check for neat finishing on the wrong side of the garment.
- The length and style of garments should suit your figure.
- Check for any adjustments that may be needed to the garment. Sometimes, you may have to adjust or alter it to get a proper fit.
- Read labels before buying to find out if the garment can be washed or if only dry-cleaning is recommended. Remember that dry-cleaning costs are high.
- Be careful with items on sale. Remember that all sale items may not be of high quality.
- Choose styles and colours that will coordinate with the rest of your wardrobe.

ACTIVITY

Visit a store that sells ready-to-wear clothing and select three outfits that you would like to purchase. Examine them and list all the factors that make you think you have made wise choices in ready-to-wear clothing.

WHERE TO SHOP

Shopping is something that we all have to do and there are many places where you can shop for clothes such as malls, department shops, boutiques and specialty shops, factory outlets, online shops, catalogues and discount shops.

ACTIVITY

Your teacher will assign a shopping location to your group. Create a pros and cons list for that shopping experience.

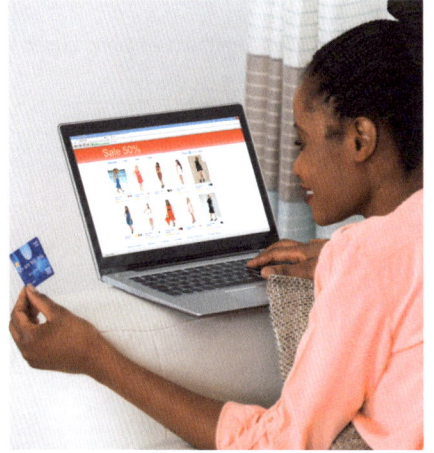

Figure 7.32 Online shopping is a whole new experience.

Seaming techniques

SEAMS AND SEAM FINISHES

A seam is made when two or more layers of fabrics are stitched together. There are different types of seams. Whichever seam is chosen, it must be strong and neat on both the right and wrong sides of the garment.

Your choice of seam will depend on the factors in Table 7.1.

Table 7.1 Choice of seams

THE TEXTURE OF THE FABRIC	THE TYPE OF GARMENT	THE SHAPE OF THE SEAM	THE POSITION OF THE SEAM
For example, for fine and loosely woven fabrics that fray badly, the seam should be enclosed to prevent unravelling of the fabric.	Clothes that are hard-wearing need seams that can withstand strain in wear and laundering, for example, a double-stitched seam.	It is difficult to sew corners and curved areas with certain types of seam, for example, a French seam. A plain seam might be more suitable.	Straight edges, like the side seam of shirts and blouses, are more suited to French seams than the curved armhole of the same garment.

General rules for working seams

- Threads used must be suitable for the material.
- The width of the seam depends on the texture of the material. The finer the material, the narrower the seam should be.
- All seams of the same type on a garment must be of similar widths.

TYPES OF SEAMS

Plain seam

This is a flat seam that is also known as a dressmaker's seam or machine-stitched seam. It can be used on almost any garment and fabric. The stitching is done by machining and is not visible on the right side of the garment. There are several stages in making a machine-stitched seam (Figure 7.33).

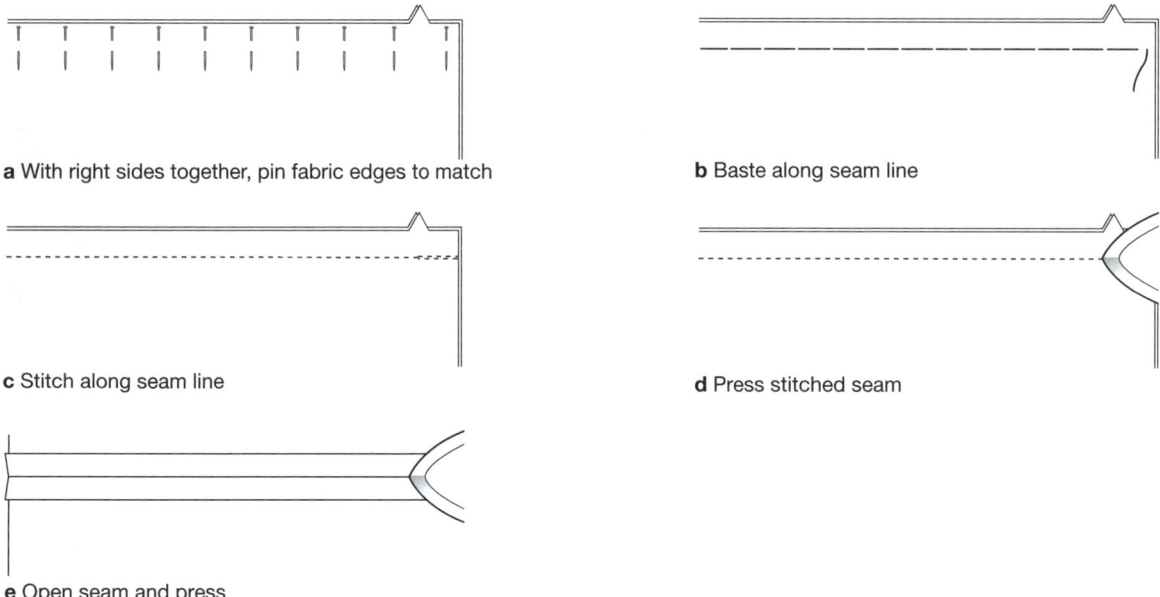

a With right sides together, pin fabric edges to match

b Baste along seam line

c Stitch along seam line

d Press stitched seam

e Open seam and press

Figure 7.33 A machine-stitched seam

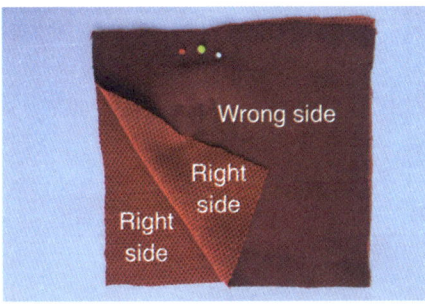

Figure 7.34 Machine-sewn seam

> **Did you know?**
> - The stitching line along the seam is called the seam line.
> - The seam allowance (SA) is the space between the fabric edge and the seam line.
> - Seams are the basic building block of a garment and form the structure of the garment and help to create the garment.
> - Seams can also be used as a decorative feature and should be carefully done for a beautifully finished garment.
> - The machine should be adjusted correctly to the fabric for stitch length, tension and pressure. Thread should be properly matched to fabric.

How to make a plain seam

1. With right sides together, pin the fabric with edges matching.
2. Baste or tack just inside the seam line, within the seam allowance.
3. Remove the pins, and machine stitch along the seam line.
4. Remove tacking and press the stitched seam.
5. Open the seam and press again.

French seam

This is a strong but bulky seam. The edges are enclosed so there is no need to neaten. It is particularly suitable for sheer and lightweight fabrics, on straight edges of blouses, slips and children's wear.

How to make a French seam

The seam is first stitched on the right side.

1. Put the two wrong sides together, pin and tack 1 cm (⅜ in) from the edge. Remove the pins.
2. Machine stitch close to the tacking thread. Press the seam together.
3. Trim the seam to 3 mm (⅛ in); remove the tacking and press open.
4. Fold to the wrong side on the stitching line. Tack and stitch on the fitting line.
5. Remove the tacking stitches, and press the seam towards the back (Figure 7.35).

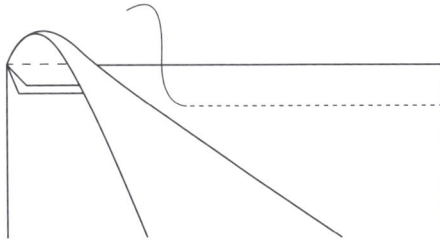
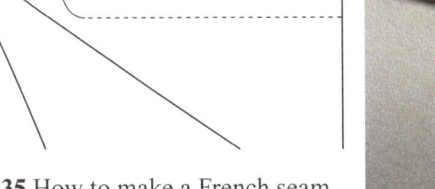

Figure 7.35 How to make a French seam

Double-stitched seam

This is a flat and strong seam used on light and medium weight fabrics. The raw edges are enclosed and it is comfortable worn close to the skin. It is suitable for underwear, pyjamas, shirts, jeans and overalls.

How to make a double-stitched seam

1 Work on the right side of the fabric. With wrong sides together, pin and tack close to the fitting line.
2 Remove the pins and machine stitch on the seam line.
3 Remove the tacking and press the seam open.
4 Trim the back or the left-hand side of the seam to 6 mm (¼ in). Fold the wider seam allowance in half and take it over to the narrower one. Pin and tack the seam to the garment.
5 Machine stitch close to the fold. Remove the tacking threads and press. This seam should have two rows of stitching on the right side (Figure 7.36).

> **Did you know?**
> French and double-stitched seams are 'enclosed seams' because the seam allowance is within the seam finish, making it invisible.

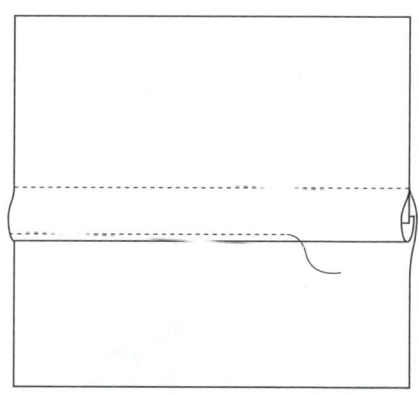

Figure 7.36 Double-stitched seam

Overlaid seam

This is a decorative seam with the stitching visible on the right side. Braids, frills and loops may be stitched between the layers of material to give a decorative effect. It is particularly useful on yokes, bands and difficult shapes (Figure 7.37).

How to make an overlaid seam

1 The smaller section is usually stitched over the larger one. Fold the seam allowance of the top section to the wrong side and tack.
2 Place the wrong side of the section with the folded edge to the right side of the under section to match the fitting line.
3 Pin and tack. Machine stitch close to the folded edge.
4 Trim and neaten the seams together.

Seam finishes

A seam must be finished neatly for several reasons.

1 It prevents raw edges from fraying.
2 It strengthens the seam.
3 It gives a neat, professional look to the garment.

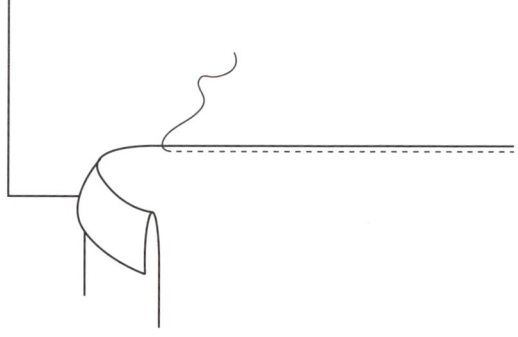

Figure 7.37 Overlaid seam

Types of seam finishes

A seam can be finished in one of the following of ways (Table 7.2 and Figure 7.38) depending on the type of sewing machine you have.

Table 7.2 Types of seam finishes

SEAM FINISH	USE
Pinked	Suitable for fabrics that do not fray. Use pinking shears and trim to the desired width.
Stitched and pinked	Stitch 6 mm (¼ in) from each raw edge. Trim close to the stitching with pinking shears.
Overcast	Used on any type of fabric. Trim the seam. Work overcasting stitches by hand along the cut edges.
Edge stitched	This method is suitable for light and medium weight fabrics. Turn the raw edges under 3 mm (⅛ in). Machine stitch close to the folded edges.
Machine zigzag	Used only on firmly woven fabrics. Machine a regular zigzag stitch just inside the raw edge of the seam. Trim close to the stitching line.
Bound	Makes use of crossway strips or bias binding. Used on thick and loosely woven fabrics. Suitable for unlined jackets. Press open one edge of the bias strip. Place it on the right side of the seam. Pin, tack and stitch. Turn to the wrong side and hem to the stitching.

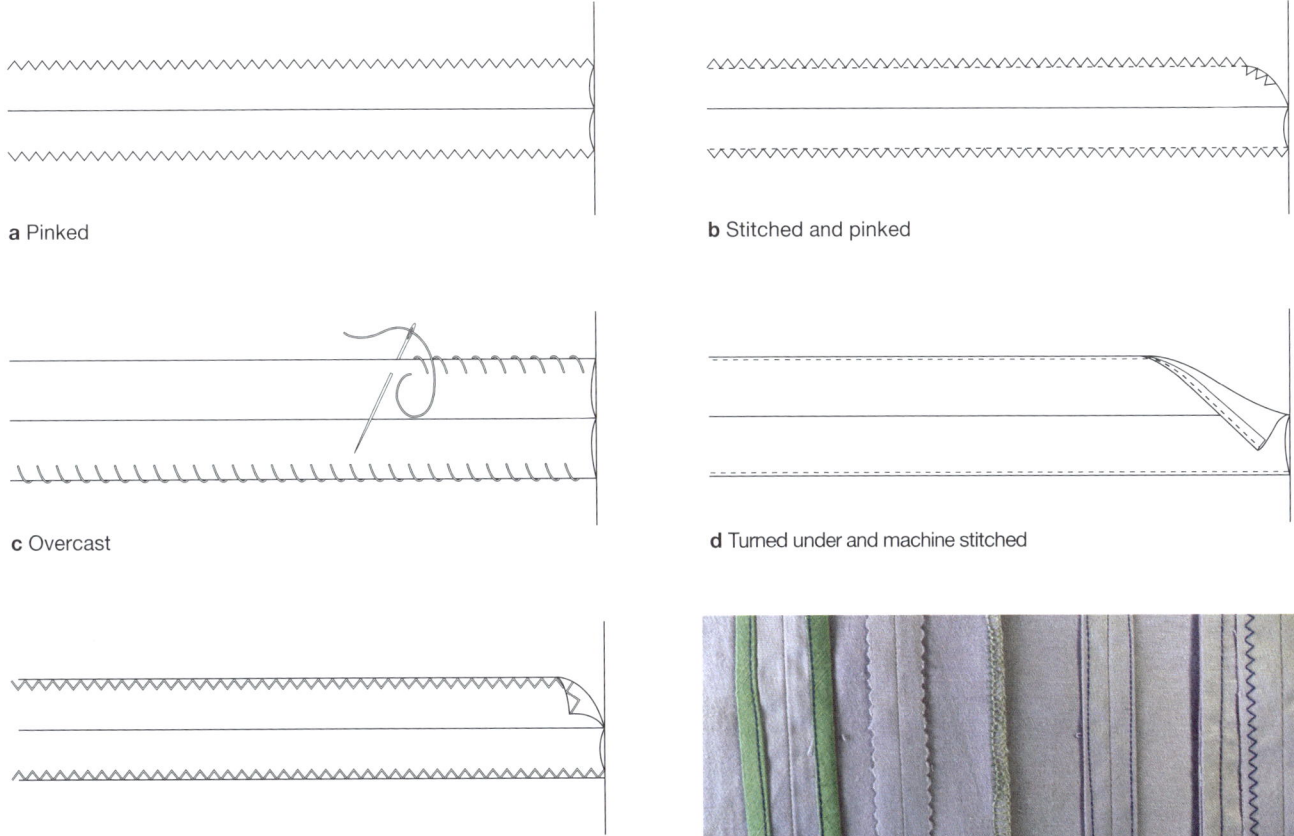

a Pinked

b Stitched and pinked

c Overcast

d Turned under and machine stitched

e Zigzagged

Figure 7.38 A seam can be finished in one of several ways.

ACTIVITIES

1. Use the ends of fabric and practise making the different types of seams.
2. Mount your specimens of seams in a scrapbook. Next to each, state (a) the name of the seam, (b) the type of fabric on which it is done, (c) the area of a garment where it may be used.

FIBRES

In Book 1, you read about the different types of fibres and about the natural fibre, cotton. In this section, you will find information about another natural fibre (linen), the types of human-made fibres, and about a human-made fibre called polyester.

Linen

Linen is a cellulosic fibre that comes from the stem of the flax plant. The flax plant has slender stems, blue flowers and grows to a height that ranges from 91 cm to 1.2 m (3 to 4 ft). The plant requires a cool damp climate, and is grown chiefly in Russia, Belgium, Ireland and parts of the USA.

The stems of the plant are processed to produce soft, strong fibres that are used for manufacturing linen yarns.

Linen fibres produce a strong fabric that is cool to wear, especially in tropical climates.

Linen fibres are not as elastic as cotton fibres, therefore linen fabric creases badly.

Linen fabric is also very expensive.

You may wish to learn about linen and polyester alongside cotton, found in Book 1 of the Home Economics in Action series.

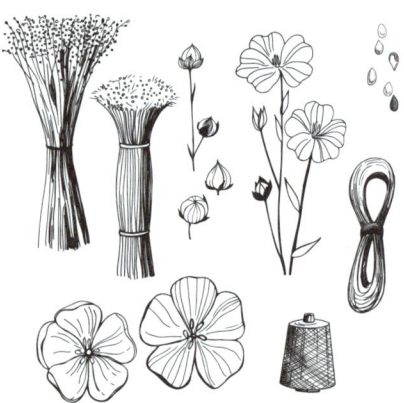

Figure 7.39 Linen made from the flax plant

Figure 7.40 A linen swatch

Human-made fibres

The term 'human-made' is used to describe all fibres that are not found in the natural environment. By using chemicals only, or combined with natural materials, scientists are able to produce staple and filament fibres that can be made into fabrics. Fibres made in this way are called 'synthetic', 'manufactured' or 'artificial' fibres.

Figure 7.41 Polyester chips are made into thread

Chapter 7 Clothing and textiles

Human-made fibres have a wide range of uses. Not only are they used to make fabrics for uniforms and everyday clothing, but they are also used for protective clothing, home textiles, floor coverings, medical and surgical products, transportation, computers, cables, ropes, space travel and agriculture. They are of different types, depending on the raw materials used in the manufacturing process.

Types of human-made fibres

Human-made fibres can be divided into two types:

Synthetic. These are made from chemicals found in air, coal, tar, salt, natural gas, water and petroleum products. The popular synthetics include polyester, nylon, saran, acrylic, modacrylic and spandex, among others.

Regenerated. These are made from the cellulose of cotton and wood pulp, and are called regenerated cellulosics. Examples are rayon, acetate and triacetate.

Figure 7.42 Examples of human-made fibres

Polyester

Polyester fibres are long-chain filament fibres made from elements of coal, air, water and petroleum. These substances are combined with an alcohol and an acid to form complex molecules called polymers. The processes for the manufacture of polyester filament fibres include:

- heating or dissolving the chemical solution to form a thick liquid called the spinning solution
- forcing the liquid through spinnerets (small holes) to form long continuous strands called filaments
- stretching the filament yarns between a series of rollers to obtain the thickness desired
- winding the filaments onto bobbins for use in constructing fabrics.

Polyester fabrics

Manufacturers give different names to the range of fabrics they produce for the textiles market. These are called trade names. There are many trade names for polyesters, and there are many varieties of polyester fabric. Some polyester fabrics include Dacron (pronounced day-kron), Kodel, Fortrel, Vycron, Trevira and Tetrex.

Blends and mixtures

Blends, mixtures and combinations form a significant part of today's fibres. The terms refer to the way in which different fibres are used to make yarns and fabrics. The type of yarns that are combined to make a fabric determines the appearance, strength, quality, **texture** and feel of the particular fabric. Therefore, while some fabrics may be more expensive, they have improved qualities. Several fibres can be blended together, for example, polyester with silk and cotton.

Blended fibres are a mixture of different fibres spun together as one yarn. Blended fabrics are made of yarns in which two or more different fibres are mixed before the yarn is spun. Natural fibres can be blended with other natural fibres, or with human-made or synthetic fibres. For example, linen blended with cotton is called 'union'. Linen may also be blended with silk, wool, polyester and other human-made fibres.

Wool fibres are often blended with cotton, polyester, nylon and viscose rayon. Silk fibres may be blended with wool, nylon or human-made fibres. Staple rayon fibres can be blended with other short fibres such as cotton and wool to make spun yarns that are called blends. Blended rayon yarns are also made with polyester, acetate or nylon fibres.

Acetate fibres are often blended with rayon, wool or cotton, and can be 'crimped' during the manufacturing process to resemble wool.

Some of the polyesters may be blended or combined with cotton or any other fibre. When polyester is blended with cotton, the properties of both fibres are combined. Where one fibre is deficient in a specific quality, it is enhanced by the qualities of the other fibre with which it is blended. Wool, for example, adds elasticity and absorbency to blended fabrics. Silk fibres add lustre and strength.

Combination fabrics make use of only two different types of yarn, which are twisted together to form ply yarns. A combination yarn is one that has two different fibre strands twisted together to make a ply yarn.

A mixture is a fabric that has yarns of one fibre forming the warp threads and yarns of a different fibre forming the weft or filling threads.

ACTIVITIES

1. Visit a fabric store and read the labels on the fabric bolts to identify 10 blended fabrics. Record the name given to the fabric by the manufacturer, the type of fabric and the percentage of each fibre in the blend.
2. At the fabric store, identify five fabrics that are 100% polyester, and give the trade name under which each is sold.

Taking body measurements

MEASURING AND MEASUREMENTS

In clothing, **measuring** is the process of obtaining accurate proportions. These may be obtained using either the imperial system or the metric system. Body measurements are the actual measurements of different areas of your body. Before shopping online or making any garment, whether it is a shirt, pants, dress, blouse or skirt, you need to check your body measurements.

Did you know?

The tape measure is the only measuring tool that can be used for taking accurate body measurements. It has the imperial system on one side and the metric system on the other side.

Figure 7.43 A tape measure

Taking body measurements

1. Take measurements every time you want to make a garment, since you are constantly growing during adolescence and as a result, your measurements change.
2. Some measurements are difficult for you to take on your own, so ask a friend to help you.
3. Make sure you are wearing well-fitting undergarments.
4. Do not measure yourself wearing thick or bulky clothing. Wearing close-fitting clothing will be ok.
5. Tie a string around your waist to find your natural waistline.
6. Stand straight with arms at your sides. Let the person stand slightly at your right-hand side, then take measurements and write them down. Figures 7.44 and 7.45 show how to measure the body for girls' clothes, the extra body measurements you will need for making pants, and the leg measurements for boys' pants.
7. Take measurements closely, but not tightly.
8. If you are making pants, you will also need the measurements for crotch depth and pants length, as shown in Figure 7.46.

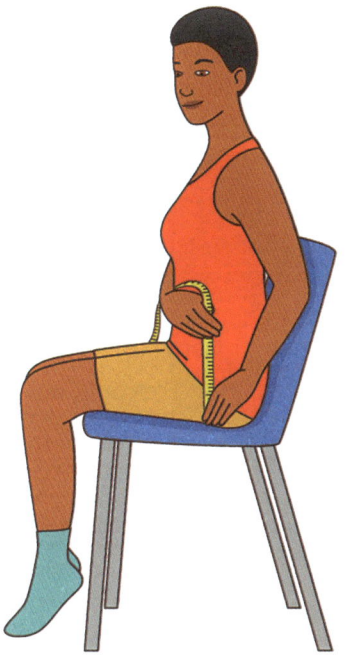

Figure 7.44

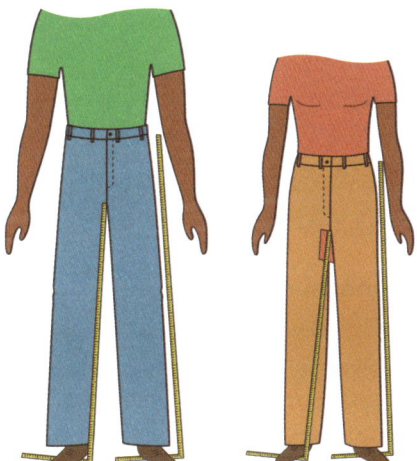

Figure 7.45

Figure 7.56 Correct method of measuring

How to measure

Table 7.3 explains how to take body measurements. Figure 7.47 and Figure 7.48 illustrate how to do this.

Table 7.3 How to take body measurements

Bust	Pass the tape around the fullest part of the bust (chest for boys), with the tape just below the shoulder blades and two fingers inside.
Waist	With the string tied snuggly around your natural waistline, move the tape back and forth so that it sits in the smallest part of the waist, then measure closely, but not tightly.
Hips	Pass the tape around the fullest part of the hips, about 23 cm (9 in) below the natural waistline.
Neck (collar)	Measure around the base of the neck.
Back width	Measure straight across the back about 10 cm (4 in) down from the base of the neck. Measure from armhole to armhole.
Back-neck to waist	Measure from the lower bone at the back of the neck, down to the natural waistline.
Back skirt length	Hold the tape at the natural level of the waist and measure down to the desired length.
Crotch length	Sit straight on a flat surface and measure from the waist at the side to the seat.
Pants length	Stand upright; measure from waist to floor (Figure 7.47).

Figure 7.47 Measuring the length of pants

To measure your height

1 Stand without shoes against a wall.
2 Place a book flat on your head, and ask a friend to mark the place on the wall where the book meets your head.
3 Take a tape measure and measure from this point on the wall to the floor. This is your height.

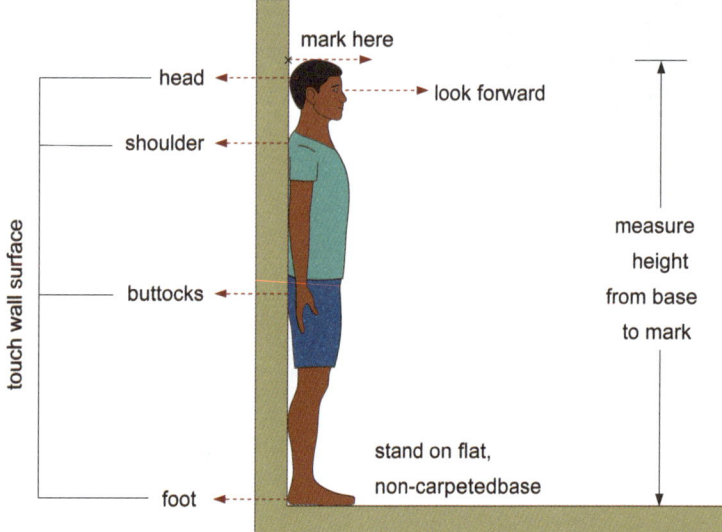

Figure 7.48 How to measure correctly

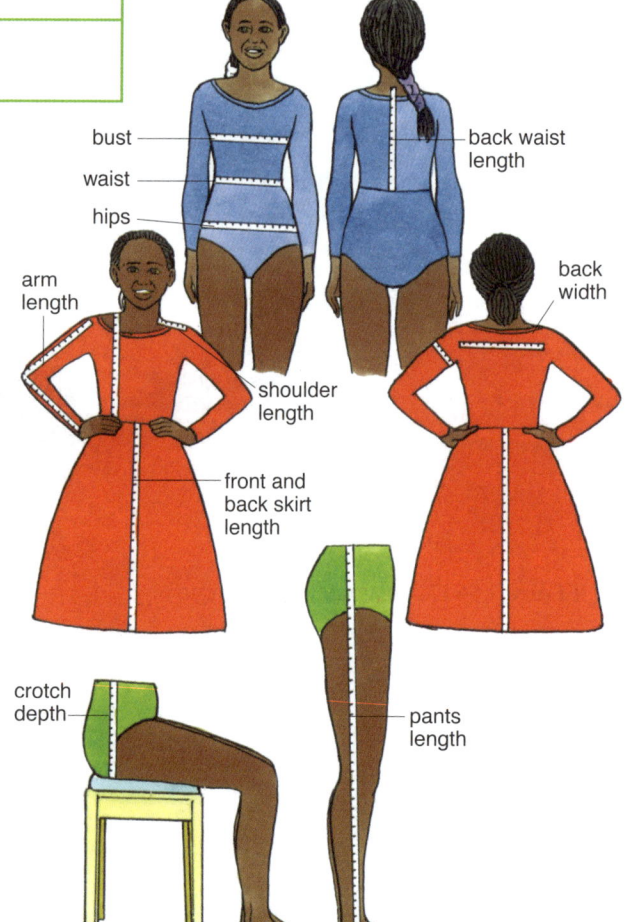

Chapter 7 Clothing and textiles

> **ACTIVITY**
>
> Select a partner and take body measurements, both in centimetres and inches. Record the measurements in a list on your special notepad for measurements. Name it, 'My body measurements'. You will need to use the measurements when choosing commercial patterns.

Figure types

Figure types refer to the natural shape or silhouette of the body. Bodies come in many different shapes and sizes, as you can see in Figure 7.49.

> **Did you know?**
> Body measurements and height are used to determine figure type and size.
> To look your best, choose styles and fabric designs that will enhance your figure.

Figure 7.49 Figure types

Table 7.4 Most figure types can be categorised into five broad types and are named after geometric shapes or fruits.

FIGURE TYPE	CHARACTERISTICS	FASHION TIPS DIFFERENT TYPES OF WOMEN'S BODY SHAPES AND FIGURES
1 Rectangle (also known as straight or banana)	• Bust and hips are basically the same size (balanced) • Waist is slightly smaller than the bust and hips (undefined) • Not many curves • Straight hips and bottoms • Well aligned shoulders and hips	Add curves by defining your shoulders, hips and your waist. Do wear: • shoulder pads to emphasise your shoulders and give you a feminine body figure (but please do not do it in excess) • semi-fitted clothes • short-sleeved and sleeveless tops and dresses if you don't have a very small upper arm • medium to high neckline dresses • dresses that wrap or flow through the waistline • straight to gently flared flat-fronted pants • A-line shirts. Do not wear: • clingy fabrics and fitted clothes, because they will make you look very straight • low necklines will emphasis your flat bust so avoid them • baggy tops and baggy pants are not good choices • narrow skirts will emphasise your flat bottom and are not flattering (avoid them).

Taking body measurements

2	Triangle (also known as pear, bell or spoon) 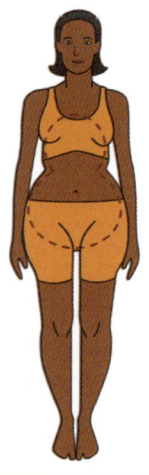	<ul><li>Full hips and thighs</li><li>Rounded shoulders with a smaller bust</li><li>Hips are larger than the bust</li><li>Waist is defined, it gradually slopes out into the hips</li><li>Rounded bottom</li></ul>	Your style aim is to balance your top half to bottom half by creating the appearance of a wider upper body. Do wear:<ul><li>accessories and designs to draw attention to your upper body</li><li>short-sleeved tops</li><li>shoulder pads to broaden your shoulders</li><li>medium to high necklines</li><li>garments to emphasise your waist</li><li>skirts and dresses that are straight or slightly flared</li><li>low rise pants to avoid gaping at the waist</li><li>bootleg and straight pants.</li></ul>Do not wear:<ul><li>baggy garments and garments that add bulk to your hips (hems or design lines at hip-line will only add more size to your hips)</li><li>pleated skirt or pants.</li></ul>
3	Hourglass (also known as X shape) 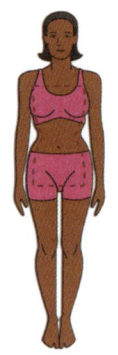	<ul><li>Full bust</li><li>Bust and hips are balanced</li><li>Defined narrow waist that curves out to the hips</li><li>Rounded bottom</li><li>Curvy body</li></ul>	Emphasise your curves, especially your waist, without adding bulk. Do wear:<ul><li>fitted and semi-fitted clothes</li><li>soft, clingy, flowing fabrics</li><li>low to medium-low necklines</li><li>dresses with defined waistlines</li><li>straight and gently flared pants</li><li>straight and gently flared shirts</li><li>accessorise your waist with a belt to flatter your figure</li><li>anything that is comfortable for you.</li></ul>Do not wear:<ul><li>bulky fabrics or baggy styles, because they will hide your figure.</li></ul>
4	Inverted triangle (also known as athletic or apple) 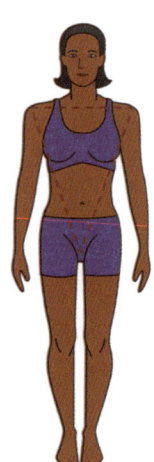	<ul><li>Proportionally larger upper body</li><li>Broad shoulders and a wide back</li><li>Average to big bust</li><li>Less defined waist</li><li>Narrow hips</li></ul>	For you to dress to flatter your inverted triangle body shape, your main style aims are to create the illusion of the perfect hourglass body shape by balancing your lower body to your upper body, and to draw attention away from your upper body. Do wear:<ul><li>flowing fabrics</li><li>V-necklines</li><li>three-quarter length sleeves</li><li>well-adjusted bra</li><li>tops and dresses that flow through the waist</li><li>A-line skirts</li><li>flared pants</li><li>skirts with satin, denim and tweed fabrics, because they create interest to your lower body.</li></ul>Do not wear:<ul><li>bulky fabrics and styles that will emphasise your shoulders</li><li>high necklines</li><li>big collared shirts</li><li>tapered skirts and pants.</li></ul>

| 5 | Round 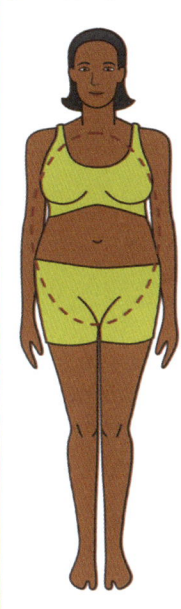 | • Large bust
• Narrow hips
• Full midsection
• Waist is undefined and largest part of the figure
• Full shorter neck and full face | Draw attention upwards towards your shoulders and face.
Do wear:
• earrings, necklaces and other focal points designed to draw an observer's eyes up towards your shoulders and face
• semi-fitted and loose-fitting clothing
• very fitted bras and support underwear to minimise your stomach
• tops and bottoms in the same colours are better worn together
• low necklines
• un-tucked tops that do not emphasise the rounded stomach
• tops and dresses that flow through the waistline
• straight pants in soft, flowing fabric are a good choice.
Do not wear:
• clingy fabrics
• tight-fitted clothes
• fabric with large patterns
• high necklines
• tucked-in tops
• pleated skirts, as they add more volume to your figure. |

ACTIVITIES

1. Examine fashion magazines and collect pictures of six different designs that are suitable for the following figure types: (a) short figure, (b) slim figure, (c) tall figure, (d) plump figure.
2. Mount the pictures you collected in a folder and label clearly.
3. Use your body measurements and identify:
   a Your figure type
   b Your pattern size. Study Table 7.4 on pages 217–219 about figure types and sizes. Also study the wall chart if there is one in your class.

Subject link

Decisions about clothing choices and personal appearance are relevant to Science, Mathematics, Visual Arts and Computer Technology.

Career corner

Jobs in the garment industry

The garment and textile industries provide several job opportunities for the student of Clothing and Textiles. The opportunities available depend on several factors:

- the number of people that can be employed
- the skills of the existing staff, and the skills needed
- the size of the staff
- the nature of the business.

A small garment industry might have employees who are multi-skilled. For example, there might be an employee who is skilled in several areas, such as designing, pattern-making and stitching. This would reduce the number of staff to be hired. Also, the staff of a small garment industry may at times interchange jobs, depending on the demands of the business at the time. Table 7.5 outlines some jobs in the garment and textile industry.

Table 7.5 Some jobs in the garment and textile industry

Manager	Oversees the entire running of the business; is accountable for the staff, machinery and production.	
Supervisor	Supervises staff; is usually responsible for a small section of the business, such as production or cutting. If the business is very small, there is usually only one supervisor.	
Designer	Designs the clothing; makes the sketches and sometimes selects suitable fabrics for designs.	

Pattern maker	Makes the patterns for the garments.	
Sample maker	Makes a sample garment to try out the patterns.	
Cutter	Makes the lay-out plan, and cuts out the garments.	
Operators	Sometimes called 'Stitchers', they stitch the garments. If there are several operators, each may be assigned specific parts of the garment on the production line.	
Finishers	These people trim the garment and do finishing tasks, such as stitching on hooks and eyes and labels.	

Pressers	Press and iron the garments.	
Quality control staff	Check the clothing to ensure that it meets the manufacturer and marketing standards.	
Sales and marketing staff	Responsible for advertising, finding and arranging sales and for selling the items.	

Design project

Your 24-year-old sister, Debbie, is starting a new job as a Sales Supervisor for a large department store. She has a rectangle figure and has asked for your assistance in planning her work wardrobe. Recommend an appropriate basic outfit that will enhance Debbie's figure type.

Include a wardrobe extender and accessories to be worn with the basic outfit.

Create a vision board to share your ideas with your sister.

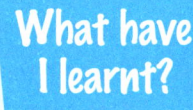

Multiple choice questions

1. The space between the fabric edge and the stitching line is called the seam _____
   A finish.
   B allowance.
   C guide.
   D line.

2. All of the following are points to consider when choosing seams EXCEPT:
   A Position on garment
   B Type of fabric
   C Length of seam
   D Shape of seam

3. Which of the following seams is best for sheer fabric?
   A Curved
   B Double stitched
   C French
   D Turned and stitched

4. The double stitched seam is mostly used on the following garments:
   A Jeans, overalls, pyjamas
   B Camisole, kids clothes, shorts
   C Pyjamas, t-shirt, jeans
   D Men's shirt, sportswear, neck ties

5. A wardrobe that contains the right type of clothes for day-to-day activities is _____
   A functional.
   B seasonal.
   C basic.
   D inspirational.

6. Important factors to consider when choosing clothes are:
   A Cost, colour, brand
   B Design, quality, colour
   C Brand, quality, design
   D Design, colour, style

7. All the following are guidelines for care of clothing EXCEPT:
   A Remove stains immediately
   B Launder clothing according to the type of fabric
   C Repair torn sections after laundering
   D Air worn clothes before storing

8. How often should body measurements be taken?
   A Weekly
   B Every three months
   C Every time you want to make a garment
   D Twice per year

9   An employee in a garment factory who makes sketches and sometimes selects suitable clothing.
    A   Sample maker
    B   Designer
    C   Operator
    D   Supervisor

Short answer questions

1   Outline any five reasons why people wear clothes.
2   List four guidelines for selecting clothing to be worn in the Caribbean.
3   Write five guidelines for dressing appropriately to make the best appearance.
4   List three guidelines to follow when purchasing ready-to-wear clothing.
5   Explain the importance of taking accurate body measurements.
6   Discuss the body measurements needed to construct the following garments:
    a   Boy's shirt
    b   Knee-length skirt
    c   A pair of long pants
7   Name the body measurements that determine figure type and size.
8   Differentiate between the following terms:
    a   Wardrobe planning and wardrobe inventory
    b   Basic garments and wardrobe extenders
9   List three key benefits of wardrobe planning.
10 Name four categories for grouping clothes when preparing an inventory.
11 List three advantages and three disadvantages of shopping for clothes online.
12 Make a list of at least 10 jobs in the garment industry and state the duties of each.
13 Complete the table.

Figure type	Bust to hips relationship	Waist description
Oval	Large bust and narrow hips	
Hourglass		Narrow
Triangle	Hips larger than bust	
Rectangle		Slightly smaller than bust and hip
Inverted triangle		Less defined

10 Match items as it relates to wardrobe planning from Column A to Column B.

COLUMN A	COLUMN B
All the clothes and accessories you have to wear	Accessories
Climate, lifestyle, needs vs wants	Wardrobe inventory
Items that accent your clothes	Multi-purpose clothing
The first step in wardrobe planning	Purpose of accessories
Gives outfits a finished look	Wardrobe
Mix and match garments	Factors to consider
Clothes that can be worn several different ways	Ways to extend wardrobe

11 a Match the body shapes to the body shape images.

BODY SHAPE

A   B   C   D   E

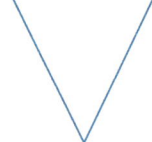  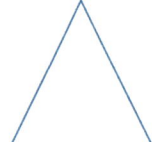 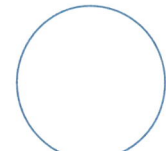 

BODY SHAPE IMAGES

(i)   (ii)   (iii)   (iv)   (v)

b 'To look your best, choose styles that will enhance your figure'.
List five pieces of fashion advice that you will give for each of the body shape images in (i) to (v).

Taking body measurements

Appendix 1 Weights and measures

In this book, quantities and measurements have been given in both metric and imperial. An exact conversion does not usually give convenient working amounts, so we have rounded off the metric measures into units of 25 grams. Do not mix metric and imperial in the same recipe.

The tables below show the recommended equivalents between metric, imperial and American/Canadian (not British) standard measuring cups and spoons.

Weights and equivalent measures

METRIC	IMPERIAL	CUPS OF FAT (E.G. BUTTER)	CUPS OF FLOUR	CUPS/SPOONS OF SUGAR
1 kg	36 oz (2 lb 4oz)			
560 g				$2\frac{1}{4}$ cups (brown)
500 g	18 oz (1 lb 2 oz)			2 cups (granulated)
450 g	16 oz (1 lb)	2 cups		
350 g	12 oz ($\frac{3}{4}$ lb)			
225 g	8 oz ($\frac{1}{2}$ lb)	1 cup		
100 g	4 oz ($\frac{1}{4}$ lb)	$\frac{1}{2}$ cup	1 cup	
50 g	2 oz	$\frac{1}{5}$ cup	$\frac{1}{2}$ cup	
30 g				2 tbsp (granulated)
25 g	1 oz	$\frac{1}{8}$ cup	$\frac{1}{4}$ cup	

kg means kilogram(s); g means gram(s); oz means ounce(s); lb means pound(s)

Volume

METRIC	CUPS/SPOONS	IMPERIAL
1 000 ml (l litre)	4 cups	32 fl. oz (2 pints)
500 ml	2 cups	16 fl. oz (1 pint)
250 ml	1 cup	8 fl. oz ($\frac{1}{2}$ pint)
125 ml	$\frac{1}{2}$ cup	4 fl.oz ($\frac{1}{4}$ pint)
50 ml	$\frac{1}{5}$ cup	2 fl.oz ($\frac{1}{8}$ pint)
30 ml	$\frac{1}{8}$ cup	1 fl. oz ($\frac{1}{16}$ pint)
15 ml	1 tbsp	
5 ml	1 tsp	

ml means millilitre; fl oz means fluid ounce; tbsp means tablespoon; tsp means teaspoon

Miscellaneous measurements

DESCRIPTION	METRIC	IMPERIAL
1 cup rice	225 g	8 oz
1 stick margarine	100 g	4 oz
1 dash	$\frac{1}{2}$ ml	$\frac{1}{8}$ sp
1 pinch	$\frac{1}{4}$ ml	$\frac{1}{16}$ tsp

Length

METRIC	IMPERIAL
1 m	39 inches
900 mm	36 inches (1 yard)
300 mm	12 inches (1 foot)
100 mm	4 inches
25 mm	1 inch

m means metre; mm means millimetre
Note that there are 10 millimetres in one centimetre and 1000 millimetres in one metre

500 ml = 2 cups = 16 fl. oz (1 pint)

Appendix 2 Nutrition tables

Summary of nutrients for use in the Caribbean

Water–soluble vitamins							Minerals					
Thiamine mg	Riboflavin mg	Niacin NE[g] mg	Ascorbic acid mg	Pyridoxine B_6 mg	Folacin[h] µg	Vit B_{12} µg	Calcium mg	Magnesium mg	Iron[i] mg	Sodium[j] mg	Potassium[k] mg	Zinc mg
0.3	0.4	4	25	0.1	40	0.3	400	50	6	120	500	5
0.3	0.4	5	25	0.1	40	0.3	400	50	6	120	500	5
0.4	0.4	5	30	0.2	60	0.3	500	60	10	200	700	5
0.5	0.4	7	50	0.2	60	0.3	500	60	10	200	700	5
0.6	0.7	9	60	0.3	100	0.8	500	150	10	225	1000	10
0.5	0.6	9	60	0.3	100	0.8	500	150	10	225	1000	10
0.7	1.0	12	60	0.3	100	0.9	500	200	10	300	1400	10
0.7	0.9	11	60	0.4	100	0.9	500	200	10	300	1400	10
0.8	1.2	14	60	0.4	100	1.0	600	250	10	400	1600	10
0.7	1.0	12	60	0.7	100	1.0	600	250	10	400	1600	10
1.0	1.3	16	60	0.7	200	1.5	700	300	12	500	2000	15
0.8	1.1	13	60	0.8	200	1.5	700	250	15	500	2000	12
1.0	1.3	18	60	0.7	200	1.5	900	350	12	500	2000	15
0.9	1.1	15	60	0.8	200	1.5	900	250	15	500	2000	12
1.2	1.3	20	60	0.7	200	1.5	700	350	10	500	2000	15
0.9	1.1	15	60	0.8	200	1.5	700	250	15	500	2000	12
1.1	1.3	19	60	0.7	200	1.5	700	350	10	500	2000	15
0.9	1.1	15	60	0.8	200	1.5	700	250	15	500	2000	12
0.9	1.3	15	60	0.7	200	1.5	700	350	10	500	2000	15
0.7	1.1	12	60	0.8	200	1.5	700	250	10	500	2000	12
+0.1	+0.3	+2	+10	0.8	+200	2.3	1000	+20	30	500	2000	15
+0.2	+0.5	+3	+10	0.8	+100	2.0	1000	+50	15	500	2000	19
+0.2	+0.5	+3	+10	0.8	+100	2.0	1000	+50	15	500	2000	16

[g] 1 NE (niacin equivalent) = 1 mg niacin or 60 mg tryptophan
[h] Expressed as free folate activity
[i] Based on 15% absorption for diets containing 14–20% of energy from food from animals
[j] NRC (USA) values. Sodium values are minimum requirements; total day's intake should not exceed 1600–2000 mg.
[k] Supplementation may be required.

Source: Nutrition Made Simple, Versada S. Campbell and Dinesh P. Sinha

Summary of recommended dietary allowances[a]

Age	Gender	Body weight	Energy[b]		Protein[c]	Fat-soluble vitamins		
		kg	kcal	MJ	g	Vitamin A RE[d] µg	Vitamin D[e] mg	Vitamin E[f] α–TE
0–3 mths	MF	4.5	520	2.18	9	350	10	3
4–6 mths	MF	7.0	700	2.90	13	350	10	3
7–9 mths	MF	8.5	810	3.40	14	350	10	4
10–11 mths	MF	9.6	960	4.03	14	350	10	4
1–3 years	M	13.5	1390	5.81	16	400	10	6
	F	12.9	1295	5.42	15	400	10	6
4–6 years	M	19.7	1800	7.53	22	400	5	7
	F	18.6	1625	6.79	21	400	5	7
7–9 years	M	26.7	2070	8.66	27	400	2.5	10
	F	26.6	1825	7.64	27	400	2.5	10
10–14 years	M	45.0	2450	10.22	45	500	2.5	10
	F	45.0	2065	8.66	45	600	2.5	8
15–18 years	M	60.0	2720	11.38	57	600	2.5	10
	F	55.3	2190	9.18	52	600	2.5	8
19–29 years	M	70.0	2970	12.44	53	650	2.5	10
	F	60.0	2200	9.23	45	560	2.5	8
30–60 years	M	70.0	2870	12.02	53	650	2.5	10
	F	60.0	2160	9.04	45	560	2.5	8
> 60 years	M	70.0	2295	9.60	53	650	2.5	10
	F	60.0	1835	7.68	45	560	2.5	8
Pregnancy			+285	+1.0	+6	660	5.0	10
Lactation		0–6 mths	+500	+2.0	+11	960	5.0	12
		6+ mths			+8	960	5.0	11

[a]The allowances represent daily amounts of energy and nutrients sufficient for the maintenance of health in nearly all people in the Caribbean.

[b]BMR × PAL (Physical Activity Level) for 10-year-olds and above

[c]Adapted from World Health Organization based on egg protein assuming complete digestibility, but adjustment may be necessary for diets based on high vegetable protein.

[d]RE = Retinol Equivalents. 1µ g RE = 1 µg retinol (3.3 IU or 6 µg β carotene (10 IU)

[e]1 µg = 40 IU

[f]α–tocopherol equivalents: 1 mg d–α–tocopherol = 1 α–TE

Appendix 3 Height and weight tables

Height and weight table for women

Weight in kilograms and pounds according to frame in indoor clothing weighing 5 lb

HEIGHT			SMALL FRAME		MEDIUM FRAME		LARGE FRAME	
feet	inches	cm	lb	kg	lb	kg	lb	kg
4	9	148	102–111	46.4–5.06	109–121	49.6–55.1	118–131	53.7–59.8
4	10	150	103–113	46.7–51.3	111–123	50.3–55.9	120–134	54.4–60.9
4	11	152	104–115	47.1–52.1	113–126	51.1–57.0	122–137	55.2–61.9
5	0	155	106–118	48.1–53.6	115–129	52.2–58.6	125–140	56.8–63.6
5	1	157	108–121	48.8–54.6	118–132	53.2–59.6	128–143	57.8–64.6
5	2	160	111–124	50.3–56.2	121–135	54.9–61.2	131–147	59.4–66.7
5	3	162	114–127	51.4–57.3	124–138	55.9–62.3	134–151	60.5–68.1
5	4	165	117–130	53.0–58.9	127–141	57.5–63.9	137–155	62.0–70.2
5	5	168	120–133	54.6–60.5	130–144	59.2–65.5	140–159	63.7–72.4
5	6	170	123–136	55.7–61.6	133–147	60.2–66.6	143–163	64.8–73.8
5	7	173	126–139	57.3–63.2	136–150	61.8–68.2	146–167	66.4–75.9
5	8	175	129–142	58.3–64.2	139–153	62.8–69.2	149–170	67.4–76.9
5	9	178	132–145	60.0–65.9	142–156	64.5–70.9	152–173	69.0–78.6
5	10	180	135–148	61.0–66.9	145–159	65.6–71.9	155–176	70.1–79.6
5	11	182	138–151	62.1–68.0	148–162	66.6–73.0	158–179	71.2–80.7

Adapted from: Metropolitan Life Insurance Company, 1983 *Metropolitan height and weight table for women*

Height and weight table for men

Weight in kilograms and pounds according to frame in indoor clothing weighing 5 lb

HEIGHT			SMALL FRAME		MEDIUM FRAME		LARGE FRAME	
feet	inches	cm	lb	kg	lb	kg	lb	kg
5	1	158	128–134	58.3–61.0	131–141	59.6–64.2	138–150	62.8–68.3
5	2	160	130–136	59.0–61.7	133–143	60.3–64.9	140–153	63.5–69.4
5	3	162	132–138	59.7–62.4	135–145	61.0–65.6	142–156	64.2–70.5
5	4	165	134–140	60.8–63.5	137–148	62.1–67.0	144–160	65.3–72.5
5	5	168	136–142	61.8–64.6	139–151	63.2–68.7	146–164	66.4–74.7
5	6	171	138–145	62.9–66.2	142–154	64.8–70.3	149–168	68.0–76.8
5	7	173	140–148	63.6–67.3	145–157	65.9–71.4	152–172	69.1–78.2
5	8	175	142–151	64.3–68.3	148–160	66.9–72.4	155–176	70.1–79.6
5	9	178	144–154	65.4–70.0	151–163	68.6–74.0	158–180	71.8–81.8
5	10	180	146–157	66.1–71.0	154–166	69.7–75.1	161–184	72.8–83.3
5	11	183	149–160	67.7–72.7	157–170	71.3–77.2	164–188	74.5–85.4
6	0	185	152–164	68.7–74.1	160–174	72.4–78.6	168–192	75.9–86.8
6	1	188	155–168	70.3–76.2	164–178	74.4–80.7	172–197	78.0–89.4
6	2	190	160–172	71.4–77.6	167–182	75.4–82.2	176–202	79.4–91.2
6	3	193	162–176	73.5–79.8	171–187	77.6–84.8	181–207	82.1–93.9

Adapted from: Metropolitan Life Insurance Company, 1983 *Metropolitan height and weight table for men*

Appendix 4 Fashion silhouettes

Dresses

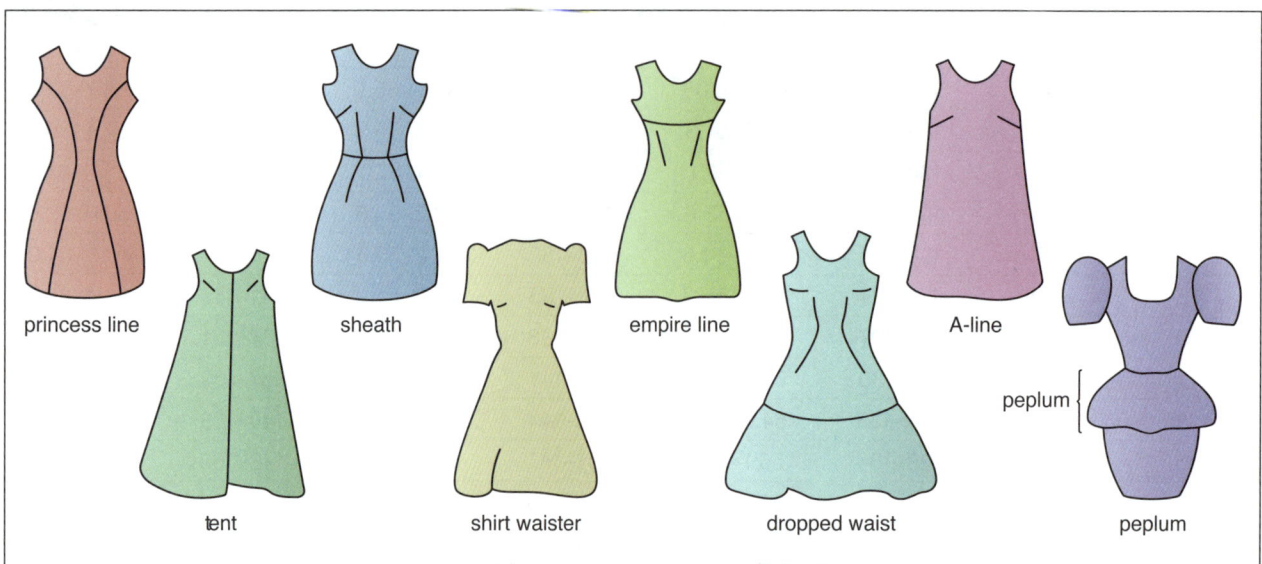

Skirts

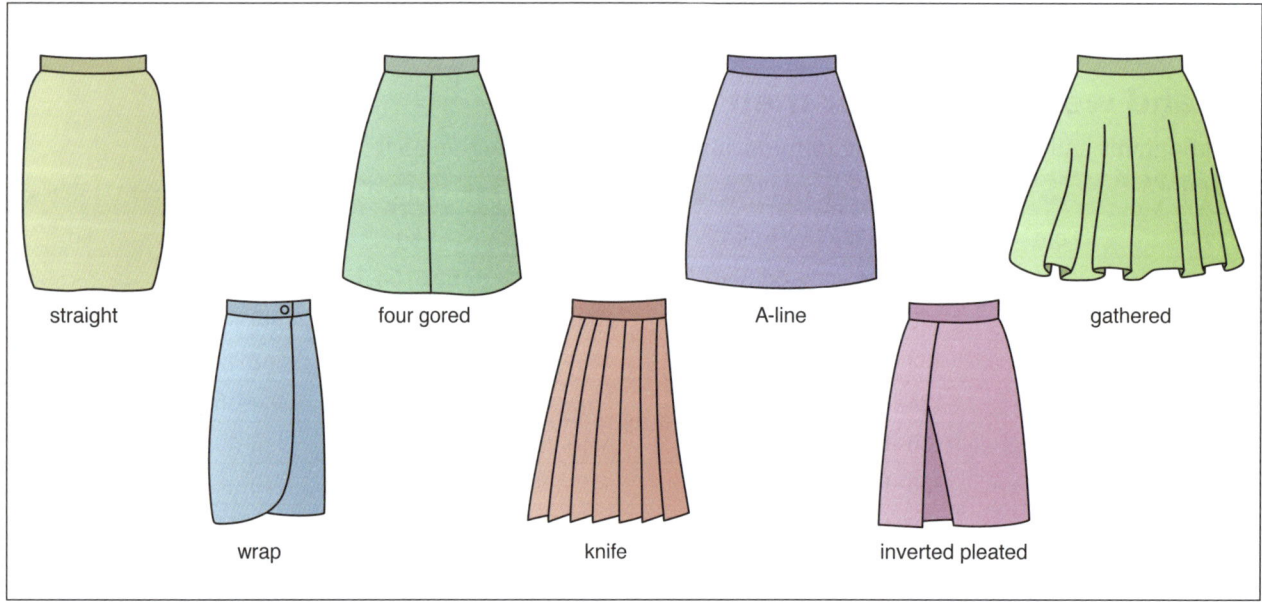

Sleeves

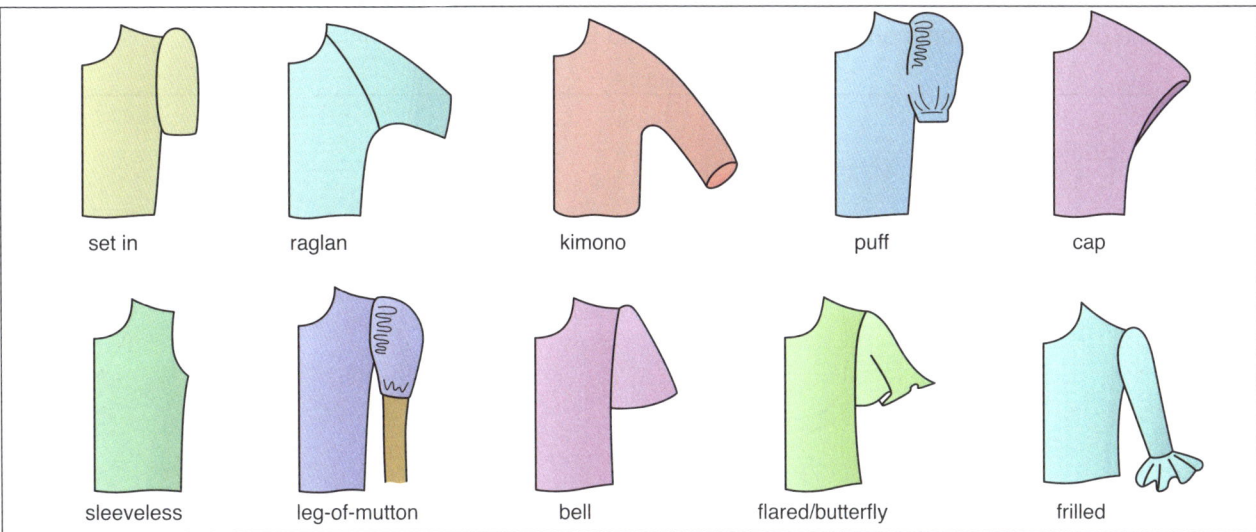

Necklines

Collars

Appendix 5 Glassware

These are some of the more common types of glasses used to serve different drinks:

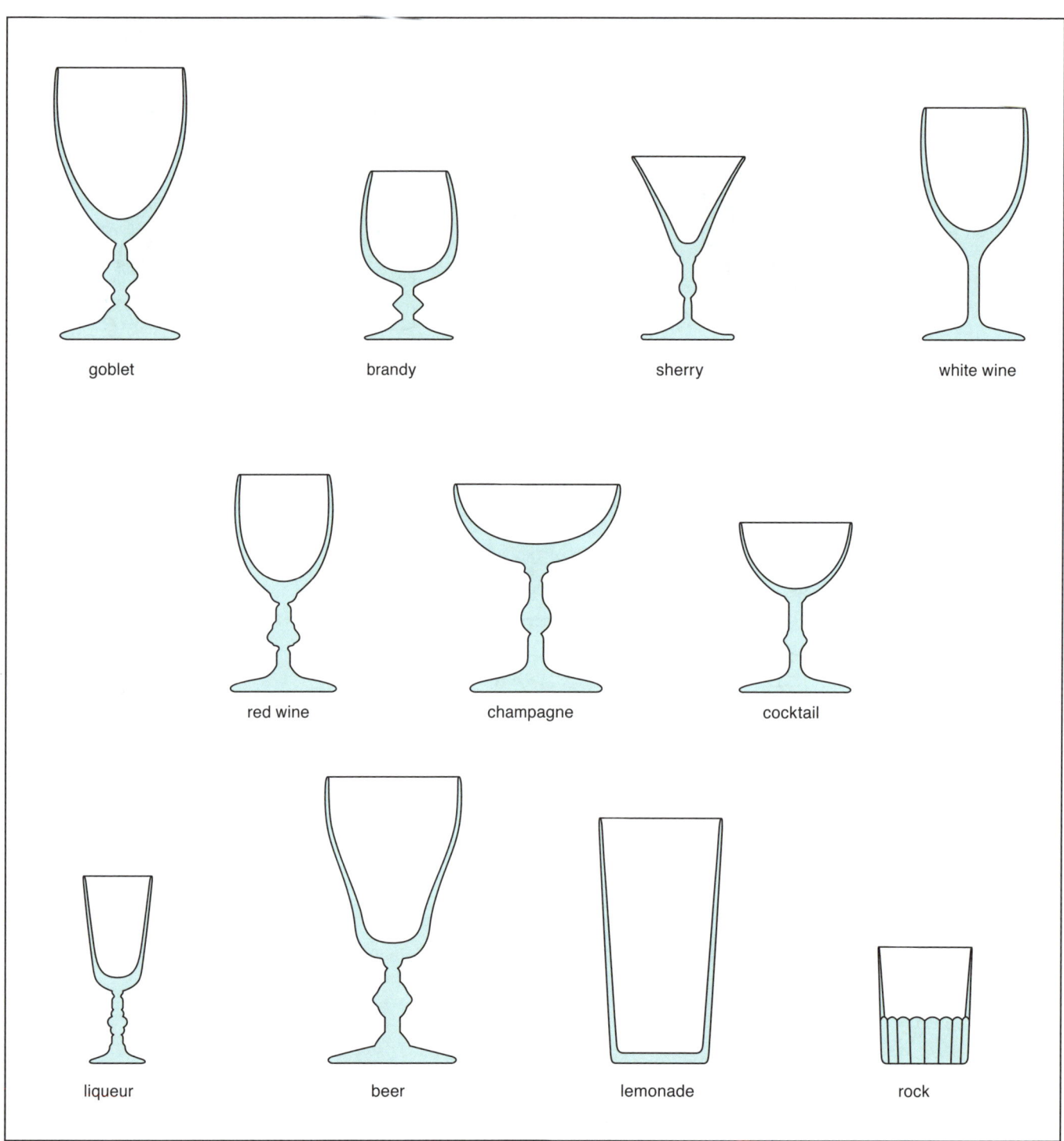

Cookery terms

Au gratin A food with a browned surface, usually obtained by covering with a sauce, sprinkling with breadcrumbs, and then grilling

Batter A mixture of flour and liquid, usually egg and milk, beaten until smooth, and then fried or baked

Bakes A quick bread that can be fried or baked; also known as Johnny cakes or fried dumplings

Brown To bake, fry or toast food until the surface is brown in colour

Carambola A fruit which can have a variety of names: Chinese star apple (Barbados), coolie (Grenada), tamarind (Trinidad and Tobago), pommer canelle (St. Lucia)

Carite Type of white fish, also called Spanish mackerel

Chill To cool food in a refrigerator or cold place

Coat To cover food with a layer of thick liquid, e.g. beaten egg, batter, or egg and breadcrumbs, to protect it when cooking

Dot To scatter small bits of ingredients, usually margarine or butter on top of food.

Sauté To toss lightly in a little fat while frying

Season To add salt, pepper or other ingredient to make food taste better

Steep To extract flavour, colour or another qualities from a substance by leaving it in water just below boiling point

Stock A liquid in which bones, meat or vegetables have been boiled for some time and which can be used for soups and stews

Zest The thin outer rind of fruit such as oranges or lemons

Glossary

acquired immunity immunity acquired when the body produces antibodies, as a result of immunisation or a non-fatal attack of the disease

amino acid the small molecules that join together to make proteins

amniotic sac the fluid-filled bag in which a baby develops

basal metabolic rate (BMR) the amount of energy your body needs to carry out involuntary activities such as breathing while it is at rest

blended fibres a mixture of different fibres spun together as one yarn

budget any plan for spending income

census an official counting by government officers of the number of people in an area or country

combination fabrics fabric made using two different types of yarn twisted together to form a ply yarn

communicable diseases diseases that can be spread from one person to another

conception when a sperm unites with an ovum; the beginning of a pregnancy

contagious diseases diseases spread by direct or indirect contact with people or other organisms

crude birth rate the number of live babies born in one year for every 1000 people in the population

crude death rate the number of deaths in one year for every 1000 people in the population

crystal a fine, expensive type of glassware

degenerative the deterioration and loss of function in the organs or tissues

dextrin a short polysaccharide molecule – the brown substance formed when bread is toasted

disaccharide a double sugar, made up of two monosaccharides joined together

disease a condition that prevents the body or part of it from working properly

dividend a share of profits paid in proportion to share of ownership

embryo a mass of cells that develops from a fertilised ovum

emigrants people who leave a country to go and live somewhere else

energy the power to do work and other activities

epidemic an outbreak of a disease that spreads rapidly and infects lots of people

essential amino acids the amino acids that are essential for growth and health of humans

expenditure the money that is spent by a family or individual

fertilisation when a male cell unites with a female cell to produce an embryo

foetus an embryo after the age of 8 weeks, when organs and features are developing

flatware cutlery; knives, forks, spoons, serving utensils

fontanelle the soft spot in a baby's skull, covered by a tough membrane, where the bones have not yet joined up, allowing the brain to go on growing

frying cooking food in hot fat or oil

glassware drinking glasses, glass serving dishes, etc. used at a meal

health insurance scheme a scheme for saving money on a regular basis so that any necessary healthcare bills can be paid

Heimlich manoeuvre a first-aid technique to remove an obstruction from someone's throat

hydrogenation the process by which liquid plant oils are changed to solid or semi-solid fats such as margarine and shortening

immigrants people who move into a country from another country

immunity the ability of the body to fight and kill invading organisms without becoming ill

immunisation the process of making people immune to disease

income money that is paid to a worker in exchange for labour

infection the invasion of the body by harmful micro-organisms (pathogens)

infestation the invasion of the body by parasites

inorganic waste waste that will not decay, such as plastic or glass

kilocalorie the amount of energy that is required to raise the temperature of one kilogram of water by 1°C

liquidity the ease with which an individual can turn invested assets (like savings) into cash in hand

measuring the process of obtaining accurate measurements

microorganisms tiny living things that cannot be seen by the naked eye

monosaccharide a simple, single-molecule sugar

natural immunity immunity that is inherited from parents or ancestors

net migration the difference between the number of people who enter a country and the number of people who leave it

non-communicable diseases diseases that cannot be spread from one person to another

organic refuse perishable waste such as leftover food

ovum an egg cell

packed meal a meal prepared at home and taken in a container to be eaten away from home

pandemic an epidemic of disease that spreads to several countries

parasitic worms worms that live in the human body and harm it

pathogens microorganisms that harm the human body

polysaccharide a complex carbohydrate such as starch, made up of many simple sugar molecules joined together

population education the study of the relationship between people and their environment

recovery position the recommended position for an unconcious body to prevent choking to death

retail shop a shop that buys goods from manufacturers or wholesalers and sells them to consumers

salary monthly payment for work done; income

savings bond a promise from a corporation or government to pay the investor a certain amount of money, plus interest, at a specific time in the future

silverware flatware made from or plated with silver

snacks light refreshments eaten between meals

soaking immersing a fabric in liquid for a few hours, to remove stains

sponging using a damp sponge or piece of absorbent fabric such as a towel to remove a stain from fabric

stain an unwanted discolouration on a fabric, usually caused by an accident

steaming cooking food in the steam that rises from a boiling liquid

texture describes how a fabric looks or feels

toiletries items that are used for regular personal body care

toxin a poison; a substance produced by a pathogen that harms the body

trace elements minerals found in food in very small quantities that are essential for good health

vector any insect or other animal that carries disease-causing organisms from one person or animal to another

vitamins nutrients found in food in very small quantities that are essential for good health

wage weekly payment for work done; income

weaning the transition from breast-feeding or liquid bottled milk to eating solid food

Index

acquaintance(s) 25–6, 40
acquired immunity 91, 111
adolescence 28, 101, 215
adoption 22, 25
adult
    becoming an 28–31 see also stress
adulthood 29–30, 100, 194 see also self-expression
advertising 74, 82–3, 222
airborne transmission 89-90 see also disease(s)
amino acids 118–9, 124 see also protein(s)
amniotic sac 99
apartment(s) 49, 72
artificial respiration 69
ascorbic acid 125 see also Vitamin C

baby's
    arrival 20, 36–7
    bed 105
    bones 102
    clothing 38, 109
    habits and routine 38
    head 101–3, 108
    physical progress 103–5
    room 37
    teeth 102–3
bacteria 53, 55, 61, 88, 146, 150
    harmful 59, 154, 160
bacterial growth 150, 156
baking 78, 160, 164–5, 173
baking tins 183–4
bank transfer 74
bank(s) 79–81, 84, 196
basal metabolic rate (BMR) 130, 228 see also energy
bathing 38, 89, 108
bathroom and toilet 61
bedroom 58–9, 62
birth control 35
birth rate 33, 40
bleach 59, 61, 63–4
blended fibres 213–4
blends and mixtures 213 see also polyester
blood calcium levels 123
blood cells 91, 127–8
blood pressure 127
blood sugar level 116
bloodstains 62, 73
bloodstream 90
bond 25–6
bones 68, 122–3, 127, 160–1, 166, 171–2
    baby's 102
bottle-feeding 106–7, 111
breast-feeding 106–7, 111
breathing 30, 66, 68, 130

mouth-to-mouth 69
budget 74–5, 78–9, 85, 188, 197
budgeting 74–5, 145, 189
burns and scalds 67
butter cream 150, 182

cake-making 145, 177–84, 189, 190 see also recipes
    common faults and causes in 184
    creaming method 180
    general guidelines for 183
    main ingredients 177
    melted fat method 181
    methods of 177–84
    qualities of a good cake 183
    recipes 178–183 see also recipes
        rubbing-in method 178–9
        whisking method 182–3
calcium 102, 123, 126–7, 171, 227 see also minerals
carbohydrates 32, 114–7, 123–4, 127–8, 130–1, 141–2, 159
carbon dioxide 32
career corner
    bank teller 80
    creative development professional 83
    community nutrition officer 136
    cutter 221
    designer 220
    finishers 221
    food safety and quality assurance supervisor 155
    manager 220
    operators 221
    pattern maker 221
    pressers 222
    professional chef 188
    quality control staff 222
    real estate agent 50
    sales and marketing staff 222
    sample maker 221
    social worker 39
    supervisor 220
census 31, 33, 40
checklist 44, 71
    guidelines for writing recipes 157
    preparation of food 153
    serving and consuming food 153
chef 188
cheque(s) 74–5, 80, 82, 84
chewing gum 63, 199
child growth and development 98–110
childcare 105–10
    baby's clothing 109
    bathing the baby 108
    crying 109
    feeding 106–7
    immunisation 110
    sleeping 105

    sleeping position 105
    the baby's bed 105
    toilet training 109
    weaning 107
childhood 28, 110
chocolate 63, 136, 142–3, 159
choking 68
cleaning 38, 54–61, 73, 76, 92–4, 111
    dry- 82, 207
cleaning agent(s) 61, 94, 148
clothes 23, 28, 37, 56, 58, 76–7, 82, 192–3, 198, 200–2
    baby's 109
    purchasing 203–4
    reasons for wearing 194–6
coal pot 54, 60
cobalamin 124 see also vitamin B_{12}
cocoa 64, 138, 140
coffee 64, 67, 138, 140
cola 63
combination fabrics 214
commercial banks see under bank(s)
conception 98, 111 see also fertilisation
condominium 49, 72
cons see pros and cons
consumer goods 83, 84
consumer safety inspectors 155
consumer(s) 16, 74, 81–5, 146
contraception 35 see also family planning
cooker(s) 51–6, 59–60, 76, 78, 83, 127
    coal pot see coal pot
    electric 54–5, 60
    gas 54–5
    kerosene 54, 60
    slow 153
    split-level 55
cooking
    methods of 160–8
    moist methods of 160–4
cooking equipment 54–5
cooking fish 171, 173–4
co-operatives 81
courtesy 24–5
credit card 84
credit unions 80 see also savings institutions
crude birth rate 33 see also population growth
crude death rate 33 see also population
crystal 187 see also glassware
cutlery 56, 153, 185 see also flatware
cuts and scratches 67 see also first aid

daily care 59–61
danger zone 149–150, 156 see also bacteria
death rate 33
debit card 84

decision(s) 8, 14, 25, 27, 29, 42, 44, 65, 70, 77, 80
    clothing 192–6
    independent 28
    major management 50
    meal planning and preparation 171
    responsible 34
decision-making 47
deficiency 126–7, 129, 141
deficiency and excess 117–8, 121–5 see also minerals and vitamins
designer 11, 12, 220
design project 39, 70, 85, 110, 141, 188, 222
dextrin 116 see also polysaccharide
diet 102, 114, 116–9, 121, 125, 144, 171, 175, 227
    balanced 113, 143
    healthy 31, 40, 77, 111
    importance of fats and oils in the 176
    mother's 102
    vegetarian 124
dietary allowance 228
dietary fibre 114, 116–7
dietary needs 148
dining room 59
dinnerware 53, 185–7, 190
disaccharides 115, 141 see also sugars
disease(s)
    causes of 87–8
    communicable 86, 88–91
    contagious 88, 90
    deficiency 91, 113, 126
    degenerative 87-8
    natural defence against 90–1
    non-communicable 88, 146
    non-contagious 88
dividend 80
do it yourself 12–8, 39
drink(s) 68, 139, 152
    fruit 138, 140, 143, 187
    high-energy 115
    soft 63, 148
drink(s) warm 67 see also shock
drinking glasses 187, 189 see also glassware
drinking water 89, 96, 127, 129
dusting 57, 59, 92–3 see also hygiene in the home

electrocution 69 see also first aid
embryo 98–9, 111 see also ovum and fertilisation
emigrants 33 see also immigrants
energy 47, 114, 121
    clean 40
    how important is 129
    measuring 130–1
    release of 123, 127
    source of 115, 117
    time and 34, 42, 48, 50, 57

energy/fuel efficiency 54
energy-giving nutrients 123–4, 130
energy needs 129–30
energy production 114, 118
environment 20, 48, 52, 70, 92, 97, 105
environment damp/moist 88
    healthy 86, 96
    natural 31–2, 212
    social 50, 201
environment work 200
environmental factor(s) 50, 78
epidemic 90, 111 see also disease(s)
essential amino acids 119 see also amino acids and protein(s)
expenditure 74–8, 85

fabric(s)
    absorbent 63 see also stain removal
    blended 213–4
    bulky 218
    clingy 217–9
    combination 214
    constructing 213
    cotton 109 see also baby's clothing
    flowing 218–9
    lightweight 209
    linen 185, 192, 198, 212
    non-washable 63
    polyester 213
    synthetic 198
    tweed 218
    washable 63
    woven 208, 211
family income 28, 75–9
family life 21–3, 41
family life cycle 36
family life in the past 21–2
family planning 34–5, 40
family relationship(s) 25, 29, 36
fast fashion 201
fats 114, 117, 124, 128, 130, 141
    animal 131
    hydrogenated 118, 176
    liquid 118
    saturated 118
    solid 118, 152
    unsaturated 118
fats and oils 145, 175–6
feeding 36, 38, 41, 105, 106–7
fertilisation 98 see also embryo
fibres, blended 213
first aid 65–9
    artificial respiration 69
    burns 67, 69, 167, 194
    choking 68–9
    cuts 67, 90
    electrocution 69
    falls 68
    first-aid box/kit 65–6
    food poisoning 89, 144, 146, 154
    poisoning 67–8

    scalds 67
    scratches 67, 89–90, 194
    shock 66–7, 69
    suffocation 68–9
    how to apply basic 66–9
    box/kit 65–6
first aid technique see Heimlich manoeuvre 68, 73
fish 127, 140, 145, 171–5
    oily 122–3
    types of 171–3
flatware 185–7, 189–90
fluorine 127 see also minerals
foetus 98–9, 127 see also embryo
fontanelle 102 see also baby's bones
food groups 132–4, 145
    Caribbean 131
    six 76, 131
food handling 144, 147
food poisoning see under first aid
food preparation 52, 56, 144–5
    uses of fats and oils in 175
foods
    buying and storing 147–50
    high-energy 130
food safety see under safety
food storage 52, 55, 147–50, 152
friendship 24–7
    ending a 27
    keys to a good 24–5
fructose 115–6 see also sugars
fruit juice 64, 107, 139–40
frying see methods of under cooking
fuel 54, 77–8, 162, 164–5
furniture 37, 50, 57–8, 70, 75, 104
furniture polish 92–3
furniture, kitchen 51

galactose 115 see also sugars
garment industry 220–2, 224
glassware 185, 187, 190, 232
glucose 115–6 see also sugars
grease 53, 59, 64, 93, 163, 165, 178–82
grill(ing) 54–5, 160, 173
growth 55, 86, 90, 94
growth and development after the birth 100–4
growth chart 100
guideline(s) 50, 55, 161, 165, 186
    bathing the baby 108
    bottle-feeding 107
    general 53, 59, 140
    safety 155
    saving 80, 85
    storage of fish 171, 173
    wardrobe inventory 202
guidelines for
    cake-making 183
    caring for clothing 205, 223
    packing meals 139
    purchasing ready-to wear 207

removing stains 62–4
selecting clothing 198–9, 224
shopping 83, 147
storing food 148
toilet training 109
writing recipes 157

healthcare 76–8, 154, 195
health insurance scheme 77
Heimlich manoeuvre 68, 73
hire purchase 84
hot plate or burners 54–5
household cleaning materials 56
household tasks 42, 57–62, 73
housing 31–2, 34, 42, 48, 77, 48–50, 76–7
hydrogenation 118
hygiene 77, 91, 97, 147
hygiene in the home 92–5
hygiene in the surroundings 96–7

ice cream 28, 64, 150–1 see also stain(s)
ideas storming 9, 13–4, 141, 145
immigrants 33
immunisation 91, 97, 110–11
immunity 91, 110–11, 154
income 28, 74–6, 79, 85, 131, 201 see also budget
industry 191, 206, 224
    textile 192, 220
infection 90–1, 108, 111, 122, 125 see also microorganisms
    tetanus 67
infestation 57, 90, 111
inorganic waste 94–5
iodine 64, 66, 127, 171 see also minerals and stain removal
iodine deficiency 141
iron 87, 118, 125, 127, 134, 171 see also marasmus

kerosene 54–6, 60, 67
kilocalorie 116–17, 129–31 see also energy
kitchen 48, 50–6, 59–61, 72
kitchen bins 59–61
kitchen counter 48, 50
kitchen equipment 53–5
kitchen garden 96, 135
kitchen hygiene 147
kitchen layout 52, 54, 70
kitchen planning 51–5
kitchen safety features 53

lactation 102, 228 see also breast-feeding
lactose 115–6 see also sugars
lard 169, 176
lay-away plan 84
light meals 139–40, 145
linen 185, 190, 192, 198, 212–3

bed 58–9
household 56
table 185
liquidity 80 see also savings
living room 59
living together 23

machine operators 195
macro-nutrients 113–21, 130
malnutrition 87–8, 91, 117, 121, 141–2
maltose 115 see also sugars
management process(es) 42–5, 49, 70–1 see also time management
manager 43, 47, 195, 220
manufacturer 55, 66, 82, 214, 222
manufacturer's instructions 107, 205
marasmus 87 see also iron
margarine see hydrogenation and shortening
marketing 206, 222
marriage 25, 79
meal planning 78, 113, 131–7, 145, 148, 171
measuring 70, 101, 130, 157, 214–16
micro-nutrients 113, 121–7
microorganisms 55, 88–90, 154 see also pathogens
mildew 56, 64
milk 64, 68, 128, 139, 152, 160 see also calcium, galactose, glassware, lactose and vitamin(s)
    breast 106, 119
    coconut 161
    cow's 107
    evaporated and sterilised 149
milk dishes 151
milk powder 150
milk teeth 102
minerals 91, 121, 126–7, 130, 160, 227
molecules 115, 213
monosaccharides 115, 141
mopping 59, 92–93
motion mindedness 48
multi-mix principle 113, 131 see also meal planning

net migration 33
niacin 124, 227 see also vitamin B_3
nutrients 88, 90, 102, 106, 128–9, 160, 164, 227 see also macro-nutrients and micro-nutrients
    energy-giving 123
    high in 76
    right 131

organic refuse 94
overpopulation 34
ovum 98

packed meals 137–9, 145
    guidelines for 139

suitable containers for 138
suitable foods for 137–8
paint(ing) 27, 53, 57–8, 64,
pandemic 90 see also epidemic
parasites 88, 90, 111, 154 see also disease(s)
pathogens 88, 90–1, 111, 146 see also disease(s)
payment 77, 79, 83
    methods of 84
peanut butter 119, 127, 142
peers 24, 27, 188
personal hygiene 77, 91 see also hygiene
personal needs 77
phosphorus 102, 118, 123, 126–7 see also minerals
plastic 53, 55, 118, 137, 185
plastic bag(s) 68–9, 94, 138, 149, 151–2, 205
plastic wrap 138–9, 151–2, 173
plasticware 186–7
poisoning 67–8, 89, 144, 146, 154 see also first aid
polyester 185, 192, 212–4
polysaccharides 115–6 see also sugars
population census 31
population education 20, 31–2
population growth 31–3, 40
potassium 126–7, 227 see also minerals
pregnancy 98–9, 102, 105, 111, 125, 228
    teenage 35, 39
problem statement(s) 10–13
problem-solving 10, 36
problem-solving tips 8, 12, 14, 17, 18
pros and cons 8, 49, 188
pros and cons list 14, 207
protein(s) 114, 117–21, 124, 127–8, 130–31, 138, 171–2, 228
    complementary 119–20, 143
prototype 9, 15–8
prototype model 15
prototype testing 16

quality control 18, 222
questions
    multiple choice 40, 71, 85, 141, 189, 223
    short answer 41, 73, 85, 111, 142, 189, 224

recipe(s) 118, 135, 144, 157, 176, 177
    cassava bakes 156
    cheesy cornmeal muffins 181
    citrus sponge squares 182
    coconut cake 179
    corn-crusted trout fillets 175
    evaluate a basic 157-8
    fish broth 166
    fish soup 174
    French toast 170
    interpret and use a basic 157

pancakes 169
patriotic pudding 163-4
pumpkin fritters 170
rock buns 178
salted codfish fritters 171
spicy pound cake 180
steamed fish 163
true sponge cake 183
recovery position 69 see also first aid
refrigerator 48, 52, 55–6, 59, 83, 135, 149–53, 156, 173 see also danger zone
   care of 60
   how to pack the 151–2
relationships 20, 24, 29, 44
   types of 25–7
responsibilities 20, 22, 28–9, 36, 38, 44, 97, 136
   key 155
retinol 122, 228 see also vitamin A
riboflavin 124, 227 see also vitamin B_2
roasting 160, 164–6
rule(s) 30, 131, 185, 187 see also multi-mix principle and table setting
   2-hour 153
   5-second 146
   hygiene 97
rules for
   frying 168
   keeping a first-aid box/kit 66
   safe storage 56
   steaming 162
   working seams 208

safety 42, 79
   clothing 194
   food 144–5, 146–7, 153, 155
safety equipment 155
safety features see under kitchen 53
safety in the home 65–70
safety of your water system 97
safety precaution (oven) 55
salary 136, 155
sales 77, 82–3, 222
sample maker 224
saturated fats 118
saving 54, 76, 78
savings and investments 78–81
savings bonds 80, 85
savings guidelines 79
savings institutions 79–81
scorecard 158–9
scrubbing 57, 59, 92–4
seam allowance 62, 209–10
seam finishes 192, 208, 210–1
seaming techniques 208–11
shares 80
shock 66–7, 69 see also first aid
shopping 53, 70, 78, 144–5, 147–8, 150
   going 83–4

grocery 11, 76
   online 207, 224
shopping list 76, 83, 148, 152, 189–90
shortening 118, 149, 175–6
silverware 186
sink(s) 51–3, 56, 59
   weekly care of 59–61
slavery 21–2, 41
sleeping 30, 38, 105, 193
snack(s) 132, 137–41, 145, 176–7
   mid-morning 128, 170
social environment 50, 201
specification(s) 9, 13, 16–18
sponging and soaking 63 see also stain(s)
stain removal 62–4
stain(s) 59, 61, 205, 223
   ball point ink 63
   blood 62–3, 73
   chewing gum 63
   chocolate 63
   cocoa 64
   coffee 64
   cola 63
   egg 64
   fruit juice 64
   grass 64
   gravy 94
   grease from food 64
   guidelines for removing specific 63–4
   ice cream 64
   iodine 64
   lipstick 64
   mildew 64
   milk 64
   mud 64
   mustard 64
   nail polish 64
   oil from machinery 64
   paint 64
   protein-based 63
   rust 64
   scorch marks 64
   shoe polish 64
   soft drinks 63
   tar 64
   tea 64
steaming 160–2, 164, 173
storage in the home 56
stress 30–1, 40, 46–7
sucrose 115–6 see also sugars
suet 176
suffocation and choking 68–9 see also first aid
sugars 114–16
supervisor 155, 220, 222, 224
sweeping 57–9, 92, 116

table mats 59, 185, 187
table napkins 185, 187

table setting 144–5, 185–7, 190
tar 64, 213 see also stain(s)
tea 64, 138, 140 see also stain(s)
technique(s) 77
   lifesaving 69
   seaming 208–11
   work simplification 42
work simplification and motion mindedness 48
teenager(s) 20, 27, 30, 39, 141, 194, 203
teeth 117, 122–3, 127, 143 see also vitamins
   baby's 102–3
   false 68 see also first aid
texture 116, 140, 157–9, 165, 175–6, 183–4
thiamine 123–4, 227 see also vitamin B_1
time management 45–7
toilet 61
toilet training 109–10
toiletries 76, 77, 83, 148
toxins 88, 90, 138,
trace elements 126 see also minerals
transport 31, 78, 130, 137
   fat-soluble vitamins 117
   hot beverages 138
   nutrients 129

unsaturated fats 118

vacuum cleaner 93
vector 90–1 see also pathogens
vegan 120
vegetable oils 131, 176
vegetarian 120, 122, 124–5, 133–4, 142
vermin 92, 94, 96, 148
   getting rid of 95
vitamins 91, 121–5 see also minerals and nutrients
   A 122, 126, 228 see also retinol
   B complex 121, 123–4
   B_1 123–4, 126, 227 see also thiamine
   B_{12} 124 see also cobalamin
   B_2 124, 227 see also riboflavin
   B_3 124, 227 see also niacin
   C 126, 149 see also ascorbic acid
   D (cholecalciferol) 102, 122–3
   fat-soluble 117–8, 121, 176, 228

wages 21–2
wardrobe 77, 192, 197–8, 205, 207, 222
wardrobe planning 200–3, 224–5
waterborne germs 89
water needs 128–9
weaning 107, 111
work routine 57–60
work simplification 42, 48, 71
work surfaces 51–3

Acknowledgements

Photo acknowledgements

p. 6 *cc*, **p. 19** *cc*, **p. 112** *cc*, **p. 191** *cc* © Kirill/stock.adobe.com; **p. 6** *cc* © Cienpies Design/stock.adobe.com; **p. 7** *tc* © Rawpixel Com/stock.adobe.com; **p. 8** *cc* © Robu S/stock.adobe.com; **p. 10** *tr* © Vector Mine/stock.adobe.com; **p. 10** *cl* © Vlad Chorniy/stock.adobe.com; **p. 11** *tl* © Marek Photo Design.com/stock.adobe.com; **p. 13** *br* © Freshidea/stock.adobe.com; **p. 14** *cl* © Baurka/stock.adobe.com; **p. 17** *cr* © Uladzislau/stock.adobe.com; **p. 18** *cl* © Freeslab/stock.adobe.com; **p. 19** *cr* © Graphics Dunia4u/stock.adobe.com; **p. 20** *tc* © Good Studio/stock.adobe.com; **p. 21** *tr* © Archivist/stock.adobe.com; **p. 26** *tr* © Salmonnegro-Stock/Shutterstock.com; **p. 28** *cr* © Africa Studio/stock.adobe.com; **p. 32** *ll* © Angelov/stock.adobe.com; **p. 37** *cl* © New Africa/stock.adobe.com; **p. 39** *cr* © Prostock-studio/stock.adobe.com; **p. 42** *tc* © Harvepino/stock.adobe.com; **p. 44** *bl* © EKH Pictures/stock.adobe.com; **p. 52** *bl* © Toyakisfoto Photos/stock.adobe.com; **p. 52** *bc* © Three Di Cube/Shutterstock.com; **p. 52** *bc* © Toyakisfoto Photos/stock.adobe.com; **p. 52** *br* © Chris/stock.adobe.com; **p. 61** *cr* © Andriano CZ/stock.adobe.com; **p. 62** *cr* © Africa Studio/stock.adobe.com; **p. 65** *bl* © Elenabsl/stock.adobe.com; **p. 71** *cr* © Roman/stock.adobe.com; **p. 84** *cr* © Vector Icons/stock.adobe.com; **p. 86** *tc* © Tartila/stock.adobe.com; **p. 89** *cr* © Horizonphoto/stock.adobe.com; **p. 91** *cl* © Vector Juice/stock.adobe.com; **p. 91** *br* © Riccardo Niels Mayer/stock.adobe.com; **p. 92** *tr* © YG Studio/stock.adobe.com; **p. 92** *cr* © Andrey Popov/stock.adobe.com; **p. 93** *tr* © Pixel-Shot/stock.adobe.com; **p. 93** *cr* © Prostock-studio/stock.adobe.com; **p. 93** *cl* © Freedomz/stock.adobe.com; **p. 93** *cr* © Lightfield Studios/stock.adobe.com; **p. 94** *tr* © Kirsten D/peopleimages.com/stock.adobe.com; **p. 94** *cr* © Ronstik/stock.adobe.com; **p. 94** *bl* © Aisha Graphix/Shutterstock.com; **p. 95** *cl* © Suchkova Anna/Shutterstock.com; **p. 95** *cl* © Makro Betz/stock.adobe.com; **p. 95** *br* © Macrovector/stock.adobe.com; **p. 96** *bl* © Fottoo/stock.adobe.com; **p. 97** *tl* © C5 Media/stock.adobe.com; **p. 98** *bl* © Alla 72/stock.adobe.com; **p. 100** *cc* © Good Studio/stock.adobe.com; **p. 100** *bl* © Piscine 26/stock.adobe.com; **p. 101** *cl* © Monkey Business/stock.adobe.com; **p. 101** *bl* © Michael Jung/stock.adobe.com; **p. 102** *tr* © Anatta Tan/stock.adobe.com; **p. 102** *cr* © Artemida-psy/stock.adobe.com; **p. 102** *cr* © Надія Коваль/stock.adobe.com; **p. 103** *tr* © Rawpixel.com/stock.adobe.com; **p. 103** *cl* © Laura Dwight/Alamy Stock Photo; **p. 103** *cc* © Laura Dwight/Alamy Stock Photo; **p. 103** *cr* © Evgenia/stock.adobe.com; **p. 103** *bl* © Microgen/stock.adobe.com; **p. 104** *cl* © Yuri Arcurs/Alamy Stock Photo; **p. 104** *cr* © Prostock-studio/stock.adobe.com; **p. 104** *br* © Brocreative/stock.adobe.com; **p. 105** *br* © Monkey Business/stock.adobe.com; **p. 106** *bl* © Pikselstock/stock.adobe.com; **p. 108** *bl* © Chomplearn 2001/stock.adobe.com; **p. 109** *cr* © Anja/stock.adobe.com; **p. 109** *br* © PeopleImages.com Yuri A/Shutterstock.com; **p. 112** *cc* © Gstudio/stock.adobe.com; **p. 113** *tc* © Sunny Forest/stock.adobe.com; **p. 119** *cr* © Rohit Seth/stock.adobe.com; **p. 119** *bl* © Karen Roach/stock.adobe.com; **p. 119** *br* © Andrewgorbi/stock.adobe.com; **p. 131** *br* © Nextuz/stock.adobe.com; **p. 131** *br* © Doomu/stock.adobe.com; **p. 131** *br* © Kolesnikovserg/stock.adobe.com; **p. 131** *br* © Zcy/stock.adobe.com; **p. 131** *br* © Maxim/stock.adobe.com; **p. 131** *br* © GS Design/stock.adobe.com; **p. 131** *br* © Bells 7/stock.adobe.com; **p. 131** *br* © Olvius/stock.adobe.com; **p. 131** *br* © Malshak Off/stock.adobe.com; **p. 131** *br* © Annguyen/stock.adobe.com; **p. 131** *br* © Ahikun Sun/stock.adobe.com; **p. 131** *br* © Natika/stock.adobe.com; **p. 131** *br* © Images My/stock.adobe.com; **p. 131** *br* © Volff/stock.adobe.com; **p. 131** *br* © Ruzz/stock.adobe.com; **p. 132** *tl* © Bigc Studio/stock.adobe.com; **p. 132** *bl* © Elena Schweitzer/stock.adobe.com; **p. 133** *cr* © Tupungato/stock.adobe.com; **p. 144** *tc* © Artur/stock.adobe.com; **p. 149** *cr* © Colleen Michaels/stock.adobe.com; **p. 149** *bl* © Sergii Moscaliuk/stock.adobe.com; **p. 153** *bl* © Vector Mine/stock.adobe.com; **p. 155** *tl* © Microgen/stock.adobe.com; **p. 156** *tr* © Jutia/Shutterstock.com; **p. 158** *bl* © Arena Creative/stock.adobe.com; **p. 160** *cr* © Zigzagmtmart/stock.adobe.com; **p. 161** *br* © Ekramar/stock.adobe.com; **p. 163** *tr* © HL Photo/stock.adobe.com; **p. 163** *cr* © CDK Productions/stock.adobe.com; **p. 164** *br* © New Africa/stock.adobe.com; **p. 166** *cr* © SE/stock.adobe.com; **p. 166** *br* © Foma A/stock.adobe.com; **p. 168** *tr* © Arto Barto/stock.adobe.com; **p. 169** *tr* © Joshua Resnick/stock.adobe.com; **p. 169** *cr* © Виктория Котлярчук/stock.adobe.com; **p. 170** *tr* © Mariusz Blach/stock.adobe.com; **p. 170** *cr* © Qqwartm/stock.adobe.com; **p. 171** *tr* © Lipe/stock.adobe.com; **p. 172** *tr* © Vladimir/stock.adobe.com; **p. 172** *cr* © Timolina/Shutterstock.com; **p. 172** *bc* © Evgenyb/stock.adobe.com; **p. 173** *cr* © Idambeer/stock.adobe.com; **p. 173** *cr* © Shaiith/stock.adobe.com; **p. 173** *br* © Wuttichok/stock.adobe.com; **p. 174** *cr* © Augar 0607/stock.adobe.com; **p. 175** *tr* © Design Pics/Alamy Stock Photo; **p. 178** *cr* © Photo Everywhere/stock.adobe.com; **p. 179** *tr* © Agneskantaruk/stock.adobe.com; **p. 180** *cr* © Radachynskyi/stock.adobe.com; **p. 181** *cr* © Liliya Trott/stock.adobe.com; **p. 182** *cr*, **p. 209** *tl*, *bc*, **p. 210** *br*, **p. 211** *br* © Hachette; **p. 183** *tr* © Anikonaann/stock.adobe.com; **p. 185** *tr* © Ekaterina Senyutina/stock.adobe.com; **p. 186** *tr* © Viktor/stock.adobe.com; **p. 186** *cr* © Spicy Truffel/stock.adobe.com; **p. 188** *tr* © Moodboard/stock.adobe.com; **p. 191** *cc*, **p. 192** *tc* © Friends Stock/stock.adobe.com; **p. 193** *tl* © Sofiko 14/stock.adobe.com; **p. 193** *br* © Krakenimages.com/stock.adobe.com; **p. 194** *tr* © Vaksmanv/stock.adobe.com; **p. 194** *cl* © Nipastock/stock.adobe.com; **p. 194** *br* © Studio Romantic/stock.adobe.com; **p. 195** *tr* © Monkey Business/stock.adobe.com; **p. 195** *bc* © Pharanyu - stock.adobe.com; **p. 196** *cc* © Ladadik Art/stock.adobe.com; **p. 197** *tl* © Deagreez/stock.adobe.com; **p. 197** *bl* © Serhiibobyk/stock.adobe.com; **p. 197** *br* © Vitalii Vodolazskyi/stock.adobe.com; **p. 198** *cr* © Marina/stock.adobe.com; **p. 198** *br* © Marinabh/stock.adobe.com; **p. 199** *bc* © Creative Juice/stock.adobe.com; **p. 200** *cl* © Molly Ferguson Art/stock.adobe.com; **p. 200** *cr* © The img/stock.adobe.com; **p. 201** *tl* © Yingyaipumi/stock.adobe.com; **p. 201** *tc* © H Ko/stock.adobe.com; **p. 201** *tr* © Andrey Popov/stock.adobe.com; **p. 203** *bl* © Seventyfour/stock.adobe.com; **p. 204** *tr* © AS Photo Family/stock.adobe.com; **p. 204** *cr* © Bogdych/stock.adobe.com; **p. 204** *bl* © New Africa/stock.adobe.com; **p. 205** *tr* © Andri Wahyudi/Shutterstock.com; **p. 205** *cr* © Rawpixel.com/stock.adobe.com; **p. 205** *bl* © H Ko/stock.adobe.com; **p. 205** *bc* © New Africa/stock.adobe.com; **p. 205** *br* © Triocean/stock.adobe.com; **p. 206** *bl* © Sorbis/Shutterstock.com; **p. 207** *br* © Andrey Popov/stock.adobe.com; **p. 210** *cr* © Veniamin Kraskov/Shutterstock.com; **p. 212** *bl* © Rraya/stock.adobe.com; **p. 212** *cc* © Ju See/stock.adobe.com; **p. 212** *bc* © Recycle Man/stock.adobe.com; **p. 213** *tr* © Viktoriia Borovska/stock.adobe.com; **p. 214** *bc* © Stockphoto-graf/stock.adobe.com; **p. 215** *cl* © Amorn/stock.adobe.com; **p. 216** *tr* © Viktoria/stock.adobe.com; **p. 217** *cl* © Good Studio/stock.adobe.com; **p. 220** *cr* © Bnenin/stock.adobe.com; **p. 220** *cr* © Michael Jung/stock.adobe.com; **p. 220** *br* © Pressmaster/stock.adobe.com; **p. 221** *tr* © Friends Stock/stock.adobe.com; **p. 221** *cr* © Stasique/stock.adobe.com; **p. 221** *cr* © Sergey Klopotov/Shutterstock.com; **p. 221** *cr* © Yurakrasil/stock.adobe.com; **p. 221** *br* © Fotoproff/stock.adobe.com; **p. 222** *tr* © Drazen/stock.adobe.com; **p. 222** *cr* © Michael Jung/stock.adobe.com; **p. 222** *cr* © Sofiko 14/stock.adobe.com; **p. 225** *bc* © Ola-ola/Shutterstock.com.

t = top, *b* = bottom, *l* = left, *r* = right, *c* = centre